SYMPOSIA OF THE ZOOLOGICAL SOCIETY OF LONDON NUMBER 54

Advances in
Animal Conservation

SYMPOSIA OF THE ZOOLOGICAL SOCIETY OF LONDON NUMBER 54

Advances in Animal Conservation

The Proceedings of a Symposium
held at the Zoological Society of London
on 31st May and 1st June 1984

Edited by **J. P. HEARN**

and **J. K. HODGES**

Institute of Zoology, The Zoological Society of London, Regent's Park, London, England

Published for **THE ZOOLOGICAL SOCIETY OF LONDON**

by **CLARENDON PRESS · OXFORD**

Oxford University Press, Walton Street, Oxford OX2 6DP

Oxford New York Toronto
Delhi Bombay Calcutta Madras Karachi
Kuala Lumpur Singapore Hong Kong Tokyo
Nairobi Dar es Salaam Cape Town
Melbourne Auckland

and associated companies in
Beirut Berlin Ibadan Nicosia

Oxford is a trade mark of Oxford University Press

Published in the United States
by Oxford University Press, New York

Reprinted 1988

British Library Cataloguing in Publication Data

Advances in animal conservation: the proceedings of a symposium held at the Zoological
Society of London on 31st May and 1st June 1984.——(Symposia of the Zoological Society of
London; no. 54)
1. Wildlife conservation
I. Hearn, J.P.   II. Hodges, J.K.   III. Zoological Society of London   IV. Series
639.9   QL82

ISBN 0-19-854002-7

Library of Congress Cataloging in Publication Data

Main entry under title:
Advances in animal conservation.
(Symposia of the Zoological Society of London; no. 54)
"Celebrates the 80th birthday of Professor Lord Zuckerman"—Pref.
Includes bibliographies and index.
1. Wildlife conservation—Congresses.   I. Hearn, J.P.   II. Hodges, J.K.   III. Zuckerman,
Solly Zuckerman, Baron, 1904– .   IV. Zoological Society of London.   V. Series.
QL1.Z733 no. 54   591 s   85–22104
[QL81.5]   [333.95'4]

ISBN 0-19-854002-7

Set by Promenade Graphics Ltd, Cheltenham
Printed and bound in Great Britain by
Antony Rowe Limited, Chippenham, Wiltshire

Preface

The preservation of genetic diversity and the conservation of rare and endangered species are objectives held by many people but understood by few. The extinction of animal species seen in this century, largely due to the increase in human populations, has little to do with the natural processes of evolution and extinction. The problem will not go away, as a further doubling of the human population can be expected in the next 50 years.

More and more, conservation of animals depends on a sound understanding of the fundamental limiting factors in animal survival, involving genetics, disease, nutrition, reproduction, and veterinary care. In future, animals in captivity and in the wild will need to be managed as one stock. The time constraints already apparent lend little hope for leisurely pursuit. We have detailed knowledge of only about 40 of the 4000 species of mammals, among them those on which we depend for much of our agriculture, food production, and biological research, as well as for our domestic pets. Our detailed knowledge of birds, reptiles, and other animals is even smaller.

In recent years, great strides have been made in our understanding of the many scientific disciplines that are relevant to animal production, conservation, and management. Translation of this knowledge to assist in the preservation of exotic species in captivity and in the wild is the aim of this symposium. Four topics are considered, namely conservation in the wild, conservation in captivity, conservation and comparative medicine, and government and conservation.

This symposium celebrates the 80th birthday of Professor Lord Zuckerman, OM, KCB, DSc, FRS. Lord Zuckerman's close association with the Zoological Society of London for over 55 years, and his service as Secretary and then as President over the past 30 years, has stimulated fundamental change and initiative in the Society and in the broader field of animal conservation. He founded the Institute of Zoology, the *Symposia of the Zoological Society of London*, and the *International Zoo Yearbook*. His drive and energy have helped introduce hard science into the field of animal conservation. His great fund-raising capacity modernized and transformed much of London and Whipsnade Zoos and put the scientific activities of the Society on a firm footing. This symposium is a small mark of our appreciation of his leadership.

We are honoured that HRH The Prince Philip, Duke of Edinburgh, took part in our celebration and introduced the scientific programme. His Royal Highness is President of the World Wildlife Fund (International) and a past

President of the Zoological Society of London. His tireless efforts in the cause of conservation of the environment are well known.

I am grateful to the *Journal of Reproduction and Fertility* for financial support for the symposium, to Dr J. K. Hodges who is co-editor of this volume, and to Miss Unity McDonnell and Miss Constance Nutkins for a great deal of help in its production. Finally, and far from least, I am grateful to the President of the Zoological Society of London, Sir William Henderson, FRS, to the Chairmen of the four scientific sessions and to the speakers who have made this a valuable and memorable occasion.

London   J. P. H.
June, 1984

Contents

Conservation in the wild

Conservation in captivity

The impact on conservation of animal disease 103

W. M. HENDERSON

Zoos of the future 111

R. WHEATER

Conservation and comparative medicine

Embryo manipulation and genetic engineering 123

C. POLGE

Contents xi

Lactation and neonatal survival of mammals 183

A. S. I. LOUDON

Government and conservation

The cost of conservation 211

F. B. O'CONNOR

Contents

Contributors

H.R.H. THE PRINCE PHILIP, Duke of Edinburgh, KG, KT: President, World Wildlife Fund International; Vice-President, International Union for the Conservation of Nature.

BENIRSCHKE, K., Director of Research, San Diego Zoo, PO Box 551, San Diego, California 92112, USA

BRAMBELL, M. R., Director, Chester Zoo, The North of England Zoological Society, Zoological Gardens, Chester CH2 1LH, England

HALLE, M., Assistant Director, Conservation for Development Centre, IUCN, Avenue du Mont-Blanc, CH-1196 Gland, Switzerland

HEARN, J. P., Director, Institute of Zoology, *and* Director of Science, The Zoological Society of London, Regent's Park, London NW1 4RY, England

HENDERSON, W. M., FRS, President, The Zoological Society of London, Regent's Park, London NW1 4RY, England; *and* Yarnton Cottage, High Street, Streatley, Berks RG8 9HY, England

HODGES, J. K., MRC/AFRC Comparative Physiology Research Group, Institute of Zoology, The Zoological Society of London, Regent's Park, London NW1 4RY, England

JONES, D. M., Director of Zoos, The Zoological Society of London, Regent's Park, London NW1 4RY, England

JUNGIUS, H., Director, Regional and Project Services, IUCN, World Conservation Centre, Avenue du Mont-Blanc, CH-1196 Gland, Switzerland

LAWS, R. M., CBE, FRS, Director, British Antarctic Survey, NERC, High Cross, Madingley Road, Cambridge CB3 0ET, England

LOUDON, A. S. I., MRC/AFRC Comparative Physiology Research Group, Institute of Zoology, The Zoological Society of London, Regent's Park, London NW1 4RY, England

MOORE, H. D. M., MRC/AFRC Comparative Physiology Group, Institute of Zoology, The Zoological Society of London, Regent's Park, London NW1 4RY, England

O'CONNOR, F. B., Director (England), Nature Conservancy Council, Calthorpe House, Calthorpe Street, Banbury, Oxon OX16 8EX, England

POLGE, C., FRS, AFRC Institute of Animal Physiology, Animal Research Station, 307 Huntingdon Road, Cambridge CB3 0JQ, England

RAWLINS, C. G. C., Chief Executive Officer, The Zoological Society of London, Regent's Park, London NW1 4RY, England. *Present address*: Birchgrove, 64 Earl Howe Road, Holmer Green, nr. High Wycombe, Bucks HP15 6QT, England

SANDBROOK, J. R., International Institute for Environment and Development, 3–4 Endsleigh Street, London WC1H 0DD, England

SKINNER, J. D., Director, Mammal Research Institute, Department of Zoology, University of Pretoria, Pretoria 0002, South Africa

WHEATER, R. J., Director, The Royal Zoological Society of Scotland, Scottish National Zoological Park, Murrayfield, Edinburgh EH12 6TS, Scotland

ZUCKERMAN, S., OM, KCB, FRS, Past President, The Zoological Society of London, Regent's Park, London NW1 4RY, England. *Present address*: The University of East Anglia, Norwich NR4 7TJ, England.

Organizer of symposium

PROFESSOR J. P. HEARN, Director, Institute of Zoology, *and* Director of Science, The Zoological Society of London, Regent's Park, London NW1 4RY, England

Chairmen of sessions

SIR WILLIAM HENDERSON, FRS, President, The Zoological Society of London, Regent's Park, London NW1 4RY, England; *and* Yarnton Cottage, High Street, Streatley, Berks RG8 9HY, England

DR R. M. LAWS, CBE, FRS, Director, British Antarctic Survey, NERC, High Cross, Madingley Road, Cambridge CB3 0ET, England

DR R. RILEY, FRS, Agricultural Research Council, 160 Great Portland Street, London W1N 6DT, England

SIR JAMES GOWANS, CBE, FRS, Secretary, Medical Research Council, 20 Park Crescent, London W1N 4AL, England.

Introduction

H. R. H. THE PRINCE PHILIP, DUKE OF EDINBURGH, KG, KT

'Advances in Animal Conservation' has a fine ring about it; and speaking as the President of the World Wildlife Fund International, as well as a Vice-President of the International Union for the Conservation of Nature, it is exactly the sort of thing that I would like to hear, because as you can imagine I spend much of my time listening to horror stories, and watching the size of the Red Data Books of endangered species getting bigger by the month. I get endless reports about such things as pollution, like the great oil spill in the Arabian Gulf, which is threatening marine species of all sorts and particularly the fragile dugong population; and then stories about poaching, which, apart from using extremely cruel methods, is threatening rhino-ceroses and elephants in Africa, amongst many other species. Then there is commercial fishing and whaling, which are threatening many wild fish stocks and dwindling whale populations. And then there is the continued use of persistent pesticides, and now the release of PCBs, which threaten whole food chains and particularly migrating bird species. Then there is illegal trade in wildlife and wildlife products and acid rain, which threatens forests and lakes and of course their inhabitants.

Behind all this, like an immense and threatening hurricane, is the menace of the ever-growing human population of the world. It is already neutraliz-ing virtually all economic development projects in the less-developed world, and it will inevitably consume all the world's renewable resources faster than they can possibly regenerate. Just to illustrate the scale of these prob-lems, let me give you some figures on the world trade in wildlife and wildlife products which were produced for the meeting of the WWF Council in Washington recently because there was a discussion about this particular subject. These, I may say, are *minimum* estimates, and include both legal and illegal trade. Fifteen million fur skins, plus another 35 million from captive-bred animals. Two and a half million live reptiles, 10 million raw skins and 20 million products. Ten million cacti; one million orchids—and both of those mostly taken from the wild. Three hundred and fifty million ornamental fish, mostly tropical, and many taken from the wild. Three million live birds; half a million parrots alone, from a relatively small area in South America. Forty thousand primates, most of which are used for bio-medical research. Seven hundred thousand kilograms of raw ivory and 28 million ivory products; and just to remind you, it takes roughly 95 elephants to produce 1000 kg of ivory, so if you have got a pocket calculator you can figure out what that means. The total value of all wildlife trade in the United

States alone is estimated to be between $800 million and $1 billion annually. And these figures, of course, do not include the value of commercial sea fishing or the number of wild fish taken at sea or in lakes and rivers.

Now I mention all this just as a reminder that advances in aminal conservation depend upon a great many factors beyond the scope of scientific research and beyond solution by captive breeding.

The difficulty is that animal conservation cannot be seen in isolation from the world's natural processes. One of the remarkable features of these processes is that they can be abused for years without any noticeable effect and then suddenly there is a major disaster. The effect of acid rain, for instance, and the collapse of the herring population in the North Sea are only two examples. Destroyed or degraded habitat also threatens the extinction of animal species just as effectively as commercial over-exploitation or extermination in the name of disease control. Captive breeding of endangered species will always be worth while but it is a bit discouraging if meanwhile the natural habitat has been destroyed.

It is unfortunately the case that even development projects, in the form of drainage schemes, dams for hydro-electric and irrigation projects, machinery for the exploitation of forests and forest products, and improved fishing techniques and equipment, can all create serious conservation problems. All such projects are potentially destructive unless they are based on the long-term sustainable yield of the resources exploited, and unless their long-term influence on the local ecology, including wild plant and animal populations, is taken into consideration. Furthermore, if such projects only result in yet further growth in the human population the problems are compounded. Developers may not like the idea, but as population numbers increase, the proportion of poor in the population is not likely to decrease, so that the total number of poor is actually increased.

Needless to say, the conservation of nature cannot be achieved by any single programme. It depends on a mass of detailed tactical programmes and research efforts, all of which should fit into the framework of the World Conservation Strategy. And this is why the increasingly successful efforts by zoos to breed endangered species in captivity and the work undertaken in comparative medicine is so extremely important.

I would like to congratulate and to thank the London Zoological Society for organising this important symposium and to welcome the distinguished contributors. I believe that this meeting represents a major offensive on this sector of the front line of the world conservation campaign and I wish it every possible success.

Finally, I note that this symposium celebrates the 80th birthday of Lord Zuckerman. He has provided leadership and initiative in this field for over 50 years. Perhaps he should consider changing the spelling of his name to Lord Zookerman.

Conservation in the wild

Symp. zool. Soc. Lond. (1985) No. 54: 3–23

Animal conservation in the Antarctic

R. M. LAWS

British Antarctic Survey
NERC
Madingley Road
Cambridge CB3 0ET

Synopsis

The Antarctic continent and surrounding Southern Ocean comprise a tenth of the Earth's surface. Ice covers 99 per cent of the land, terrestrial life is virtually confined to the remaining 1 per cent, and many of the most suitable sites for scientific bases are close to seal and bird colonies. So far, there are few terrestrial conservation problems, but future commercial developments would cause greater impacts. Some problems arise from the introduction of alien species to the sub-Antarctic islands.

A vast unplanned experiment has been in progress since the beginning of this century as modern whaling expanded by means of pelagic factory ships throughout the Southern Ocean. Interactions within the oceanic ecosystem are centred on the very abundant key species krill, *Euphausia superba*, the staple food of whales, seals, birds, fish, and squid. With the decline of the whales these other groups increased in abundance and the 'surplus' of krill made available by the decreased consumption by baleen whales has now been largely taken up. Commercial whaling has virtually ended, but fishing for fish and krill has greatly increased over the past two decades and now represents the most immediate threat.

A series of far-sighted, internationally agreed, and uniquely based measures have been introduced by the Antarctic Treaty nations, to conserve the terrestrial animals and plants, seals, and marine living resources. The International Whaling Commission has been responsible for whale conservation.

Introduction

The two polar regions are strikingly different. The Arctic is essentially a mediterranean sea—a deep ocean basin—surrounded by wide continental shelves and by the northern continents which are populated and administered by developed nations. The Antarctic remained undiscovered until the 19th century and lacks indigenous peoples. It carries an ice cap up to 4 km thick in places, making it the world's highest continent, and the weight of ice depresses the underlying land so that the continental shelf is unusually deep. The continent of Antarctica is surrounded by a wide, deep ocean, which separates it from the other southern continents, and is characterized by relatively simple circumpolar currents.

Despite the absence of an indigenous human population, and very low

ZOOLOGICAL SYMPOSIUM No. 54
ISBN 0–19–854002–7

transient populations involved with scientific research activities, there have already been major historical conservation problems, due to overhunting of fur seals and elephant seals in the 19th century which brought these populations near to extinction, and in this century the development and decline of the Antarctic whaling industry. However, the region is now subject to a range of conservation agreements which are potentially, and so far actually, as successful as any that apply elsewhere. This chapter first characterizes the land, inland water, and marine ecosystems and then outlines the development of the unique series of conservation measures that are in force.

The ecosystems and animals to be conserved

Land and inland waters

The environment

The land area is about 14 million km², of which only 1 per cent or 142 000 km² is ice free. Much of this is bare or lichen encrusted rock with little or no soil and other vegetation. As the ice has receded since the last glacial maximum c. 18 000 years ago, coastal areas have been most affected and soil formation, vegetation, and fauna have undergone most development there.

Smith (1984) has defined the sub-Antarctic and Antarctic regions in geobotanical terms which are also appropriate in terms of the fauna. The sub-Antarctic (South Georgia and the southern islands north of the Antarctic Convergence of the south Pacific and south Indian Ocean) is characterized by a cool oceanic climate, the mean monthly temperature of the coldest month rarely falling below −2°C. The maritime Antarctic (mainly South Sandwich, South Orkney, South Shetland Islands, the west coast of the Antarctic Peninsula and offshore islands to c. 70°S) has a cold maritime climate, mean monthly temperatures rarely falling below −10°C in winter (northern) or −15°C (southern). For continental Antarctica the zone colonized by animals is essentially the coastal fringe south of 70°S and on the east coast of the Antarctic Peninsula south of 63°S, and three more southerly islands. Temperatures are lower and rain is rare.

Natural fauna

The invertebrate land fauna has been described by Block (1984). There is no indigenous human population and the dominant macroscopic land fauna (excluding bird and seal colonies which, though conspicuous, are marine based), is composed of arthropods—insects and arachnids. The largest insects are chironomid midges, the wingless *Belgica antarctica* and winged *Parochlus steinenii*; the largest arachnid is the oribatid mite *Alaskozetes antarctica*, adults of which reach a length of c. 1 mm. Larger forms occur in the sub-Antarctic. Other arthropods include Collembola, feather lice on birds and sucking lice on seals, as well as bird fleas. Oligochaetes (mainly in the sub-Antarctic) and Mollusca (gastropod land snails of the sub-Antarctic) are larger. Beetles are considered to be introduced species and are better represented in the sub-Antarctic. Spiders and three species of Lepidoptera are restricted to the sub-Antarctic, as are a few species of Myriapoda. The microscopic invertebrates comprise protozoans, rotifers, tardigrades, and nematodes, but the biology and ecology of most of these animals is rather poorly understood. The species that have received most attention are the collembolan *Cryptopygus antarcticus* and the mite *Alaskozetes antarcticus*. According to Block (1984) the terrestrial ecosystems in the Antarctic, being devoid of large above-ground herbivores and containing mainly decomposer-orientated communities, provide ideal test-beds for examining perturbation effects. Such experiments provide information necessary to evaluate environmental impacts due to human activities.

The majority of inland waters have arisen from glacial retreat and their development has been described by Heywood (1977a, 1984). If they occupy even 1–2 per cent of the land area they may represent a total surface area of only some 2 000 km². Many are proglacial lakes and many of the others are saline, both these types containing no fauna, although some, thought to be of marine origin, contain a few species of copepods. In the unusual epishelf lakes of Ablation Point, Alexander Island, fresh water overlies sea water. The fresh water layer probably contains Protozoa, rotifers, tardigrades, and nematodes, and a small population of a copepod, *Pseudoboeckella poppei*, was present; in the saline layer a marine copepod and the marine fish *Trematomus bernachii* occurred (Heywood 1977b).

The freshwater lakes constitute only a fraction of the total inland water surface area—at most perhaps a few hundred square kilometres. Their evolution from the proglacial stage involves trophic change from hypo-oligotrophy to oligotrophy and they may be mesotrophic or even eutrophic in coastal areas where bird and seal colonies transfer nutrients from the marine ecosystem by excretion and moulting. An area such as Signy Island, South Orkney Islands, contains examples of all stages of this evolution (Heywood, Dartnall & Priddle 1980). Benthic algal felts and aquatic mosses support Protozoa, a few species of Turbellaria, Gastrotricha, Nematoda, Tardigrada, one enchytraeid worm, 24 Rotifera species, and seven species of Crustacea (Copepoda, Cladocera, Ostracoda, Anostraca). Enrichment of the lakes results in increased productivity with decreased diversity, and some lakes may be thought of as polluted by seal excreta (Heywood 1984). The limited crustacean fauna reflects the short time since the last glaciation. These lakes can be regarded as closed boxes for eight months of the year when they are frozen over, containing simple ecosystems that are easily perturbed.

Introduced animals and their effects

Of the invertebrates, beetles are considered to be wholly introduced by man (Block 1984) and enchytraeid worms and chironomid flies have inadvertently been introduced at Signy Island (Burn 1982). But there are conspicuous mammal introductions on the sub-Antarctic islands which like many introductions have caused serious conservation problems. Not all have succeeded and there are none in the maritime Antarctic or continental Antarctica.

Bonner (1984a) has recently reviewed the status of mammals introduced to various sub-Antarctic islands and represented by surviving populations, The mammal species involved are the black and brown rats, *Rattus rattus* and *R. norvegicus*, mice, *Mus domesticus*, rabbits, *Oryctolagus cuniculus*, reindeer, *Rangifer tarandus*, cats, *Felis catus* and mouflon, *Ovis ammon musimon*. Various domestic animals (cattle, goats, pigs, horses, and sheep) have been introduced, but only sheep have become established (at Iles Kerguelen and Iles Crozet).

The brown rats at South Georgia probably have some impact on burrow nesting petrels, but have greater effect on the South Georgia pintail, *Anas georgicus*, and appear to have largely eradicated the Antarctic pipit, *Anthus antarcticus*, in areas which they have colonized. Rabbits have had substantial effects on the ecosystems of some sub-Antarctic islands (Macquarie, Kerguelen, and Crozet). Current management policy at Macquarie Island is to eliminate them using myxoma virus.

Reindeer have been introduced to South Georgia and Iles Kerguelen, the first introductions occurring in 1911 and 1956 respectively. There are now three herds at South Georgia and two at Kerguelen. The problem at South Georgia is better understood through research undertaken by the British Antarctic Survey. These three herds are at different stages of an eruptive oscillation, but have not shown the classic cycle of rapid increase followed by a population crash that characterized the islands of St. Matthew and St. Paul in the Bering Sea. This is thought to be due mainly to the different food resources, particularly in the presence of rich and accessible tussock grass in winter at South Georgia. The reindeer populations have had a major impact on the environment through selective overgrazing of macrolichens, short grasses, and eventually tussock grass. Currently the deer appear to be reaching a balance with their habitat but the habitat is changing in response to the deer (Leader-Williams 1980; Bonner 1984a).

Cats are established on Iles Kerguelen and Crozet, and on Marion and Macquarie Islands, having been introduced in the 19th century on Macquarie and Crozet, reintroduced in 1951 or 1952 at Kerguelen and introduced in 1949 at Marion Island. The cats are successful predators, feeding opportunistically on rabbits and mice (where they co-exist), on nocturnal burrowing petrels of several species, and occasionally on penguins. They have had a considerable impact. At Marion Island the population of 2139 cats in 1975 was estimated to take 455 000 birds each year. The disappearance or rarity of some bird species has been attributed to cats. Attempts have therefore been made to eliminate the cats, most recently by biological control introducing the virus of feline panleucopaenia (FPL) in 1977. Since then the trend of the cat population has been downwards, although it is unlikely that FPL will eliminate the cats from Marion Island (Van Aarde & Skinner 1982).

Marine

The environment

On an equal area projection of the world the Southern Ocean is seen to occupy a vast area, from c. 40–70°S. The Antarctic Convergence, where cold northward-flowing Antarctic surface water meets the southward-moving warmer sub-Antarctic water, is a circumpolar faunal boundary within the Southern Ocean at an average latitude of about 55°S. The seas south of this boundary have an area of 36 million km² or about a tenth of the world ocean. It is a wide, deep circumpolar ocean that effectively isolates the Antarctic continent from the rest of the world. The current systems are driven by the winds, flowing predominantly westward at higher latitudes and eastward north of about 60°S. Floating ice shelves fringe the continental shores, most of them about 200 m thick; they account for about 40–45 per cent of the coastline. A zone of pack ice reaching about 20 million km² at maximum extent in winter and contracting to about 4 million km² in summer is a partial barrier to whales and a haul-out platform for seals and penguins (Foster 1984).

Major animal components and interactions in the marine food web

Zooplankton species are largely circumpolar in distribution in broad latitudinal zones, and the zooplankton standing crop is higher than in tropical and temperate regions, averaging about 105 mg m^{-3}. A single species, the Antarctic krill, *Euphausia superba*, accounts for about half of this biomass and is the central organism in the marine food web—the staple food of squids and vertebrates (Fig. 1)—but it is absent north of the Antarctic Convergence. Other zooplankton includes copepods, amphipods, other euphausiids, chaetognaths, salps, siphonophores, pelagic gastropods, and ichthyoplankton (Everson 1984a). Although krill is circumpolar in distribution there appear to be several areas of concentration which may represent separate stocks (Mackintosh 1973). It occurs in large swarms, sometimes in 'superswarms' comprising as much as 2.1 million tonnes in 450 km², but it is not known what proportion of the stock is more dispersed. Its total biomass has ben estimated at 500–750 million tonnes and annual production

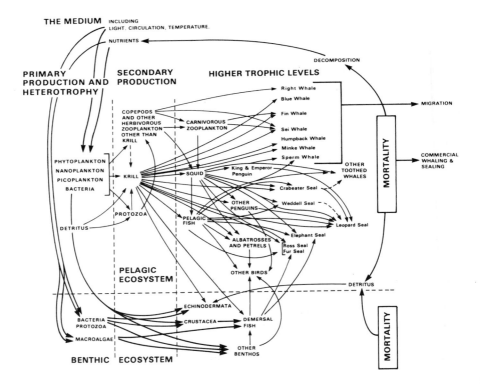

Fig. 1 Simplified diagram to indicate complex interactions (shown by the arrows) within Antarctic marine food webs. (Modified from Everson 1977).

may be as high as 750–1350 million tonnes (Siegfried, Condy & Laws, 1985).

Oceanic squids are another important group including more than 20 Antarctic species which occur in large numbers, most about 1–4 m long, and feeding largely on krill. The larger squid appear to feed on fish at depth. It is estimated that some 20 million tonnes of squid are consumed annually by birds, seals, and whales; the squid in turn probably consume *c*. 100 million tonnes of krill (Fig. 1). About 120 species of fish of 29 families occur in the seas south of the Antarctic Convergence and the dominant group is the

Nototheniiformes which make up nearly three quarters of the coastal fish species (Everson 1984*b*). Some species spend their early years in inshore waters feeding on benthos and later become pelagic feeders on krill (e.g. *Notothenia rossii*); others migrate seasonally in summer to feed on Antarctic krill (e.g. *Micromesistius australis*). Small bathypelagic fish, mainly Myctophidae, may be abundant year round in the open ocean but there are no dense shoals of counterparts to the herring of the north. Overall fish may take some 100 million tonnes of krill annually (Siegfried *et al.*, 1985).

Almost all Antarctic birds are seabirds, mainly albatrosses, petrels and penguins. Their ecology has recently been reviewed by Croxall (1984). South of the sub-Tropical Convergence 64 species breed and 37 of these breed south of the Antarctic Convergence (six penguins, six albatrosses, 18 petrels, one shag and four skuas, gulls, and terns). Their distributions are greatly influenced by oceanographical and environmental features and, except for the emperor penguin, *Aptenodytes forsteri*, by the accessibility of ice-free ground for nesting. Foraging ranges during the breeding season range from *c*. 30 km in the gentoo penguin, *Pygoscelis papua*, to *c*. 500 km in the king penguin, *Aptenodytes patagonica*, and from *c*. 300 km in petrels to 2650 km in the wandering albatross *Diomedea exulans*. The penguins have much greater feeding depths, from *c*. 45 m in the chinstrap penguin, *Pygoscelis antarctica*, to 265 m in the emperor penguin. Ecological separation is promoted by the birds' exploitation of distinctive feeding areas and depths and by morphological and behavioural adaptations. They feed mainly on crustaceans (krill, copepods, amphipods), squid, fish, and carrion. Krill amounts to about 75 per cent of all bird food and in terms of biomass and food consumption virtually all Antarctic birds are penguins, two thirds of them Adelie penguins, *Pygoscelis adeliae*. In the sub-Antarctic, penguins amount to 80 per cent of bird biomass and half of these are macaroni penguins, *Eudyptes chrysolophus*. Breeding success varies from year to year and appears to be correlated with availability of krill. Three species, chinstrap, Adelie, and macaroni penguin, account for 90 per cent of Antarctic bird biomass with total populations of about 80–120 million; total Antarctic bird numbers are about 350 million (Clarke 1983) and they consume about 130 million tonnes of krill both directly and indirectly through their other prey (Figs 2 and 3).

There are seven species of seals represented in the Southern Ocean and their biology has been reviewed by Laws (1984*b*). The southern elephant seal, *Mirounga leonina*, has a world population of about 750 000, breeding mainly on sub-Antarctic islands. Also breeding in the sub-Antarctic is the Kerguelen fur seal, *Arctocephalus tropicalis*, population about 50 000; the Antarctic fur seal, *A. gazella*, breeds almost exclusively south of the Antarctic Convergence and now numbers over a million. The crabeater seal, *Lobodon carcinophagus*, is by far the most abundant seal in the world (*c*. 30

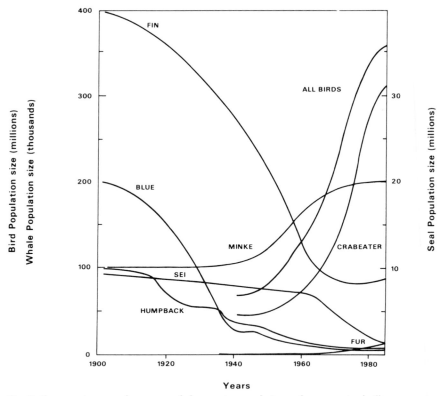

Fig. 2 Current views on the nature of changes in populations of some major krill consumers. Bird, fur seal, and crabeater seal curves are obtained by extrapolating percentage annual increases backwards in time from current estimates of abundance. Whale curves after Beddington (in Mitchell & Sandbrook 1980).

million); the leopard seal *Hydrurga leptonyx* numbers *c*. 440 000 and preys on the crabeater; the Weddell seal, *Leptonychotes weddellii*, numbers *c*. 800 000; and the Ross seal, *Ommatophoca rossii*, numbers *c*. 220 000. The last four species breed on the floating sea ice. Ecological separation is promoted by differing geographical distributions, haul out habits, different feeding depths and morphological differences. Crabeater and leopard seals and Antarctic fur seals take a great deal of krill at shallow depths (to 70 m); elephant, Ross, and Weddell seals tend to take fish and squid at greater depths (to 600 m).

In the 19th century wide-ranging sealing expeditions almost exterminated the fur seals and the elephant seals, but from the population sizes given above it can be seen that with protection they made a dramatic recovery (Bonner 1984*b*). Currently there is concern about a reported decline of

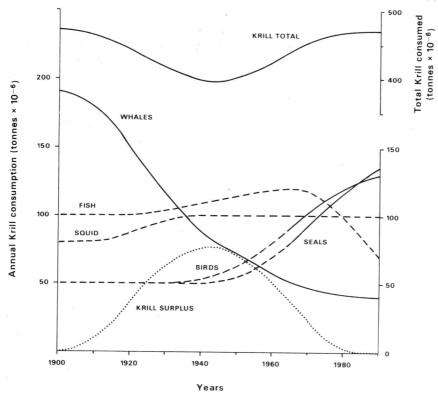

Fig. 3 Conceptual model of changes in consumption of krill by the major predator groups, 1900–1985. Curves for birds, seals and whales derived from applying published annual food consumption values to the curves in Fig. 2. Fish and squid curves are hypothetical. The purpose is to demonstrate how an earlier krill 'surplus' may well have been eliminated by the 1980s.

elephant seal populations in the Indian Ocean sector (Laws 1984*c*). The stocks of Antarctic and sub-Antarctic seals probably now total at least 33 million, with a biomass of about 7 million tonnes and eating more than 130 million tonnes of krill (Fig. 3), at least 6 million tonnes of squid and at least 8 million tonnes of fish.

Baleen whales are very mobile and undertake large scale seasonal migrations across the Antarctic Convergence between the tropical and sub-tropical breeding grounds and polar feeding grounds; so do adult male sperm whales. There are six species of baleen whales ranging from the 9 m (maximum length) minke whale, *Balaenoptera acutorostrata*, to the 30 m blue whale, *B. musculus*. The largest toothed whale is the sperm whale, *Physeter macrocephalus*, to 18 m, and there are 11 small toothed whales found in Antarctic waters, including the killer whale, *Orcinus orca*, the southern white-sided dolphin, *Lagenorhynchus cruciger*, and the beaked whales *Berardius arnuxi* and *Hyperoodon planifrons*. Twenty small toothed whales are recorded from the sub-Antarctic seas. Apart from the sperm whale very little is known about the biology of the toothed whales, but they all feed on fish and/or squid.

The major food of baleen whales is krill, but the more northerly species principally take copepods (Fig. 1). The average annual feeding period south of the Antarctic Convergence is *c*. 120 days and the feeding zone is about 19 million km^2 in October–December, decreasing to 15 million km^2 in January–March, reflecting the progressive 'grazing' on krill, by immigrant baleen whales, as it is exposed by the retreat of the pack ice (Laws 1977). Thus, the krill zone contracts and shifts southwards during the summer. The larger species of whales and within species the larger, and older, individuals tend to reach high latitudes. Different feeding mechanisms, behaviour, and distributions again tend to promote ecological separation.

The Antarctic baleen whales and sperm whale have been the object of a fishery since 1904 when their numbers are estimated to have been about 1.1 million, with a biomass of about 45 million tonnes, eating each year an estimated 190 million tonnes of krill, 12 million tonnes of squid and nearly 5 million tonnes of fish. Competition for the available food probably limited sizes and numbers. By 1973 their numbers had declined through overhunting to about half a million, weighing 9 million tonnes and eating about 43 million tonnes of krill, 5 million tonnes of squid and 130 000 tonnes of fish (Laws 1977). Figure 2 shows the probable changes in population sizes of key species of baleen whales.

The enormous reduction of the whales means that more than 100 million tonnes of krill formerly eaten by whales had probably become available to the remaining stocks of whales and to other predators (Fig. 3). An indication of the importance of this resource is given by reference to the total annual yield from all the world's fisheries, which is about 70 million tonnes. It has been suggested that some of the krill 'surplus' could be safely harvested by man, while allowing the depleted stocks of whales to increase to a reasonable level. A proviso is that management is soundly based and the rate of growth of the krill fishery is slow enough to allow the ecosystem gradually to come into a new balance, involving a change in numbers of krill consumers other than man, towards their former levels of abundance. This requires quantitative knowledge of the interactions within the food web. The central position of krill in the Antarctic ecosystem is clear (Fig. 1) and so are the dangers to the natural krill predators of an uncontrolled commercial exploitation of krill, which has now begun. The technological problems of catching and processing krill have been overcome, and if larger markets can be established catches are likely to increase rapidly.

Squid may have benefited from whaling in two ways. First, they should have enjoyed the greater krill abundance following the depletion of their competitors, the baleen whales. Secondly, heavy exploitation of sperm whales (and baleen whales) has probably resulted in a decrease in the level of predation on squid from about 12 to 7 million tonnes annually. There seems little or no prospect of the early development of an Antarctic squid fishery. Reported commercial catches of fish, mainly from South Georgia and Kerguelen, surpassed 400 000 tonnes in the 1969/1970 season, but had declined to c. 28 000 tonnes in 1979/1980 and c. 74 000 tonnes in 1980/ 1981 (FAO Fishery Statistics, I. Everson, pers. comm.). These catches may have exceeded 80 per cent of the standing stocks, which have been depleted. Estimates of maximum sustainable yields at the two main fishing grounds, South Georgia and Kerguelen, total under 160 000 tonnes annually (Everson 1977).

Turning now to the birds, three species, chinstrap, Adelie, and macaroni penguins, are much the most abundant in terms of biomass. Their distinctive breeding colonies can be counted and an allowance made for immature age groups not represented. The chinstrap is a northerly species, most abundant in the Scotia Sea where it has shown, over 30 years, average annual increases in the colonies monitored of 6–10 per cent. The more northerly macaroni penguin at South Georgia has also shown large increases, of up to 9 per cent annually, in the two decades from 1957 to 1977. Adelie penguins account for two thirds of Antarctic bird biomass, and they have also increased at northerly sites in the Scotia Sea, where they feed on *Euphausia superba*; at Signy Island, South Orkney Islands over 31 years, 1947–78, the annual increase averaged 2–3 per cent (Croxall & Prince 1979). Conversely, there is no indication of an increase in Adelie penguins in the Ross Sea, but little competition for food between whales and other groups is to be expected in this area (Laws 1977).

The crabeater seal off the west coast of the Antarctic Peninsula apparently experienced an advancement of the age at maturity from about 4 years in the 1950s to $2\frac{1}{2}$ years by the early 1960s and subsequently a reversion to the earlier level (Bengtson & Laws, 1985). This may be the result of increased growth rates and may be associated with an increased reproductive rate leading to an increase in numbers. The 14–17 per cent annual increase for the South Georgia fur seal population is unusually high—for other marine mammals 8–10 per cent is the rule—and is possibly also related to the increased abundance of krill accompanying the reduction of the whale stocks (Laws 1984a).

Ecological separation between the pack-ice seals and baleen and sperm whales is probably only partial, even though their distributions tend to be complementary—the seals requiring pack ice as a platform for breeding, basking and moulting, and the whales generally avoiding it. There appears to have been an increase in the pregnancy rates of fin and sei whales and an apparent (but controversial) decrease in their age at maturity; in the case of the sei this may have preceded large scale exploitation of this species which began in the 1960s. If these changes are real they would strengthen the conclusion that an indirect effect of whaling is involved, presumably through greater availability of food to the survivors. The minke whale age at sexual maturity also appears to have declined from 14 years to 6 years (although this too is controversial) and it may have expanded to fill partially the vacuum created by the removal of the blue whale. The present minke whale population levels could be double or treble the numbers before whaling began, although estimation of abundance is exceedingly difficult and trends of abundance can only be determined over a long time scale (Laws 1977).

It seems not unreasonable to conclude, at least as a working hypothesis for conservation purposes, that there have been increases over the past 30 years or more in many species, particularly those penguins dependent on *E. superba*, the crabeater seal, and the minke whale; and larger than expected increases in the Antarctic fur seal. These all appear to be due to increased food availability, especially of krill. Potential increases in krill-feeding fish would be expected to be nullified or reversed by the intensive commercial fishing activities. An attempt is made, in Figs 2 and 3, to quantify these changes, on the basis of published work cited earlier. It is in the Atlantic sector that the responses to a 'surplus' of krill are likely to have been greatest, for this is the region where there is the most overlap in the feeding distributions of the whale, seal and bird populations. It is unlikely that there is any large current 'surplus' of krill (Fig. 3) and at some point man may begin to compete significantly with the populations of squid, fish, birds, seals, and whales.

Conservation and management measures

In the sub-Antarctic islands north of 60°S national conservation legislation formulated by the UK (Falkland Islands Government), South Africa, France, and New Zealand applies. In general it appears to be adequate and the measures in force at South Georgia are modelled on the Agreed Measures under the Antarctic Treaty (see below) with in addition a Seal Fisheries Ordinance and the scheduling of Sites of Special Tourist Interest. So successful have these measures been that fur seals have recovered under protection from a few hundred survivors to over a million today and the situation regarding other seal and bird populations is healthy. The sub-Antarctic will not be further discussed here and the account which follows deals with conservation measures that apply to the Antarctic Treaty region south of 60°S and the high seas to the south of the Antarctic Convergence.

The absence of human populations has made it possible to make the

Antarctic proper, under the provisions of the Antarctic Treaty (1961), a demilitarized, nuclear-free region with unparalleled international co-operation in scientific research. A series of conservation agreements and conventions have been concluded under the Antarctic Treaty system (Auburn 1982). The region still remains in almost pristine condition (with the important exception of the historical exploitation of seals and whales) and pollution and other human impacts have so far been minimal. Unusually for such a large area, it has conservation measures that appear so far to be working well. Regrettably, they can be expected to come under great strain in the future, as exploitation develops in response to world economic forces.

Agreed Measures for the Conservation of Antarctic Flora and Fauna (1964)

Much of the success so far has been due to the fact that the vast area south of 60°S comes under the aegis of the Antarctic Treaty involving 32 nations, and the Agreed Measures for the Conservation of Antarctic Flora and Fauna apply; they apply only to land areas and ice shelves south of 60°S, and are under continuous review. Additions and amendments are made by recommendations from Antarctic Treaty Consultative meetings, usually after taking advice from the non-governmental Scientific Committee on Antarctic Research (SCAR), of the International Council of Scientific Unions (ICSU). SCAR played an important part in drafting these measures.

The Agreed Measures (text in Auburn 1982) prohibit within the Treaty Area 'the killing, wounding, capturing or molesting of any native mammal or native bird, or any attempt at any such act, except in accordance with a permit . . . to be drawn in terms as specific as possible and issued only for limited purposes'. These are 'to provide indispensable food for men or dogs', 'to provide specimens for scientific study or scientific information', or 'to provide specimens for museums, zoological gardens, or other educational or cultural institutions or uses'. Specially Protected Species of animals and birds are designated. Permits may be 'issued for a compelling scientific purpose', provided that the actions permitted 'will not jeopardize the existing natural ecological system or the survival of that species'.

Specially Protected Areas (SPAs) are designated, which are afforded special protection, and permits for activities in them may only be issued 'for a compelling scientific purpose which cannot be served elsewhere, and . . . the actions permitted thereunder will not jeopardise the natural ecological system existing in that Area'. Sites of Special Scientific Interest (SSSIs) were later designated which have management plans and are also subject to protective measures. Subsequently, provision was made for marine SSSIs. Examples of harmful interference are defined, and participating governments are required to take 'all reasonable steps towards the alleviation of pollution of the waters adjacent to the coast and ice shelves'. The introduction of non-indigenous species, parasites, and diseases is prohibited and certain precautions to this end are specified.

Provision is made for the annual exchange of information between participating governments, including records of permits issued and statistics of the numbers of each species killed or captured annually in the Treaty Area. There are arrangements for discussion of the status of species and their need for protection. Finally provision is made for amendment by unanimous agreement of the participants.

The Agreed Measures are generally working well and statistics on seals and birds are exchanged and published by SCAR in the SCAR Bulletin (*Polar Record*). However, a recent decision by France to build an aircraft runway at Pointe Geologie, Adelie Land, has stimulated protests because of the alleged effects of construction and operational activities on seabird colonies, including an emperor penguin rookery. It illustrates the potential conflict between the logistic needs of scientific research and the need to minimize enviromental impacts.

The International Whaling Convention (1946)

The whales are a special case with a disastrous and well-known history. The first effective restriction of pelagic whaling was for economic reasons which led to an agreement between whaling companies not to hunt whales in the 1931/1932 season. Attempts at international control were made in 1931, 1937, and 1938 and in 1944 a quota was internationally agreed in terms of Blue Whale Units (BWU), defined as equivalent to 1 blue, 2 fin, 2.5 humpback or 6 sei whales. The quota of 16 000 BWU came into operation in the 1945/46 season; then, in 1946, 14 governments agreed an International Convention for the Regulation of Whaling. The International Whaling Commission (IWC) was established under this Convention and membership has grown to 39 countries in 1984. A Scientific Committee meets annually to discuss the status of the stocks and advise the IWC; it convenes specialist meetings to address specific problems. Accounts of the population dynamics and management of whales under the Convention are given by Allen (1980), Brown & Lockyer (1984), Bonner (1984b), and Gambell (1976).

This Commission represents a different grouping of nations from the Antarctic Treaty nations, its interests extend to the whole world ocean, and the Convention to which it relates has been attacked by environmentalist groups; its main shortcoming has been that it gave undue weight to the supposed needs of the whaling industry. Also, the smaller Cetacea—dolphins and bottlenosed whales—are ignored by the IWC. For these reasons it is not widely regarded as a suitable forum for resolving other Southern Ocean conservation problems, although these are closely related to the whale problem. However, it has been successful at least in preventing the extinction of any species. The annual Antarctic catch quota is currently (1984) only 4 224 minke whales and a complete moratorium will come into force in 1986 if objections by Brazil, Japan, and the USSR are withdrawn. The role of the IWC in the regulation of whaling is reviewed by Gambell (1976).

The Convention for the Conservation of Antarctic Seals (1972)

The 'Agreed Measures' and other arrangements under the Antarctic Treaty could not give any protection to seals in the sea or on floating ice because the Treaty expressly reserves the rights of states under international law with regard to the high seas. Therefore a separate agreement outside the Treaty was needed. An International 'Convention for the Conservation of Antarctic Seals' was signed in London in 1972 and entered into force in 1978 (Auburn 1982). Again SCAR played an important role in its drafting and has a specific continuing role under the Convention as an independent international source of advice. The Convention applies to the seas south of 60°S, with provision for reporting catches made in the area of pack ice north of 60°S. It is complementary to the 'Agreed Measures' and includes comprehensive seal conservation measures. It applies to the five species of phocid seals and fur seals of the genus *Arctocephalus*.

An Annex specifies measures for 'conservation, scientific study and rational and humane use of seal resources', and these measures may be amended. Permissible annual catches are specified (crabeater seals, 175 000; leopard seals, 12 000; and Weddell seals, 5 000). The killing or capture of Ross seals, elephant seals and *Arctocephalus* species is forbidden, and in order to protect the adult breeding stock during the period when it is most concentrated and vulnerable, there is a prohibition on the taking of Weddell seals one year old or older between 1 September and 31 January. There is a closed season for all species from 1 March to 31 August. Six circumpolar sealing zones defined by longitudinal limits are listed and one is closed to sealing each year in rotation. Several Seal Reserves are designated where the killing or capture of seals is forbidden.

An annual exchange of information must be provided between contracting parties and to SCAR in the form of a summary of statistical information on all seals killed or captured, by zones and months; also details of vessels and their operating periods and of future plans. When an industry has started, frequent reports are to be made to SCAR on numbers taken and biological information provided including sex, reproductive condition, age, and other data requested by SCAR. SCAR was invited to report on methods of sealing and to recommend 'quick, painless and efficient' methods of killing, and has done so (Laws 1975, 1976).

SCAR was also invited to assess the information received, encourage exchange of data, recommend programmes for scientific research, recommend data to be collected, suggest amendments to the Annex, and to report when the harvest of any species is having a significantly harmful effect on the total stocks of the species or on the ecosystem in any locality. SCAR is also to provide an estimate in any sealing season when the permissible catch limits will be reached, if at all. Provision is made for establishing a Commission, and a scientific advisory committee if commercial sealing reaches significant proportions, and for establishing an effective system of control, including inspection.

In the event there has been no commercial sealing and the numbers of seals taken under permit have been low (Laws & Christie 1980). The very conservative permissible catch limits (currently less than 1 per cent of estimated stock size), the lack of success of experimental expeditions (Oritsland 1970) and economic considerations, have prevented the development of an industry and there are no known seal conservation problems in the area except for adverse effects of expanded fur seal populations on terrestrial environments. This is a good example of an agreement on conservation measures concluded before problems develop—in marked contrast to the IWC.

The Convention for the Conservation of Antarctic Marine Living Resources (1980)

The expanding catch of krill and overfishing of sub-Antarctic fish are of most current concern and present the most important conservation problems. Krill is a high seas resource and so lies currently outside national jurisdiction. It probably constitutes the world's largest single remaining unexploited marine living resource, and annual sustainable catches by man equivalent to at least the total world fish and shellfish catch, and possibly double this, have been suggested. Any significant commercial catch would affect other krill consumers. The main problem for the scientists, if exploitation continues, is to determine permissible catches of krill by regions, so as to maintain a reasonable ecological balance in the system. However, the closely linked interactions between the various resources are an important consideration, and it is no longer sufficient to consider krill and its vertebrate consumers as a series of separate resources. There is a growing appreciation that management strategy has to be based on knowledge of the effects of simultaneous exploitation of different members of the food web at varying levels. In each geographical region, for example, what is the level of the krill harvest at which the recovery of the whale stocks would be halted or reversed? At what level will the bird and seal populations begin to be affected? What are the best strategies for conservation or for sustainable exploitation, or what compromises should be adopted? The scientific and management problems are daunting. Traditionally, fisheries management has been concerned with separate species and ecological interactions between species or groups have tended to be ignored. A whole new multi-resource management theory and strategy needs to be developed if a huge ecological disaster is to be avoided.

Following the example of the Convention for the Conservation of Antarctic Seals, a Convention for the Conservation of Antarctic Marine Living Resources (CCAMLR) was concluded in 1980 and came into force in 1982; it covers those groups not included in the International Whaling Convention, the Seal Convention and the 'Agreed Measures'. The text of the Convention for the Conservation of Antarctic Marine Living Resources is published in Auburn (1982) and a full commentary has been provided by Edwards & Heap (1981). A brief summary follows.

The objective of the convention is the conservation (including rational use) of all Antarctic marine living resources and this was essential if the Antarctic marine ecosystem was to be conserved as a whole. For this reason the Convention applies for all practical purposes to waters south of the Antarctic Convergence, to which the boundary of the convention area approximates. Any harvesting and associated activities in the area are to be conducted in accordance with stated conservation principles. These are that no harvested population should be allowed to decrease to levels below those which ensure its stable recruitment, a level which is further defined; that ecological relationships between harvested, dependent and related populations should be maintained and depleted populations restored to the levels defined above; that prevention of changes or minimization of the risk of changes that are not potentially reversible in a few decades should be a requirement.

A Commission for CCAMLR and a Scientific Committee have been established. The stated function of the Commission is very comprehensive. It is to facilitate research; to compile data on status and changes in populations and on factors influencing population distribution, abundance and productivity; to acquire catch and effort data; to analyse, disseminate and publish information and the reports of the Scientific Committee; to identify conservation measures and analyse their effectiveness; and to implement a system of observation and inspection. The Conservation measures will be those considered necessary to conserve harvested populations and other components of the ecosystem, including: the setting up of catch quotas, by regions and sub-regions; the definition of protected species; the determination of size, age, and sex of species to be harvested; the declaration of open and closed seasons; the establishment of open and closed areas; and the regulation of fishing effort and methods of harvesting. It is required to take full account of the recommendations and advice of the Scientific Committee. The functions of the Scientific Committee cover advice on achieving the objectives and on scientific aspects of all these matters and the formulation of relevant research programmes.

Like the Agreed Measures, Antarctic Treaty recommendations, and the

Seal Convention, the CCAMLR is unusual in making conservation arrangements before the commercial activities with which it is concerned have had a significant effect. The approach based on the need to protect the integrity of the Antarctic marine ecosystem is unique in international conservation arrangements and the broadly based membership of this convention which spans the full spectrum of support for protection, conservation, and for unbridled exploitation is probably also unique. It is still too early to say whether it will be successful.

International scientific co-operation

Historically, the Antarctic has been neglected in comparison with other parts of the Earth and so it is not surprising that research activities are still developing, that applied research is not yet significant, and that many activities are still exploratory. A strong case can be made for investing in the acquisition of relevant knowledge. The increasing pace of developments means that the Antarctic is coming under increasing pressures and a minerals regime is under discussion by the Treaty powers. The next steps involve not only the Antarctic Treaty Governments, but many international organizations. These include SCAR, SCOR, ICSU, IUCN, the United Nations (IOC, FAO, UNEP, UNDP), IWC, CCAMLR, and the Law of the Sea Convention.

The Scientific Committee for Antarctic Research (SCAR) of the International Council of Scientific Unions (ICSU) has a key role. The SCAR Working Group on Biology and its sub-Committee on Conservation have general responsibilities and a recent published statement outlines the need for research, care, and protection of the environment and priorities for biological programmes in the Antarctic (Laws 1984*b*). Two Groups of Specialists, developed from Working Group on Biology sub-Committees, have specific responsibilities. First, the Group of Specialists on Seals promotes seal research and advises on matters related to the Convention for the Conservation of Antarctic Seals. Secondly, in response to the Antarctic Treaty Governments and IOC, SCAR set up a Group of Specialists on the Living Resources of the Southern Ocean in 1972 which was later co-sponsored by the Scientific Committee on Oceanographic Research (SCOR). Its remit was to assess present knowledge of the Antarctic marine ecosystem, to encourage and stimulate investigations, to advise SCAR and SCOR and to liaise with and advise other international organizations. These activities led to the development of a comprehensive research programme of Biological Investigations of Marine Antarctic Systems and Stocks (BIOMASS). The principal objective of BIOMASS is to gain a deeper understanding of the structure and dynamic functioning of the Antarctic marine ecosystems as a basis for future rational management of the potential living resources (El Sayed

1977). It is the first major international effort to co-ordinate present and future research for this purpose. Comprehensive proposals cover research on the environment, seaweeds, benthic invertebrates, krill, squid, fishes, birds, and marine mammals, with recommendations for international co-ordination and co-operation, and the provision of scientific advice for management. In 1980–81 a First BIOMASS Experiment (FIBEX) was mounted involving intensive co-operative multi-ship operations by 10 nations, probably the largest single project in biological oceanography. It included acoustic and net haul surveys (by 11 research ships) of the krill abundance in the South Atlantic and Indian Ocean sectors, which suggested a total krill standing stock biomass of 650 million tonnes for the Southern Ocean. During 1983–85 a Second BIOMASS Experiment (SIBEX) has taken place. Meanwhile the Commission and Scientific Committee of CCAMLR have held three annual meetings and are seeking advice from BIOMASS.

Conclusion

The Antarctic land and inland water ecosystems are very limited in area and have sparse, species-poor animal populations. So far there are no serious conservation problems and the Agreed Measures under the Antarctic Treaty appear to be working well. Environmental impacts are in general limited to the vicinity of scientific stations which are small and relatively few in number. This could change if mineral exploration and exploitation develop, but in the current discussions of a minerals regime environmental concerns are included.

The vast Southern Ocean is a relatively simple circumpolar system of water masses, convergences and divergences, in which the Antarctic Convergence forms a physical boundary between Antarctic and sub-Antarctic life forms. The relatively long-lived and hugely abundant Antarctic krill is an essential staple food for the large populations of squid, fish, birds, seals, and whales. Some mechanisms promoting their ecological separation have been identified, but this separation is not complete and the krill predators compete and interact. The decline of the great whales due to overhunting this century has caused a major perturbation of the southern ecosystems and other krill consumers are still in the process of adjusting to this enormous competitive release. In recent decades man has overfished the demersal fish stocks and has begun to turn his attention to the krill resource. Fortunately, the potential for ecological disaster on a grand scale has been appreciated by governments and several far-sighted international conservation agreements, incorporating new conservation principles, have been concluded among 32 nations. It is still too early to say how successful they will be, but an essential ingredient for success is the acquisition of relevant knowledge of the ecological interactions by means of well-designed national and international research programmes.

The history of whaling has demonstrated the dangers of allowing a competitive industry to develop and invest capital without international agreements. The Seal Convention was probably unique in setting up adequate safeguards in advance of the development of a fishery, but krill and fish exploitation has already begun in the Antarctic and seems poised to expand rapidly. Let us hope that CCAMLR will be effective, if the priceless Antarctic marine ecosystem, still on the whole little affected by human impact, is to be conserved, with its unique and diverse forms of life.

References

Allen, K.R. (1980). *Conservation and management of whales*. Butterworths, London.

Auburn, F.M. (1982). *Antarctic law and politics*. C. Hurst & Co., London.

Bengtson, J.L. & Laws, R.M. (1985). Trends in crabeater seal age at maturity: an insight into Antarctic marine interactions? In *Nutrient cycles and food chains*: 669–75. Siegfried, W.R., Condy, P.R. & Laws, R.M. (Eds). Springer-Verlag, Berlin.

Block, W. (1984). Terrestrial microbiology, invertebrates and ecosystems. In *Antarctic ecology* 1: 163–236. Laws, R.M. (Ed.). Academic Press, London.

Bonner, W.N. (1984a). Introduced mammals. In *Antarctic ecology* 1: 237–78. Laws, R.M. (Ed.). Academic Press, London.

Bonner, W.N. (1984b). Conservation in the Antarctic. In *Antarctic ecology* 2: 821–50. Laws, R.M. (Ed.). Academic Press, London.

Brown, S.G. & Lockyer, C.H. (1984). Whales. In *Antarctic ecology* 2: 717–81. Laws, R.M. (Ed.). Academic Press, London.

Burn, A.J. (1982). A cautionary tale—two recent introductions to the maritime Antarctic. In *Colloque sur les écosystèmes subantarctiques, 1981, Paimpont*: 521. Jouventin, P., Massé, L. & Trehen, P. (Eds). Comité National Français des Recherches Antarctiques, Paris.

Clarke, M.R. (1983). Cephalopod biomass—estimation from predation. *Mem. nat. Mus. Victoria* No. 44: 95–107.

Croxall, J.P. (1984). Seabirds. In *Antarctic ecology* 2: 533–619. Laws, R.M. (Ed.). Academic Press, London.

Croxall, J.P. & Prince, P.A. (1979). Antarctic seabird and seal monitoring studies. *Polar Rec.* 19: 573–95.

Edwards, D.M. & Heap, J.A. (1981). Convention on the conservation of Antarctic marine living resources: a commentary. *Polar Rec.* 20: 353–62.

El Sayed, S.Z. (Ed.) (1977). *Biological investigations of marine Antarctic systems and stocks*. 1: *Research proposals*. Scientific Committee on Antarctic Research, Cambridge.

Everson, I. (1977) *The living resources of the Southern Ocean*. Food and Agriculture Organisation of the United Nations, United Nations Development Programme (Southern Ocean Fisheries Survey Programme GLO/SO/77/1.), Rome.

Everson, I. (1984a). Zooplankton. In *Antarctic ecology* 2: 464–90. Laws, R.M. (Ed.). Academic Press, London.

Everson, I. (1984*b*). Fish biology. In *Antarctic ecology* 2: 491–532. Laws, R.M. (Ed.). Academic Press, London.

Foster, T.D. (1984). The marine environment. In *Antarctic ecology* 2: 345–71. Laws, R.M. (Ed.). Academic Press, London.

Gambell, R. (1976). Population biology and the management of whales. In *Applied biology* 1: 247–343. Coaker, T.H. (Ed.). Academic Press, New York.

Heywood, R.B. (1977*a*). Antarctic freshwater ecosystems: review and synthesis. In *Adaptations within Antarctic ecosystems*: 801–28. Llano, G.A. (Ed.). Smithsonian Institution, Washington D.C.

Heywood, R.B. (1977*b*). A limnological survey of the Ablation Point area, Alexander Island, Antarctica. *Phil. Trans. R. Soc.* (B) **279**: 39–54.

Heywood, R.B. (1984). Antarctic inland waters. In *Antarctic ecology* 1: 279–344. Laws, R.M. (Ed.). Academic Press, London.

Heywood, R.B., Dartnall, H.J.G. & Priddle, J. (1980). Characteristics and classification of the lakes of Signy Island, South Orkney Islands, Antarctica. *Freshw. Biol.* **10**: 47–59.

Laws, R.M. (1975). SCAR Group of Specialists on Seals. *Polar Rec.* **17**: 451–4.

Laws, R.M. (1976). SCAR Group of Specialists on Seals. *Polar Rec.* **18**: 317–8.

Laws, R.M. (1977). Seals and whales in the Southern Ocean. *Phil. Trans. R. Soc.* (B) **279**: 81–96.

Laws, R.M. (1984*a*). Seals. In *Antarctic ecology* 2: 621–715. Laws, R.M. (Ed.). Academic Press, London.

Laws, R.M. (Ed.) (1984*b*). Biological research in the Antarctic. *Polar Rec.* **22**: 221–6.

Laws, R.M. (1984*c*). SCAR Group of Specialists on Seals. *Polar Rec.* **22**: 242–5.

Laws, R.M. & Christie, E.C. (1980). Seals and birds killed or captured in the Antarctic Treaty area, 1973–75. *Polar Rec.* **20**: 195–8.

Leader-Williams, N. (1980). *Ecology of introduced reindeer on South Georgia.* PhD. thesis: University of Cambridge.

Mackintosh, N.A. (1973). Distribution of post-larval krill in the Antarctic. *Discovery Rep.* **36**: 95–156.

Mitchell, B. & Sandbrook, R. (1980). *The management of the Southern Ocean.* International Institute for Environment and Development, London.

Oritsland, T. (1970). Sealing and seal research in the South-west Atlantic pack ice, September–October, 1964. In *Antarctic ecology* 1: 367–76. Holdgate, M.W. (Ed.). Academic Press, London.

Siegfried, W.R., Condy, P. & Laws, R.M. (Eds) (1985). *Antarctic nutrient cycles and food webs.* (Proc. Fourth SCAR Symp. Antarctic Biol.) Springer-Verlag, Berlin.

Smith, R.I.L. (1984). Terrestrial plant biology of the sub-Antarctic and Antarctic. In *Antarctic ecology* 1: 61–162. Laws, R.M. (Ed.). Academic Press, London.

Van Aarde, R.J. & Skinner, J.D. (1982). The feral cat population at Marion Island: characteristics, colonization and control. In *Colloque sur les écosystèmes subantarctiques, 1981, Paimpont*: 281–8. Jouventin, P., Massé, L. & Trehen, P. (Eds). Comité National Français des Recherches Antarctiques, Paris.

Symp. zool. Soc. Lond. (1985) No. 54: 25–46

Wildlife management in practice : conservation of ungulates through protection or utilization

J. D. SKINNER

Mammal Research Institute
University of Pretoria
Pretoria 0002
South Africa.

Synopsis

The early history of conservation through protection of square-lipped and hook-lipped rhinoceroses, Cape mountain zebras, sable and roan antelope, bontebok, tsessebe and black wildebeest is discussed. Results of research and management in re-establishing these species are considered and details are given of their present status and life histories. On the other hand, the role of utilization for promoting conservation of ungulates is described using blesbok, springbok, impala, kudus, eland and giraffes as examples. Considerable progress has been made with research on farming with game. Results are discussed in the context of increasing productivity per hectare. The status and life histories of these six species farmed are also tabulated.

Introduction

Game conservation has been recognized for the past two and half decades as a profitable field for scientific research. This has been fortunate indeed, particularly in southern Africa where several animal species have faced extinction. It is only since the advent of research followed by effective management that populations have increased. This chapter will first reflect on the measures taken to guarantee the survival of selected threatened species, some of the research that followed, and the management measures implemented. Secondly, it will discuss the role that game farming has played in the conservation of some of the more plentiful ungulate species in South Africa.

There is no doubt that individuals and small groups of farmers were, in the first instance, responsible for conserving certain ungulates. South Africa seemed characterized by the wanton destruction of game. From the middle of the 19th century, trade in game skins provided an important source of revenue. In 1866, for example, one firm in the central Orange Free State exported 157 000 wildebeest and blesbok skins. Similarly in 1870/71 nearly half a million blesbok, wildebeest and zebra skins were exported from Dur-

ZOOLOGICAL SYMPOSIUM No. 54
ISBN 0–19–854002–7

ban. The eastern Orange Free State is still referred to as 'Riemland' ('Rawhide-thong-land') (Von Richter 1971a). This unchecked exploitation drastically reduced the great herds of plains ungulates.

The endemic blue antelope *Hippotragus leucophaeus* was last recorded before 1800 and it was thus the first African antelope to be recorded as extinct (Klein 1974). Immense herds of quaggas (*Equus quagga*) recorded south of the Vaal River by Harris in 1837 (Harris, 1838) survived in the Orange Free State until about 1878 (Flower & Lydekker 1891, in Skead 1980), then became extinct. Lichtenstein's hartebeest *Alcelaphus lichtensteini* also became extinct in South Africa, and seems to be endangered elsewhere in Africa as a result of drought and poaching. The first report in 1895 by the game warden H. F. Van Oordt, of the Pongola Game Reserve, mentions both hartebeest and tsessebe (Pringle 1982). As he recognized the difference, this must have been Lichtenstein's hartebeest since the area is ecologically unsuitable for the red hartebeest *A. buselaphus*.

Other species have faced some critical periods. In the Cape Province the distributional range of African elephants *Loxodonta africana* has shrunk from the time they were first reported at Mossel Bay by Vasco da Gama in 1497 to their present situation with a small herd in the Addo Elephant Park and only three individuals in the Knysna forest (Skead, 1980). On the other hand, in the Kruger National Park elephants are cropped annually following strict guidelines set down by scientists to maintain populations at manageable levels to conserve all the fauna and flora in the Park. Indeed, this approach to management through utilization of such elephant populations in restricted areas was outlined by Laws (1968) and will not therefore be discussed again here.

Ungulates were conserved by farmers in small isolated pockets and these tiny sanctuaries were scattered throughout the country. Later it was recognized that the concentration of the surviving members of a species in itself posed a threat to their future survival. Such a population could easily be wiped out by an epizootic or other natural catastrophe. Strenuous efforts were therefore directed at both breeding and defining habitat requirements so that individuals could be relocated to other state sanctuaries and privately owned nature reserves to reduce this risk.

Game animals, although regarded as an important source of food, had little commercial value during the early part of this century. Trophy hunting was a pastime that everybody could enjoy and farmers gave little thought to the conservation of their game, which by law was the property of the State until shot. Conservation departments only came into existence in the late 1940s and early 1950s and hunting permits were issued at a nominal fee. Game still existed in the remote inaccessible areas where it was difficult to apply the law. The profitability of farming game had also never reached a level comparable to that achieved by conventional animal husbandry (D. M.

Joubert 1968). As a result there was a general decline in the numbers and distribution of ungulates until the early 1960s. It was then, through the activities of nature conservers and scientists, that the attention of farmers at large was focused on the possibility of exploiting this natural resource.

Proposals to examine the possibility of domesticating indigenous wild ruminants were made as early as 1848 by Methuen. However, domestication is the bringing of an animal species into subjection to or dependence on man over extended periods. The only two species of African animals which, to the present author's knowledge, have been domesticated are the guinea fowl *Numidia meleagris* and the ostrich *Struthio camelus*.

Nevertheless, by 1950, two antelope species, the springbok *Antidorcas marsupialis* and the blesbok *Damaliscus dorcas phillipsi*, were no longer regarded as strictly feral. This was because farmers could exercise ownership by enclosing them in paddocks used for enclosing domestic stock. In addition, in the 1960s farmers began to enclose certain species of browsers using 2.3 m high fencing.

Despite resistance from those with vested interests in conventional agriculture, game farming has made inroads into all the more extensive farming areas in South Africa. This has been encouraged by the provincial nature conservancies, who allow farmers to exercise ownership of the game on their farms provided fencing conforms to certain standards. A major stimulus, however, has been the enormous increase in the intrinsic value of game for venison production, trophy hunting or even aesthetic purposes. The situation will be discussed (pp. 36–40) with respect to the farming of the five most prominent bovid species plus the giraffe *Giraffa camelopardalis* which, because of the niche it occupies and its temperament, could be a prime species for 'domestication' in the future.

Conservation of endangered species

The glamour of the big game of Africa is exemplified by the so-called 'big five' of which the rhinoceros has always been a prominent member. The glamour of conservation is best epitomized in the saga of saving the square-lipped rhinoceros *Ceratotherium simum* in South Africa from extinction. This species probably came closest to joining the other extinct species in South Africa. Renshaw (1904, in Smithers 1983) recorded that at the turn of the century there were only about 10 rhinoceroses alive in Natal and in 1916 F. Vaughn-Kirby, the first ranger appointed in Natal, estimated that there were 30 to 40 actually resident in the Umfolozi Game Reserve, with a few others living close to its boundaries (Pringle, 1982). In 1930 estimates were put at 100 inside the Reserve and some 38 outside. By 1960 an aerial count gave a total of just over 700. Since then numbers in the Hluhluwe/ Umfolozi Game Reserve Complex have more than doubled and some 2800

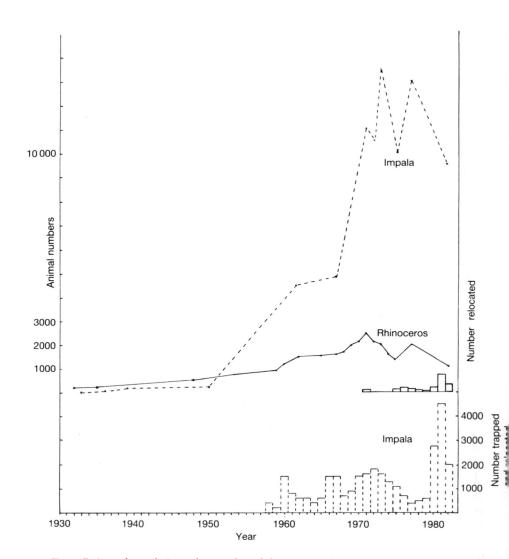

Fig. 1 Estimated populations of square-lipped rhinoceros and impala in the Hluhluwe–Umfo-lozi Game Reserve over the period 1929–82 and numbers removed annually (adapted from Brooks & MacDonald 1983).

white rhinoceroses have been relocated (see Fig. 1) (Brooks & MacDonald 1983; D. Rowe-Rowe pers. comm.).

The habitat requirements of square-lipped rhinoceroses were established at an early stage, some years before their relocation (Player & Feely 1960). They are grazers and have a marked preference for short grass; surface water is important for drinking and wallowing and there should be adequate bush cover for shade on relatively flat terrain. Bulls are territorial, and their habits have been studied in detail by Owen-Smith (1973).

The hook-lipped rhinoceros *Diceros bicornis* is somewhat smaller. Although these animals occurred on the slopes of Table Mountain in 1652 and were widespread throughout the country, they became extinct in 1853 in the Cape and 10 years earlier in the Orange Free State (Smithers 1983). In the Transvaal, the last of the species, a solitary female, was seen in the Kruger National Park in 1936 (Penzhorn 1971). They were saved from extinction by the proclamation of the Natal Game Reserves. Numbers in Natal have increased (Table I) and some 100 individuals have been relocated to other sanctuaries since 1952. An interesting translocation was that of seven hook-lipped rhinoceroses in 1961/62 from the Kenya Game Department to the Addo Elephant National Park (Penzhorn 1971). These represent the subspecies *D. b. michaeli* and, with the species now endangered in Kenya, effective steps have been taken to ensure the short-term genetic conservation of the Addo rhinoceroses which now number 16 (A. J. Hall-Martin, pers. comm.).

Table I. Approximate numbers of eight species of 'endangered' ungulates including the two rhinoceros species on national parks and provincial nature reserves in South Africa.

	Transvaal	Cape Province	Natal	Orange Free State	Total 1984
Bontebok	—	2000	—	—	2000
Tsessebe	1304	—	—	—	1304
Black wildebeest	1532	190	300	2176	4098
Roan antelope	460	—	—	—	460
Sable antelope	3348	—	—	5	3353
Cape mountain zebra	—	335	—		335
Square-lipped rhinoceros	201	—	1540	82	2423
Hook-lipped rhinoceros	106	16	455		577

Compiled from information provided by the relevant authority in April 1984.

The hook-lipped rhinoceros is a browser and requires adequate shrubs and young trees up to a height of 4.0 m (Hitchins 1968); it is dependent on surface water, and is apparently not territorial. Management of hook-lipped rhinoceros populations is increasingly viewed in an international context (Hitchins & Anderson 1983). Populations in South Africa may be the only secure ones left and should therefore be managed for maximum sustained yield with the harvestable surplus being used to establish other nuclei within the distributional range of *D. bicornis minor* in southern Africa.

Hitchins & Anderson (1983) indicate that Natal hook-lipped rhinoceros populations respond differently to different climatic cycles. During dry cycles maturation in scrub species cannot be halted, less food is available, and the rhinoceros population tends to decrease owing to a decrease in the recruitment rate. In management, there are two alternatives: the decline can be allowed or it can be pre-empted and the population reduced to levels which the changed habitat conditions can sustain. Using the latter approach 'surplus' rhinoceroses can be relocated to further conserve the species.

The Cape mountain zebras *Equus zebra zebra* are endemic to South Africa. Historically they occurred throughout the Cape mountainous areas as far north as the Suurberg and Stormberg, but by 1936 they were almost extinct, only 50 individuals occurring in one or two inaccessible mountainous areas (Pringle 1982). In 1937, the Mountain Zebra National Park was proclaimed, containing five stallions and one mare. By 1945 only two stallions and a mare remained. The mare died and the two stallions were shot before 1950, when five stallions and six mares from a neighbouring farm were introduced (Penzhorn 1984). This nucleus proved sufficient for the survival of the population, which has increased to 235 zebras, a further 35 having been relocated to other sanctuaries in the Cape Province, where they have increased. The total number of mountain zebra is listed in Table 1.

The ecology of these zebras has been extensively studied in their habitat by Penzhorn (1982*a*,*b* 1984). They are predominantly grazers. Herds usually average five individuals and remain stable for up to 15 years.

The sable antelope *Hippotragus niger* is a stately species. The type specimen was collected by Captain W. Cornwallis Harris in the Magaliesberg west of Pretoria, where the Transvaal Division of Nature Conservation reintroduced them in 1967. The southernmost limit seems to have been the Crocodile River (Pienaar 1963) which is today the southern boundary of the Kruger National Park. Their range in South Africa is much reduced and confined to the savanna woodland in the eastern and northern Transvaal where they are dependent on cover and drinking water.

Outside the Kruger Park with its inherent restrictions as an endemic foot-and-mouth disease area, the Hans Merensky Nature Reserve was the only state reserve supporting natural populations of sable antelope at the time of its acquisition in 1950. Utilizing these sable antelope the Transvaal Division of Nature Conservation has at various times established new breeding herds on Loskop Dam, Percy Fyfe and Rustenburg Nature Reserves, where their

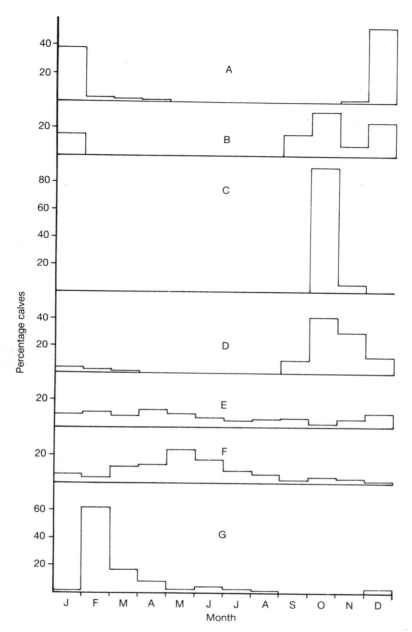

Fig. 2 Calving seasons of five former endangered ungulate species in the Transvaal, South Africa. A, black wildebeest, 408 births at S.A. Lombard Nature Reserve (from Skinner, van Zyl *et al.* 1974); B, bontebok, 96 births in the National Zoological Gardens (from Brand 1963); C, tsessebe, 45 births at P. W. Willis Private Nature Reserve (from Garstang 1982); D, tsessebe, 412 births at Percy Fyfe Nature Reserve from 1966–84; E, roan antelope, 151 births in the Kruger National Park (from S. C. J. Joubert 1976); F, roan antelope, 164 births in the Percy Fyfe Nature Reserve from 1966–84 (P. le S. Milstein, pers. comm.); G, sable antelope, 82 births in the Percy Fyfe Nature Reserve from 1968–84.

population dynamics, habitat and nutritional requirements have been studied (Wilson 1975).

The population in the Hans Merensky Reserve numbered only 30 in 1966 and increased to over 100 by 1975. This increase was due also to the release of 27 sable antelope into the area. The 11 sable antelope introduced between 1955 and 1958 into the Loskop Dam Nature Reserve increased to 53 animals by 1975. After the establishment of the seven sable antelopes at Percy Fyfe Nature Reserve in 1966, numbers increased to 26 until 1974, when 10 juvenile deaths were recorded. Sable antelope introduced to the Rustenburg Nature Reserve in 1967 numbered 10 in 1972 and increased to 27 by 1975. The calving season at Percy Fyfe Nature Reserve is illustrated in Fig. 2. Present total numbers are given in Table I.

Wilson (1975) suggested that the habitat of these reserves was marginal at best and that nutritional deficiencies were widespread. Deaths of juvenile sable and roan antelopes from protozoal parasite infection (*Cytauxzoon* sp., *Babesia* sp., and *Pneumocystis carinii*) or rickettsia (*Chlamydia*) were significantly related to body condition. In addition, competition with other grazers (zebra *E. burchelli*, waterbuck *Kobus ellipsiprymnus* and impala *Aepyceros melampus*) contributed to nutritional stress placed on sable antelope at Percy Fyfe. Furthermore, the considerable interspecific aggression displayed by sable and roan antelope may be an evolutionary adaptation to ensure sufficient range of good quality for each herd. In the absence of adequate space young sexually maturing males of two to three years are killed by the herd bull. Populations are maintained at levels where the maximum number of animals can be harvested.

The roan antelope *Hippotragus equinus equinus* is the second largest antelope in southern Africa. The species is widely distributed in Africa, but in South Africa it has reached the southernmost tip of its distributional range. In 1809 it occurred as far south as the Kuruman river (Shortridge 1934) but since then has been steadily exterminated throughout its range.

The Kruger National Park has long been considered the most important conservation area in South Africa for roan antelope, although even here they were thought to have been exterminated within the Park at the turn of the century (S. C. J. Joubert 1970). Nevertheless, they re-established themselves within the Park and by 1912 their numbers were estimated at 450. Then changes in the southern boundaries of the Park in 1923 removed some of their prime habitat. Despite this, numbers fluctuated around 400–500 until 1955 (S. C. J. Joubert 1970). Expansion of the population was probably restricted by their sensitivity to habitat changes. For example, they do not tolerate woodland where trees form a closed canopy or thickets (S. C. J. Joubert 1976).

Roan antelope are also particularly sensitive to anthrax and, since 1959, three documented epizootics (in 1959, 1960, 1970) have accounted for 83

known deaths in the Park, where foot-and-mouth disease is also endemic, preventing relocation of animals from this population to areas outside the Park. Deaths from anthrax since 1971 have been successfully contained by effective inoculation. A method was developed using a disposable projectile syringe from which a virulent spore vaccine, developed in South Africa (Sterne 1939, 1946) is administered and the antelope marked for later identification (De Vos, van Rooyen & Kloppers 1973). Despite these measures the population continued to fluctuate around 250 for two decades, but has increased to 336 in the last few years. Attempting to increase population size further in the Kruger Park would require habitat manipulation and open grassland areas have been created on an experimental basis in an attempt to achieve this.

A small population of roan antelope estimated at no more than 50 animals also persisted, despite great odds, until 1968 in an inaccessible area of the Waterberg in the Transvaal. At that time 16 animals were translocated by the Division of Nature Conservation to the Percy Fyfe Nature Reserve where they became established. A few of the Waterberg roan antelope still survive, most enclosed in the Hans Strydom Nature Reserve with a dozen on the adjoining farm (P. le S. Milstein, pers. comm.).

Roan antelope breed throughout the year (Fig. 2) which enables any population to make a rapid recovery under favourable conditions. This has been the case at the Percy Fyfe Nature Reserve where after tick toxicosis had been identified as responsible for calf mortality (Wilson 1975), the population recovered, which allowed for further introductions at Doorndraai Dam and Nylsvley Nature Reserves.

The bontebok *Damaliscus dorcas dorcas* was preserved for posterity by the action of a few farmers in the Bredasdorp district in about 1840 when 27 were enclosed on the farm Nacht Wacht. After 80 years these had increased to 180 (Fitzsimons 1919/1920). The example at Nacht Wacht was soon followed on an adjoining farm, Zeekoe Vley, but no record was kept of numbers conserved. Prior to 1920 the number of bontebok was about 300. Although previously thought to be a separate species from the blesbok, today both are considered as subspecies of *D. dorcas*.

As was the case with the extinct blue buck, bontebok were confined to an area in the winter rainfall region in the south-western Cape Province lying between Bredasdorp and Cape Agulhas (Bigalke 1955). Bontebok are almost exclusively a grazing species, and areas of short grass cover and adequate drinking water are among their essential habitat requirements (David 1973). Like the blesbok, bontebok rams hold territories (David 1975), ewes moving from one territory to the next during the breeding season in autumn (Table II).

In 1931, the first Bontebok National Park was proclaimed and 22 bontebok were relocated in the Park. The area was, however, unsuitable,

Table II. Some life history features of eight former endangered ungulate species in South Africa

Species		Mature weight (kg)	Age when first breeding (months)	Breeding season	Gestation length (days)	Time of parturition
Roan antelope	♀		(10)34.1±3.04 ♀	All year	(7)278.9±6.23	All year
	♂	270	33 ♂			
Sable antelope	♀			Mid-winter	(7)242.9±2.61	Late summe
	♂	240	16–19 ♂			
Black wildebeest	♀			Autumn	±275	Mid-summe
	♂	180				
Tsessebe			15 ♀	Late summer	238.0±4.24	Early summ
	♂	155	24 ♂	Feb–March		Mid-Sept. t Mid-Nov
Bontebok	♀			Autumn	±225	Early summ
	♂	61				
Cape mountain zebra			26 ♀	All year	±365	All year
	♂	250	60 ♂			
Square-lipped rhinoceros	♂	2300		All year	±480	All year
Hook-lipped rhinoceros	♀	884	60 ♀	All year	±450	All year
	♂	855	84 ♂			

overgrazed and copper deficient, and by 1960 the number had increased only to 84, which exceeded the carrying capacity. These animals were all then relocated to a more suitable larger habitat, where their numbers had risen to 320 by 1981. Since 1969 surplus stock have been made available to farmers and have been established on Cape Provincial Nature Reserves. This has resulted in a steady increase in total numbers (Table I) but they still remain among the least common of South African antelopes.

The tsessebe *Damaliscus lunatus lunatus* was previously distributed in South Africa as far south as the Tugela river in Natal and into the the north-west Cape as far as Kuruman (Burchell, 1824). Today its range has shrunk considerably and, apart from the Kruger National Park and adjacent private nature reserves, only two relic natural populations remained by 1973—a relatively dense population near Klaserie in the Transvaal Low-veld and a few scattered herds on farms in relatively inaccessible areas in the Water-berg (Garstang 1982). In 1965/1966, five males and 10 females were intro-duced to the Percy Fyfe and Hans Merensky Provincial Nature Reserves in the Transvaal. For the first 10 years, management was on an *ad hoc* basis. Studies in the mid-1970s by Garstang (1982) and S. C. J. Joubert (1974) indicated that tsessebe are highly dependent on open surface water within a physically open savanna habitat type, and that bush encroachment has accounted for reductions in the species' range and numbers. By means of

Birth weight (kg) ♂ ♀	Percentage of mature females calving annually	Calving interval (days)	Theoretical maximum productivity (offspring)	Age when last breeding (years)	Source
—	100	(23)318.8±17.74	15.80 based on 33 months first parturition and calving interval 317 days	14	S.C.J. Joubert (1970), Dittrich (1972), Flower (1931), Huntley (1971), S.C.J. Joubert (1976)
—	100	365	—	17	Flower (1931), Wilson (1975)
—	—	365	—	—	Skinner, van Zyl et al. (1974)
—	100	365	—	—	Huntley (1972), S.C.J. Joubert (1974), Garstang (1982)
—	—	365	—	—	David (1975), Brand (1963), Skinner, Dott, de Vos & Millar (1980)
—	32	810	7	21	B.L. Penzhorn (pers. comm.)
40 —	—	—	—	—	Owen-Smith (1973)
40 —	—	240–2670	—	—	Hitchins & Anderson (1983)

mechanical clearing, a physiognomic habitat type can be created from general woodland, taking care to leave vegetation screens for shelter and tree canopies for shade (Garstang 1982). Artificially created water supplies should be carefully camouflaged to resemble those on riverine woodland contour seeplines. On this basis a total of 328 tsessebe have now been successfully re-established at eight different localities in the Transvaal and one in Natal.

Tsessebe mate in late summer, lambing eight months later. Amongst the alcelaphines they are unique in that territorial males keep harems. Such a strategy has two disadvantages in practice. First, if the territorial male is infertile then his attendant females will not lamb. Secondly, when confined, too many attendant peripheral males interfere with breeding by constant challenging, causing a decline in the lamb crop. The lambing season for tsessebe under confined conditions tends to be longer than under natural conditions (Fig. 2).

The black wildebeest Connochaetes gnou is endemic to South Africa and in the past was confined to the open central plains. Once plentiful, by the turn of the century the species had nearly become extinct. About 600 black wildebeest remained in the Orange Free State and on one farm in the southern Transvaal by 1900, extinction only being prevented by the action of a few farmers. Restocking of nature reserves and private farms has taken place from this original nucleus over the last 60 years. As a result numbers have increased steadily and today the species is no longer endangered (Table I). In the Transvaal there were only 46 black wildebeest left in 1947 (Bigalke 1947) some of which in 1949 formed the breeding herd at the S. A. Lombard Nature Reserve. They have bred extremely successfully, and many of these have been relocated to farms in the Transvaal. In 1979 there were 1532 black wildebeest distributed amongst 75 herds, as compared with 550 animals in 39 herds nine years earlier (Fabricius & Oates, in press).

Black wildebeest are predominantly grazers, preferring short grass, and tend to remain in the same area for prolonged periods, thereby maintaining grazing pressure on the grass. Like many plains ungulates, black wildebeest in the past migrated in search of better grazing and water when climatic conditions required (Von Richter 1971a,b,c). Now that they are enclosed, no migration can take place if the condition of the veld deteriorates. This can eventually lead to overgrazing and to problems in conserving the grass cover.

Black wildebeest mate in autumn and, following a gestation period of eight and a half months, calve after the onset of the spring rains (Fig. 2; Table II) thus ensuring an adequate supply of green grass for the lactating cows (Skinner, Van Zyl & Ostes 1974). Breeding bulls are territorial, cows moving from one territory to the next. If a territorial male is denied contact with competitors, it may expend frustrated energy chasing and fighting females and calves causing mortality and lowering calving rates. Breeding herds containing less than 20 animals are seldom successful (Fabricius & Oates, in press). *C. gnou* are known to hybridize with the blue wildebeest *C. taurinus*. With relocations of both species in recent years this could prove a threat to their survival.

Conservation of species through game farming

The status of the six species of ungulates to be dealt with is given for 1973 in Table III. No estimates have been published since that time although it

Table III. Approximate numbers in 1973 of six species of ungulates used for game farming in South Africa.

Species	Approximate number
Blesbok	100 000
Springbok	275 000
Impala	350 000
Kudu	25 000
Eland	5 000
Giraffe	10 000

From Skinner (in press)

seems probable that there was a steady increase in numbers of ungulates until the severe drought of 1982–84 caused populations of all species to decline. This decline was documented in the Kruger Park where, for example, the estimated impala population decline was 23.2 per cent, that for kudu was of the order of 32.7 per cent, and that for giraffes 8.7 per cent.

Details of the life history of these species are provided in Table IV and further details for their management are provided in Skinner (1984).

Numbers have increased since the 1950s when the intrinsic value of game, both for meat production and for trophy hunting, began to rise. Unfortunately, details of population were not kept in the past, and even today estimation of such numbers is a major exercise. However, since the estimates published by Bigalke & Bateman (1962) and Kettlitz (1962), the increasing trend is apparent.

Numbers have increased largely in two regions: first, in regions unsuitable for domestic stock farming because of a high incidence of plants such as *Dicapetalum cymosum*, that are poisonous to and consumed by domestic stock; and secondly, in regions where surface drinking water is not readily available to domestic livestock. The adaptability of species such as springbok which can sustain themselves on succulent forage has long been known (Greenwald 1967).

Research has also indicated that browsing species either do not compete directly with domestic cattle and sheep (largely grazers) or compete only when the percentage lignin in grass is low (Hall-Martin 1975; Liversidge 1968; Owen-Smith, Cooper & Novellie 1983; Skinner, Monro & Zimmerman 1984). This has encouraged farmers to increase productivity of red meat per hectare by increasing the browsing species on their farms.

Available data on wild ruminants indicate that food intake in tropical regions is less than that of domestic ruminants of similar size (Rogerson 1968; Meissner & Hofmeyr 1972; Meissner 1976; Kay, Engelhardt & White 1979). Meissner (1982) approached the problem of equating wild ruminant and domestic ruminant livestock units using data published on growth, basal heat production, the efficiency of feed utilization for growth, and the nutritional niche of the species. These results were then compared with the so-called livestock unit (1 LU = one steer of two years old or six sheep, etc.). He calculated for five-year-old ungulates, for example, that a blesbok ewe or ram = 0.19 LU; a kudu cow = 0.39 LU; a kudu bull = 0.53 LU; an eland cow = 0.96 LU and an eland bull 1.19 LU.

Although for some parameters, such as milk production, wild ungulates can hardly compete with domestic livestock, it is conceded today that under the extensive range conditions pertaining in Africa they reproduce more efficiently, grow as fast, dress out at a higher percentage carcass, and yield a much higher percentage of red meat (Skinner, in press).

Although the orginal impetus for farming game arose from the thesis that

Table IV. Life history features of six prime species of ungulates used for game farming in South Africa.

Species	Mature weight (kg)	Age when first breeding (months)	Breeding season	Gestation length (days)	Time of parturition	Birth weight (kg) ♂	♀	Percentage of mature females calving annually	Calving interval (days)	Theoretical maximum productivity (offspring)	Age when last breeding (years)	Source
Blesbok	60 ♀ 70 ♂	18 ♀ ♂	Autumn	225	Early summer	7		85	365	13	15	Skinner (in press)
Springbok	37 ♀ 42 ♂	7 ♀ 12 ♂	All year	168	All year	3.2	3.4	46–100	—	24	13	Skinner, von La Chevallerie et al. (1971)
Impala	40 ♀ 55 ♂	18 ♀ ♂	Autumn	196	Mid-summer	5		90	365	13	15	Fairall (1983), Skinner (in press)
Kudu	160 ♀ 230 ♂	17 ♀	Mid-winter	212	Late summer		—	100	365	14	16	Skinner (in press)
Eland	450 ♀ 700 ♂	28 ♀	All year	271	All year	30.0	25.5	83	354.5	16.2	18	Skinner (1967)
Giraffe	828 ♀ 1190 ♂	56 ♀ ♂	All year	457	All year	95.1	89.0	48	645	10.18	23	Hall-Martin (1975)

wild ungulate species do not compete with one another for the available forage, it has been shown that there is an enormous niche overlap between species. Nevertheless, this concept has been applied in complementing domestic livestock with game. Impetus was also given to game farming by the belief that it would provide more red meat for an expanding indigenous population. This has been confounded by the demand from European gourmets and the need for an inflow of foreign currency in Africa. A third confounding factor is that farming game demands a high level of management expertise and success is only achieved where this demand is met (Fairall, in press).

The blesbok is endemic to South Africa and differs from the bontebok only in certain colour variations (Bigalke 1955). Blesbok were originally widespread, found throughout the grasslands in the Karoo, the Orange Free State, and the Transvaal as far as the Magaliesberg. Originally occurring in countless thousands, they were hunted to the point where they were seldom seen (Bryden, 1893).

Many farmers, however, conserved small herds for household use as they could be enclosed in paddocks and produced good quality meat (von La Chevallerie, 1972). Productive grazing antelope, they are today highly regarded as meat producers in the highland grasslands, dressing at 53.0 per cent, and are easily managed on a sustained yield basis. Since the 1950s numbers have increased steadily and they have been marketed in increasing numbers as the demand for and price of venison has increased (Skinner 1973). Details of their life history are provided in Table IV.

Springbok are more widespread throughout the sub-region, being found predominantly in the western arid half of southern Africa. The springbok treks were legendary (Cronwright-Schreiner 1925) and seem to have occurred largely in the north-western Cape Province in response to rainfall and consequent vegetation changes on the plains. Today these treks cannot occur because of farm fences.

The quality of springbok venison is unquestioned (Skinner, von La Chevallerie & van Zyl 1971). Moreover they are highly productive (Table IV) and are farmed extensively in combination with sheep in the Transvaal, Orange Free State and Karoo. Numbers are likely to increase even further as research into their complementary role as meat producers progresses.

The impala, *Aepyceros melampus*, is also highly regarded for game farming in the southern African woodland savanna. Its productivity has been the subject of intensive research in the past two decades (Fairall 1983; Fairall & Klein, in press; Skinner, Monro et al. 1984). Impala are selective feeders, requiring a high protein content in their diet, and are water-dependent. They graze as well as browse, but only compete with cattle to any marked degree in spring and early summer. Unlike springbok, they are seasonal breeders, lambing after the spring rains in summer. Even in game reserves they are highly productive and they frequently have to be cropped (Fig. 1) on a sustained-yield basis. Indeed, they can proliferate to such an extent that they pose problems for other species with which they compete (Melton 1978).

The kudu *Tragelaphus strepsiceros* was regarded as a reservoir for bovine tuberculosis in the eastern Cape Province and in the 1930s was the subject of intensive eradication campaigns (Thorburn & Thomas 1940). It is, however, now believed that they are very susceptible and infected by cattle. More recently they have been the cause of concern in a rabies epidemic in Namibia where many thousands were wiped out by this disease (Hassel 1982), but rabies has not occurred in kudu in South Africa. Bulls are highly regarded as trophy animals, trophies having become an important by-product of the game farming industry. Essentially browsers, they are distributed throughout the wooded savanna regions and are farmed extensively on cattle ranches.

Eland *Taurotragus oryx* are regarded as rare in the Kruger National Park, only some 700 occurring there compared to 10 times that number of kudu. Elsewhere they are not plentiful, but widespread, and particularly favour the more arid regions. They are mixed feeders and favour succulent forage. They breed throughout the year and reproductive rate can therefore be manipulated to enhance productivity (Table IV).

Although eland attracted considerable attention as potential farm animals in the 1950s and 1960s (Skinner 1967), they have proved somewhat of a disappointment in this regard, because meat quality has been variable and not as good as that of some other ungulate species (von La Chevallerie 1972) and, in addition, eland are very susceptible to tick disease and tick toxicosis in certain areas. Moreover, they are nomadic, bulls can become aggressive when confined, and they do not flourish as well as expected under confined conditions (Underwood 1975).

Productivity of giraffes has been the subject of extensive study (Hall-Martin 1975). Giraffes occur on many farms and nature reserves in the woodland savanna where they compete with few other species. They browse exclusively and this is their prime advantage, other than their docile temperament, because although they have a good carcass conformation and a high proportion of buttock, they also have disadvantages: carcasses have a relatively low fat and high bone content and the meat from mature giraffes is tough (Hall-Martin, von La Chevallerie & Skinner 1977). At present few are cropped for meat production owing to the very high demand for live giraffes. Numbers should continue to increase, as the carrying capacity of the woodland savanna is only limited by the leaf fall in favoured *Acacia* trees.

Concluding remarks

The results of studies of species and their populations are not of purely scientific interest, but have been proven essential for their effective management. The South African success in conserving endangered ungulate species stemmed in the first instance from good fortune and the foresight in all instances of a few dedicated conservation-minded farmers. Secondly, following the establishment of breeding nuclei, reintroduction of species has largely been into areas of their former range of occcurence. Care has to be taken, however, because all ecosystems are dynamic and many conservationists have long been guilty of believing habitats can be maintained in a steady state, just as many non-African biologists mistakenly believe that game farming is a panacea for solving the problems posed by low agricultural productivity in Africa.

Soon after the tide began to turn in the conservation of ungulates in South Africa and numbers began increasing in the late 1950s, an advance of enormous importance occurred with the development of techniques for the immobilization and tranquillization of ungulates (Harthoorn 1976a). Not only did this enable captured animals to be handled and transported with greater ease to new destinations and over longer distances, but it also allowed the scientist greatly to increase the scope and depth of his research. All of this has led locally to the development of an enormous trade in live ungulates, many of which are purchased purely for aesthetic reasons.

Capture and care of wild animals was still in its infancy in the early 1970s (Young 1973) and capturing in itself posed problems not previously anticipated. Harthoorn (1976b) and others turned their attention to so-called capture myopathy and made a significant contribution to establishing which prophylactic measures to adopt to minimize losses. In particular the dangers of stress resulting from chasing animals for very long distances and then restraining them have been recognized. Today ungulates are handled as little as possible, and should either be relocated immediately or given a rest-period of at least 10 days before relocation.

In addition, new techniques for disease control, as applied in the case of roan antelope, are constantly being tested. The one area where management has proved extremely difficult is in veld management and applying an effective grazing system in order to conserve veld, a practice which is so easily achieved with domestic stock. Rotational grazing has thus far proved largely impractical.

Some advances in knowledge about stocking rates have been made. Intensive studies on habitat utilization have elucidated the habits of browsers such as giraffe (Sauer, Skinner & Neitz 1982) and kudu (Owen-Smith & Novellie 1982), mixed feeders such as eland (Hofmeyr 1970), impala (Monro 1980), and springbok (Liversidge 1968) and grazers such as blesbok (Kok & van der Schijff 1973), black wildebeest (Von Richter 1971a), tsessebe (Garstang 1982), and roan and sable antelope (Wilson 1975; S. C. J. Joubert 1976), to name but a few examples. This knowledge has enabled the astute manager to adopt the right combination of species and maintain these in the right proportions according to the condition of the veld as it varies according to climatic conditions. He soon learns that the 'carrying capacity' is the most dynamic of all concepts.

The dramatic increase in numbers of ungulates has resulted in an expansion of their range within historically known limits. This has been achieved through research and applied management. A set pattern has developed since the 1950s, when management was based on *ad hoc* decisions. First a breeding nucleus was established, then the species biology was studied and finally this knowledge was applied to decisions about relocation. It has not all been easy, but today the wildlife biologist has become an indispensable factor in the conservation and management of African game, which in turn has become an important factor in the economics of many countries on the continent.

The South African success has been highlighted by the 1984 International Wildlife Conservation Award of the United States Safari Club for the conservation of white rhinoceros in Natal, roan antelope in the Transvaal, black wildebeest in the Orange Free State, and bontebok in the Cape Province. The same recipe has been followed for other species listed here, and this achievement in the conservation of animals is magnified when one considers that in some other African countries the once great herds are being decimated or destroyed by war and poaching. In the past 25 years we have fortunately never assumed that our wildlife is safely conserved for posterity. We have actively pursued a vigorous research programme to ascertain, and be able to apply, all the multiple facets of successful conservation.

Acknowledgements

I would like to thank Drs J. H. M. David, N. Fairall, A. J. Hall-Martin, S. C. J. Joubert, P. Mulder, D. T. Rowe-Rowe, and L. Stoltz and Messrs. R. Garstang, P. le S. Milstein, L. G. Oates, P. M. Norton, and R. J. van Aarde for advice.

References

Bigalke, R. (1947). The status of black wildebeest (*Connochaetes gnou* Zimmerman) in the Union of South Africa. *S. Afr. J. Sci.* 43: 213–20.

Bigalke, R. (1955). The bontebok (*Damaliscus pygargus* (Pall)) with special reference to its history and preservation. *Fauna Flora, Pretoria* 6: 95–116.

Bigalke, R.C. & Bateman, J.A. (1962). On the status and distribution of ungulate mammals in the Cape Province, South Africa. *Ann. Cape Prov. Mus.* 2: 85–109.

Brand, D.J. (1963). Records of mammals bred in the National Zoological Gardens of South Africa during the period 1908–1960. *Proc. zool. Soc. Lond.* 140: 617–59.

Brooks, P.M. & MacDonald, I.A.W. (1983). The Hluhluwe–Umfolozi Reserve: An ecological case history. In *The management of large mammals in African conservation areas*: 51–77. Owen-Smith, R. N. (Ed.). HAUM, Pretoria.

Bryden, H.A. (1893). *Gun and camera in southern Africa*. Stanford, London.

Burchell, W.J. (1824). *Travels in the interior of South Africa* 2. Longman, Hurst, Rees, Orme, Brown and Green, London.

Cronwright-Schreiner, S.C. (1925). *The migratory springbok of South Africa*. T. Fisher Unwin, London.

David, J.H.M. (1973). The behaviour of the bontebok *Damaliscus dorcas dorcas* (Pallas 1756) with special reference to territoriality. *Z. Tierpsychol.* 33: 38–107.

David, J.H.M. (1975). Observations on mating behaviour, parturition and the mother-young bond in the bontebok (*Damaliscus dorcas dorcas*). *J. Zool., Lond.* 177: 203–23.

De Vos, V., Van Rooyen, G.L. & Kloppers, J.J. (1973). Anthrax immunization of free-ranging roan antelope *Hippotragus equinus* in the Kruger National Park. *Koedoe* 16: 11–6.

Dittrich, L. (1972). Gestation periods and age at sexual maturity of some African antelopes. *Int. Zoo Yb.* 12: 184–7.

Fabricius, C. & Oates. L.G. (In press). Status of black wildebeest in Transvaal. *Fauna Flora, Pretoria*.

Fairall, N. (1983). Production parameters of the impala *Aepyceros melampus*. *S. Afr. J. Anim. Sci.* 13: 176–9.

Fairall, N. (In press). The use of non domesticated African mammals for game farming. *Acta zool. fenn.*

Fairall, N. & Klein, D.R. (In press). Protein intake and water turnover: a comparison of two equivalently sized African antelope the blesbok *Damaliscus dorcas* and impala *Aepyceros melampus*. *Can. J. Anim. Sci.*

Fitzsimons, F.W. (1919/1920). *The natural history of South Africa*. Longman, London.

Flower, S. S. (1931). Contribution to our knowledge of the duration of life in vertebrate animals. V. Mammals. *Proc. zool. Soc. Lond.* 101: 145–235.

Garstang, R. (1982). *An analysis of home range utilisation by the tsessebe* Damaliscus lunatus lunatus (*Burchell*) *in P. W. Willis Private Nature Reserve*. M.Sc. Thesis: University of Pretoria.

Greenwald, L.I. (1967). *Water economy of the desert dwelling springbok* Antidorcas marsupialis. M.S. Thesis: Syracuse University.

Hall-Martin, A.J. (1975). *Studies on the biology and productivity of the giraffe* Giraffa camelopardalis. D. Sc. Thesis: University of Pretoria.

Hall-Martin, A.J., von La Chevallerie, M. & Skinner, J.D. (1977). Carcass composition of the giraffe, *Giraffa camelopardalis giraffa*. *S. Afr. J. Anim. Sci.* 7: 55–64.

Harris, W.C. (1838). *Narrative of an expedition into Southern Africa during the years 1836 and 1837*. American Mission Press, Bombay.

Harthoorn, A.M. (1976a). *The chemical capture of animals*. Baillière Tindall, London.

Harthoorn, A.M. (1976b). *Physiology of capture myopathy*. D.Sc. Thesis: University of Pretoria.

Hassel, R.H. (1982). Incidence of rabies in kudu in South West Africa/Namibia. *S. Afr. J. Sci.* 78: 418–21.

Hitchins, P.M. (1968). Records of plants eaten by mammals in the Hluhluwe Game Reserve, Zululand, *Lammergeyer* No. 8: 31–9.

Hitchins, P.M. & Anderson, J.L. (1983). Reproduction, population characteristics and management of the black rhinoceros *Diceros bicornis minor* in the Hluhluwe/Corridor/Umfolozi Game Reserve Complex. *S. Afr. J. Wildl. Res.* **13**: 78–85.

Hofmeyr, J.M. (1970). A review of the food preferences and feeding habits of some indigenous herbivores in the Ethiopian faunal region and some studies on animal plant relationships. *Proc. S. Afr. Soc. Anim. Prod.* **9**: 89–99.

Huntley, B.J. (1971). Reproduction in roan, sable and tsessebe. *S. Afr. J. Sci.* **67**: 454.

Huntley, B.J. (1972). Observations on the Percy Fyfe Nature Reserve tsessebe population. *Ann. Transv. Mus.* **27**: 225–39.

Joubert, D.M. (1968). An appraisal of game production in South Africa. *Trop. Sci.* **10**: 200–11.

Joubert, S.C.J. (1970). *A study of the social behaviour of the roan antelope* Hippotragus equinus equinus *(Desmarest, 1804) in the Kruger National Park*. M.Sc. Thesis: University of Pretoria.

Joubert, S.C.J. (1974). The management of rare ungulates in the Kruger National Park. *J. sth. Afr. Wild. Mgmt Ass.* **4**: 67–9.

Joubert, S.C.J. (1976). *The population ecology of the roan antelope*, Hippotragus equinus equinus *(Desmarest, 1804) in the Kruger National Park*. D.Sc. Thesis: University of Pretoria.

Kay, R.N.B., Engelhardt, W. & White, R.G. (1979). The digestive physiology of wild ruminants. In *Digestive physiology and metabolism in ruminants*: 743–61. Ruckebusch, Y. & Thivend, P. (Eds). NTP Press Ltd., Lancaster.

Kettlitz, W.K. (1962). The distribution of some of the larger mammals in the Transvaal (excluding the Kruger National Park), *Ann. Cape Prov. Mus.* **2**: 118–37.

Klein, R.G. (1974). On the taxonomic status, distribution and ecology of the blue antelope, *Hippotragus leucophaeus* (Pallas, 1766). *Ann. S. Afr. Mus.* **65** (4): 99–143.

Kok, P.D.F. & van der Schijff, H.P. (1973). A key based on epidermal characteristics for the identification of certain highveld grasses. *Koedoe* **16**: 27–43.

Laws, R.M. (1968). Wildlife management in practice. *Sylva* No. 48: 21–5.

Liversidge, R. (1968). *Problems in the investigation of grazing competition between springbok and sheep*. Kimberley: Rep. McGregor Museum. (Mimeograph.)

Meissner, H.H. (1976). A note on the energy requirements of young growing blesbok. *S. Afr. J. Wildl. Res.* **6**: 51–3.

Meissner, H.H. (1982). Theory and application of a method to calculate forage intake of wild southern African ungulates for purposes of estimating carrying capacity. *S. Afr. J. Wildl. Res.* **12**: 41–7.

Meissner, H.H. & Hofmeyr, H.S. (1972). A preliminary note on the fasting metabolism and feed intake in the blesbok *Damaliscus dorcas phillipsi* and the South African mutton Merino under comparable conditions. *S. Afr. J. Anim. Sci.* **2**: 73–4.

Melton, D.A. (1978). *Ecology of waterbuck* Kobus ellipsiprymnus *(Ogilby, 1833) in the Umfolozi Game Reserve*. D.Sc. Thesis: University of Pretoria.

Methuen, H.H. (1848). *Life in the wilderness; or wanderings in South Africa*. Richard Bentley, London.

Monro, R.H. (1980). Observations on the feeding ecology of impala. *S. Afr. J. Zool.* **15**: 107–10.

Owen-Smith, R.N. (1973). *The behavioural ecology of the white rhinoceros*. Ph.D. Thesis: University of Wisconsin.

Owen-Smith, R.N., Cooper, S. M. & Novellie, P. (1983). Aspects of the feeding ecology of a browsing ruminant, the kudu, *S. Afr. J. Anim. Sci.* **13**: 35–8.

Owen-Smith, R.N. & Novellie, P. (1982). What should a clever ungulate eat. *Am. Nat.* **119**: 151–78.

Penzhorn, B.L. (1971). A summary of the re-introduction of ungulates into South African national parks (to 31 December 1970). *Koedoe* **14**: 145–59.

Penzhorn, B.L. (1982*a*). Habitat selection by Cape mountain zebras in the Mountain Zebra National Park. *S. Afr. J. Wildl. Res.* **12**: 48–54.

Penzhorn, B.L. (1982*b*). Home range sizes of Cape mountain zebras *Equus zebra zebra* in the Mountain Zebra National Park. *Koedoe* **25**: 103–8.

Penzhorn, B.L. (1984). A long-term study of social organisation and behaviour of Cape mountain zebras *Equus zebra zebra*. *Z. Tierpsychol.* **64**: 97–146.

Pienaar, U de V. (1963). The large mammals of the Kruger National Park—their distribution and present-day status. *Koedoe* **6**: 1–37.

Player, I.C. & Feely, J.M. (1960). A preliminary report on the square-lipped rhinoceros (*Ceratotherium simum simum*). *Lammergeyer* **1**: 3–22.

Pringle, J.A. (1982). *The conservationists and the killers*. Bulpin, Cape Town.

Rogerson, A. (1968). Energy utilization by the eland and wildebeest. *Symp. zool. Soc. Lond.* No. 21: 153–61.

Sauer, J.J.C., Skinner, J.D. & Neitz, A.W.H. (1982). Seasonal utilisation of leaves by giraffes *Giraffa camelopardalis* and its relationship to their chemical composition. *S. Afr. J. Zool.* **17**: 210–9.

Shortridge, G.C. (1934). *The mammals of South West Africa* **1** & **2**. Heinemann, London.

Skead, C.J. (1980). *Historical mammal incidence in the Cape Province* **1**. Dept. of Nature and Environmental Conservation, Cape Town.

Skinner, J.D. (1967). An appraisal of the eland as a farm animal in Africa. *Anim. Breed. Abstr.* **35**: 177–86.

Skinner, J.D. (1973). Technological aspects of domestication and harvesting of certain species of game in South Africa. *Proc. Wld Congr. Anim. Prod.* **3**: 119–25.

Skinner, J.D. (1984). Mating and calving seasons, sex ratios and age groups, and monitoring ungulate populations for game farming. *Proc. Symp. Game on the Farm*: 64–68. Richardson, P.R.K. & Berry, M.P.S. (Eds). Wildlife Management Association of South Africa, Pretoria.

Skinner, J.D. (In press). Selected species of ungulates for game farming in South Africa. *Acta zool. fenni.*

Skinner, J.D., Dott, H.M., de Vos, V. & Millar, R.P. (1980). On the sexual cycle of mature bachelor bontebok rams in the Bontebok National Park. *S. Afr. J. Zool.* **15**: 117–9.

Skinner, J.D., Monro, R.H. & Zimmermann, I. (1984). Comparative food intake and growth of cattle and impala on mixed tree savanna. *S. Afr. J. Wildl. Res.* **14**: 1–9.

Skinner, J.D., van Zyl, J.M.H. & Ostes, L.G. (1974). The effect of season on the breeding cycle of plains antelope of the western Transvaal Highveld. *J. sth. Afr. Wildl. Mgmt Ass.* **4**: 15–23.

Skinner, J.D., von La Chevallerie, M. & van Zyl, J.H.M. (1971). An appraisal of the springbok as a farm animal in Africa. *Anim. Breed. Abstr.* **39**: 215–24.

Smithers, R.H.N. (1983). *The mammals of the southern African subregion.* University of Pretoria, Pretoria.

Sterne, M. (1939). The use of anthrax vaccines prepared from avirulent (uncapsulated) variants of *Bacillus anthracis. Onderstepoort J. vet. Sci. anim. Ind.* **13**: 307–12.

Sterne, M. (1946). Avirulent anthrax vaccine. *Onderstepoort J. vet. Sci. anim. Ind.* **21**: 41–3.

Thorburn, J.A. & Thomas, A.D. (1940). Tuberculosis in the Cape kudu. *J. S. Afr. vet. med. Ass.* **10**: 3–10.

Underwood, R. (1975). *Social behaviour of the eland* (Taurotragus oryx) *on Loskop Dam Nature Reserve.* M. Sc. thesis: University of Pretoria.

von La Chevallerie, M. (1972). Meat quality in seven wild ungulate species. *S. Afr. J. Anim. Sci.* **2**: 101–4.

Von Richter, W. (1971a). The black wildebeest (*Connochaetes gnou*). *Nat. Cons. Misc. Publ.* No. 2: 1–30. Orange Free State Provincial Administration, Bloemfontein.

Von Richter, W. (1971b). Observations on the biology and ecology of the black wildebeest (*Connochaetes gnou*). *J. sth. Afr. Wildl. Mgmt Ass.* **1**: 3–16.

Von Richter, W. (1971c). Numerical status of the black wildebeest in South Africa. *Biol. Cons.* **3**: 234–5.

Wilson, D.E. (1975) *Factors affecting roan and sable antelope in the Transvaal with particular reference to ecophysiological aspects.* D.Sc. Thesis: University of Pretoria.

Young, E. (1973). *The capture and care of wild animals.* Human and Roussouw, Cape Town.

Symp. zool. Soc. Lond. (1985) No. 54: 47–55

Prospects for re-introduction

HARTMUT JUNGIUS

*The International Union for the
Conservation of Nature and Natural
Resources
World Conservation Centre
CH–1196 Gland
Switzerland*

Synopsis

Human influence on the distribution of species is separated into introduction (the establishment of a species in an area in which it has never occurred), re-introduction (rehabilitation of the species in an area where it has become extinct), and restocking.

In many instances, introduction has had a negative impact on the environment and is therefore rejected on principle by most scientists and conservationists. However, the world-wide destruction of species and their habitats calls for a careful review of the position on introduction. The threat to several species might soon force us to conserve them, either in captivity, or in appropriate habitats outside their range, where they can still interact with a natural environment.

Re-introduction should only be considered as one of the many, and certainly not the most important, means of supporting the conservation of the species. Efforts to prevent extinction by preserving the habitat are of paramount importance. Re-introduction has a good chance of success if scientifically planned in co-operation with the responsible political institution and the local people concerned. The reasons for the species' disappearance have to be identified and removed, and the most suitable area for re-introduction selected. Choosing an area should be based not only on the biological characteristics of the species but also on socio-economic factors such as the attitude of the people in control of the area concerned. Practical procedures to obtain and transport animals have to be developed, breeding and release techniques have to be elaborated, scientific personnel engaged, and a monitoring programme set up. Scientific planning, political support, backing from local people, adequate finances and persistence over a sustained period are all essential to ensure the success of a re-introduction project.

The history of wildlife translocation

Translocation of animals and plants by man is an old phenomenon which has led to changes in the fauna and flora of most continents. The dingo was brought to Australia by the aborigines when they settled the area some 8 000 years ago (Bellwood 1978). The fallow deer was scattered around the Mediterranean by the Phoenicians and the Romans and extended its range into central and northern Europe during the 16th and 17th centuries (Nieth-

ZOOLOGICAL SYMPOSIUM No. 54
ISBN 0–19–854002–7

ammer 1963). Colonists took animals and plants from their home countries to new places: for example, red deer and wild boar to Chile, ibex and chamois to New Zealand and the rabbit to Australia. The ancient and continuing practice of trade and exchange amongst hunters of game species like deer and falcons also led to the establishment or mixing of species populations. We also know that monks contributed to the establishment of animal populations around their monasteries in many European countries, specifically turtles and beavers, which were an important food source (Niethammer 1963).

The reasons behind these translocations were for the most part economic or cultural. Biological or ecological considerations were not taken into account with the result that many of these attempts failed. Some succeeded, and others caused disastrous effects on the environment as is the case with the rabbit in Australia. We have learned from the successes and failures of the past animal and plant translocations and most of the projects undertaken today are based on proper studies and implementation.

Re-introduction or introduction

When talking of the establishment of new animal and plant populations we distinguish between introduction, re-introduction and restocking. Re-introduction involves the establishment of a species in an area in which it became extinct in historic times. IUCN states (IUCN 1984) that re-introduction is appropriate 'where a wild species has become extinct due to human persecution, over-collecting, over-harvesting or habitat deterioration, but where these factors can now be controlled'. They should only take place where 'the original causes of extinction have been removed' and 'where the habitat requirements of the species are satisfied. There should be no re-introduction if a species became extinct because of habitat change which remains unremedied, or where significant habitat deterioration has occurred since the extinction. The species should only be re-introduced if measures have been taken to reconstitute the habitat to a state suitable for the species'.

Introduction is distinct from re-introduction: it involves the establish- of a species in an area in which it had never before occurred. It is often associated with risks of environmental disturbance and extermination of native species by the exotic. (This of course may be intended in the case of introductions for biological control purposes.) Convincing examples are introduced rats, cats, dogs, pigs, and goats, all of which have become a major environmental problem in Galapagos (Thornton 1971). The rats and pigs destroy the eggs of giant tortoises and kill the young. Cats and dogs prey on land and marine iguanas and have already exterminated populations on several islands (Kruuk & Snell 1981). Goats destroy endemic plants through overgrazing (Hamann 1975; Calvopiña & de Vries 1975) and fire ants have become one of the main predators for invertebrates and may have exterminated populations of several species before they have even been recorded. There are many similar examples from other parts of the world which will justify the reasons why introductions are rejected by most scientists and prohibited by law in many countries. However we must also realize that some introductions have enriched the environment and become a convincing success. An example is the introduction of the fallow deer to central and southern Europe where it is thriving and interacting well with the environment while it is threatened with extinction in its remaining traditional habitats in Turkey and Iran (Heidemann 1973).

A look at the IUCN *Red data books* indicates that the number of threatened and endangered species is increasing annually owing to over-utilization and destruction of their habitats. This, in my view, calls for a careful review of the position on introduction. Loss of habitat and the increasing threats to several species might soon force us to conserve them either in captivity or in appropriate habitats outside their historic range where they can still interact with a natural environment. I feel it is our responsibility to consider all possibilities to ensure that the highest possible degree of genetic diversity is being maintained. The preservation of existing habitats and animal and plant communities is certainly a top priority, but we also have a responsibility to explore ways of creating new habitats and to investigate what species and plants might thrive in areas which are totally new to them. We are already doing this to a large extent within the geographical distribution area of animals and plants which are unable to colonize new man-made environments, for instance garden ponds, quarries which are no longer in use, or lakes resulting from surface mining activities. Several categories of animals such as reptiles and amphibians and certain plants will only get to these places with man's help.

We might have to consider similar operations outside the natural distribution area of a species; for instance, for those which have been bred successfully in captivity, but whose traditional range is no longer available. This might be the case with the Formosa sika deer which lived in grasslands along the coast, rivers and foothills in the lowlands of Taiwan. It is most probably extinct in the wild because of overhunting and loss of its habitat to agriculture (IUCN 1976). Captive-bred specimens are available from deer farms in Taiwan or from other collections and could be released into a protected area elsewhere where the climate and vegetation is similar to the original habitat. Operations like this have of course to be carefully investigated and planned, and should only be carried out if the investigations show that the benefits outweigh possible disadvantages.

Re-introductions are less controversial. They are not subject to the problems facing introductions and have therefore become very popular in conservation in recent decades. Re-introduction has become the main activity of many conservation groups and several have been created for the purpose of returning species to the wild. One of the most remarkable activities in this connection was the esablishment of the International Society for the Protection of the European Bison, based on a German and Polish initiative in 1923. The activities of this Society, and particularly the energetic work of Dr Erna Mohr, Mr Jan Zabinski and others led to the successful captive breeding and final re-introduction of the species into several areas of its previous range (Mohr 1952). The largest herd of approximately 300 animals exists now in the Bialowieza Forest in Poland and Russia.

The rationale for re-introduction projects

Re-introduction needs proper planning and research. It entails the acquisition, transport and sometimes captive breeding of the species for subsequent release, and years of follow-up to ensure that a reproductive population of the species is being established in the wild. It is expensive, time-consuming and very often unsuccessful, but the number of re-introduction projects is nevertheless increasing. Important reasons for this (discussed more fully by Niethammer 1963; Holloway & Jungius 1973; Jungius 1978) are:

(i)   The re-establishment of the natural diversity in a given environment such as the addition of the European bison to the Bialowieza National Park (Mohr 1952) or the white rhinoceros to several African national parks has enhanced the value of the areas and provided greater tourist attraction (Monfort & Monfort 1984). It has also improved the scientific potential of the parks as places for study and research.

(ii)   The re-introduction of game species such as the red deer or the wild boar will improve the productivity of the area by eventually providing a surplus of game animals which could be hunted for meat and skins, or, in the case of sable in the USSR, for its fur, or the vicuña in the Peruvian Andes for its wool (Hoffmann & Otte 1977). Re-introduction of the beaver may help to improve the water regime of an area and the re-establishment of the lynx may contribute to reducing an over-population of roe deer and thus help to improve the health of a deer population or split up deer concentration and keep the animals moving, thereby reducing over-utilization of the range (Bump 1963; Lindemann 1956a, b; Nováková & Hanzl 1968; Wotschikowski 1975; Lienert 1978).

(iii)   There are also cultural reasons for re-introducing species which have been associated with man since time immemorial and are part of his history and culture. This is the case with the Arabian oryx which plays a very significant role in Arabian poetry, folklore and tradition. The animal occurred throughout the Arabian peninsula. The last herds survived in Oman where the species finally became extinct in 1972. Its extermination was not caused by local people but by outsiders. The last oryx occurred in the Jiddat al Harasis which is inhabited by a small tribe of nomads called the Harasis. These people wanted the oryx back for economic, traditional and cultural reasons. A feasibility study, commissioned by the Government, was carried out by the author. A suitable area was found and the oryx was brought back. Today there are two herds in the wild (Price 1983; Jungius, in press).

(iv)   Re-introduction of species is also considered from an ecological point of view, namely replacing a missing component of an ecosystem. This is particularly important in re-establishing the stability of fragile ecosystems such as deserts or habitats where several major species have disappeared, causing an imbalance of predation pressure. The extermination of roe and red deer may have led to increased predation by wolves on the Abruzzi chamois thus preventing the species from extending its range from a small isolated mountain area in the surrounding area of the National Park.

(v)   Re-introduction projects offer good opportunities for conservation education and fund raising because of their human appeal and action component. Dramatic events such as re-introducing confiscated orang utan to the Gunung Leuser National Park in Indonesia (Rijksen 1978), or the capture of young elephants in Rwanda to save them from a major culling operation and air-lifting them to the Akaguera National Park (Monfort & Monfort 1984) where elephants had been exterminated a long time back, captures the interest of groups of the population who were not previously associated with conservation.

(vi)   Re-introduction projects also capture the interest of the media and help establish new contacts between journalists and conservation groups. This can be extremely useful when support is needed from this body for other conservation issues.

Re-introduction has a good chance of success if it is scientifically planned, if the backing of the responsible politicians and local people concerned has been obtained and if the necessary funding is available. The author has been involved through IUCN and WWF in several re-introduction projects dealing with lynx, roe deer, red deer, bearded vulture, capercaillie, and otter in alpine areas (Holloway & Jungius 1973), in the re-introduction of the Arabian oryx in Oman and Jordan (Jungius, in press); and has advised the Chinese authorities on the re-introduction of the Père David's deer (Jungius & Loudon 1984). Below is a brief summary of the most important experiences in this field and advice on the main steps which should be followed in projects of this kind.

Implementation of re-introduction projects

The over-riding objectives for re-introduction projects must be to re-establish a free-ranging reproductive population of a species which interacts freely with its environment. To reach this aim the following activities should be carried out.

(i)   The researcher must know or acquaint himself with the ecological and behavioural characteristics of the species. He must be aware of its relation to man and needs to have a good understanding of factors favouring its reproduction and establishment in a given area.

(ii)   It must be demonstrated that the species once existed in the proposed re-introduction area.

(iii)   The reasons for the species' disappearance must be identified and it must be determined whether these have been, or can be, removed.

(iv)   An investigation must be carried out to ascertain which of the former habitats will fulfil all the species' requirements during all phases of its life-cycle. Does it provide shelter, a breeding and feeding area during the different seasons of the year, as well as during infrequent climatic extremes? Are there conflicts with other species such as predators or competitors which might have taken over the niche which the animal formerly occupied? Existing or potential threats have to be considered as well as the attitude of the local population. A thorough study of these items is crucial to the success or failure of the project. An oversight, such as failure to take into account lack of co-operation or even opposition amongst local people, or insufficient evaluation of winter and summer ranges, could destroy the best planned projects.

(v)   The most suitable re-introduction site would then be selected and a re-introduction strategy established. This will involve:

- establishing sex and age ratio and numbers of animals required
- identifying the appropriate season for transportation and release
- fulfilment of all veterinary and legal requirements
- constructing enclosures for acclimatization or captive breeding
- arranging facilities for personnel and for protection of the area
- education, information campaigns for the local people
- developing methods for the release which prevent dispersal of specimens and help to ensure that the species establishes itself in a chosen area: for instance, by releasing animals into an area which is surrounded by unfavourable habitats.

Great attention has to be given to imprinting animals on their winter, summer, and dry or wet season ranges. Use of these areas is very often based not on instinct but on tradition, which means it was learned and passed on from one generation to the next. This knowledge has been lost in captivity and techniques have therefore to be developed by the project leader to re-establish this experience. For example, when introducing ibex, bighorn sheep or caribou, special techniques need to be used to help them find and imprint on on suitable winter and summer grazing sites. This requires a good understanding of the species' biology and behaviour, imagination and the readiness to experiment patiently (Nievergelt 1966; Bergerud, 1974).

(vi) Follow-up to the release must be ensured to determine the rate of adaptation and dispersal and the need for further release, and to identify the reasons for success or failure of the project. Another important follow-up measure is the repetition of a successful release project in other areas of the species' former range with the ultimate aim of re-establishing it in all suitable habitats of its former distribution area.

Conclusion

Well planned and properly funded re-introduction projects have a good chance of success. It is therefore very tempting for conservation organisations to promote re-introduction projects because of their high publicity and education value, good fund-raising and emotional appeal. However, we must always keep in mind that re-introduction is only one of the many tools of conservation and certainly not the most important. It is a conservation contingency to be used when all other measures fail. Efforts to prevent extinction, e.g. by preserving the habitat, are of paramount importance.

When the re-introduction of a species is being considered a feasibility study should be undertaken to identify the species' former range and biological requirements, and the reasons for its disappearance. A specific area will have to be determined which would meet the species' needs and where factors which led to its extermination are no longer valid or can be controlled.

The second step of a re-introduction project would be to deal with the preparation of the programme. This would include obtaining animals of a suitable sex and age ratio, arranging transport and veterinarian requirements, selection of the site and construction of enclosures, employment and training of staff, in particular in handling animals under captive conditions (during an acclimatization or captive breeding phase). The area will have to be put under legal protection and fencing might be necessary, as well as an education campaign to obtain support from the local population.

The third step would be the release of the animals. This has to be done during the proper season. Techniques should also be developed to fix the animals to the most suitable areas after release and to prevent dispersal which would reduce the reproduction potential considerably.

The fourth phase would consist of follow-up studies to determine the development of the project and to identify at an early stage the need to intervene with additional releases or other measures to make the project a success.

Re-introduction projects must be designed as long-term activities; preparation of the project and establishment of a free-ranging, reproductive population needs time. Constant scientific and financial effort is required to complete projects successfully.

References

Bellwood, P. (1978). *Man's conquest of the Pacific*. Collins, Auckland, Sydney, Canada.

Bergerud, A.T. (1974). The role of the environment in the aggregation, movement and disturbance behaviour of caribou. *IUCN Publs* (N.S.) No. 24: 552–84.

Bump. G. (1963). Status of the Foreign Game Introduction Program. *Trans. N. Am. Wildl. Conf.* **28**: 240–7.

Calvopiña, L.H. & de Vries, T. (1975). Estructura de la población de cabras salvages (*Capra hircus* L.) y los daños causados en la vegetación de la Isla San Salvador, Galápagos. *Revta Univ. Católico, Quito* 3 (8): 219–41.

Hamann, O. (1975). Vegetational changes in the Galapagos Islands during the period 1966–73. *Biol. Conserv.* 7: 37–59.

Heidemann, G. (1973). *Zur Biologie des Damwildes* (Cervus dama *Linné, 1758*). Paul Parey Verlag, Hamburg/Berlin. (*Mammalia depicta* No. 9.)

Hoffmann, R. & Otte, U.-Ch. (1977). *Utilisation of vicuñas in Peru*. Deutsche Gesellschaft für Technische Zusammenarbeit (GTZ), Eschborn.

Holloway, C.W. & Jungius, H. (1973). Reintroduction of certain mammal and bird species into the Gran Paradiso National Park. *Zool. Anz., Lpz.* **191**: 1–44.

IUCN (1976). *Red data book* 1: *Mammalia*. IUCN, Morges, Switzerland.

IUCN (1984). *The IUCN position statement on translocation of living organisms, introduction, re-introduction and stocking*. International Union for Conservation of Nature and Natural Resources, Gland, Switzerland.

Jungius, H. (1978). Criteria for the re-introduction of threatened species into parts of their former range. In *Threatened deer*: 342–52. Holloway, C. (Ed.). IUCN, Morges, Switzerland.

Jungius, H. (In press). The Arabian Oryx, its distribution and former habitat in Oman and its re-introduction. *J. Oman Stud.*

Jungius, H. & Loudon, A. (1984). *Recommendations for the re-introduction of the Père David's Deer to China*. (Unpublished report to IUCN and WWF).

Kruuk, H. & Snell, H. (1981). Prey selection by feral dogs from a population of marine iguanas. *J. appl. Ecol.* **18**: 197–204.

Lienert, L. (1978). Erfahrungen mit der Wiedereinbürgerung des Luchses in der Schweiz. In *Der Luchs, Erhaltung und Wiedereinbürgerung in Europa*: 60–2. Wotschikowsky, U. (Ed.). Verlag Morsak, Grafenau.

Lindemann, W. (1956a). Transplantation of game in Europe and Asia. *J. Wildl. Mgmt* **20**: 68–70.

Lindemann, W. (1956b). Der Luchs und seine Bedeutung im Haushalt der Natur. *Kosmos, Stuttg.* **52**: 187–93.

Mohr, E. (1952). Der Wisent (*Bison bonasus*). *Neue Brehm Buch.* **74**: 1–75.

Monfort, A. & Monfort, N. (1984). Akagera: Rwanda's largest National Park. *Parks* **8** (4): 6–8.

Niethammer, G. (1963). *Die Einbürgerung von Säugern und Vögeln in Europa.* Paul Parey Verlag, Hamburg/Berlin.

Nievergelt, B. (1966). *Der Alpensteinbock* (Capra ibex L.) *in seinem Lebensraum.* Paul Parey Verlag, Hamburg/Berlin. (*Mammalia depicta* No. 1).

Nováková, E. & Hanzl, R. (1968). Contribution à la connaissance du rôle joué par le lynx dans les communautés sylvicoles. *J. for. suisse* **119**: 114–26.

Price, M.S. (1983). The Arabian oryx at home and free. *Swara* **6** (6): 16–19.

Rijksen, H.D. (1978). A field study on Sumatran orang utans (*Pongo pygmaeus* Lesson 1872): Ecology, behaviour and conservation. *Meded. LandbHoogesch. Wageningen* **78** (2): 1–420.

Thornton, I. (1971). *Darwin's islands. A natural history of the Galápagos.* Natural History Press, New York.

Wotschikowski, N. (1977). Der Luchs—Konkurrent oder Kumpan? *Die Pirsch* No. 19: 1144–7.

Conservation in captivity

Symp. zool. Soc. Lond. (1985) No. 54: 59–69

Zoos and conservation: the last 20 years

C. G. C. RAWLINS

*The Zoological Society of London
Regent's Park
London NW1 4RY**

Synopsis

Twenty years ago, in 1964, the first formal international meeting on the subject of zoos and conservation took place. Since then it has become the major theme of zoo discussions and publications. Have zoos made a real contribution to animal conservation?

Zoos can contribute in two ways: by breeding more of their own animals, particularly those of endangered species, and by educating public opinion to support conservation.

The animal breeding and management performance of the world's zoos in the last 20 years has been good and getting better; every measure, whether dealing with all species or only those which are rare or endangered, has shown an improvement in zoo breeding at a generally increasing rate. This has meant a decreasing demand by zoos on wild stocks.

Whether such performance does really make a contribution to conservation in the long term is tested against formulae produced in 1972 by Perry, Bridgwater & Horsemen to measure the self-sustaining capacity of zoo stocks of endangered species. The results of the last 10 years show a four-fold improvement on the position in 1972 and indicate that this improvement will continue.

Co-operation among zoos and among national and international zoo organizations has greatly increased and the attitude of zoos to co-operative effort for conservation purposes, against a more difficult economic background and with increased controls on the movement of animals between countries, has similarly improved.

Zoos have complemented other forms of public information, in particular the Press and TV, in educating the public about the need for conservation and arousing their enthusiasm for the cause. Seeing an actual live animal of an endangered species in a good zoo is more likely to bring this home to the ordinary man in the street than even the finest TV film. Sympathy for the difficulties that animals like giant pandas and gorillas face in their wild habitats is fostered by the public's knowledge of these animals in their zoos.

Finally zoos have at last got across the message that, ultimately, they may provide the last refuge for many species of animals which face extinction in the wild.

By a nice historical coincidence, this Symposium takes place almost exactly 20 years after one with the title 'Zoos and Conservation', held in this Society's old Lecture Hall in June 1964. Halfway between then and now, in

---

* Present address: *Birchgrove, 64 Earl Howe Road, Holmer Green, nr. High Wycombe, Bucks HP15 6QT, England.*

ZOOLOGICAL SYMPOSIUM No. 54
ISBN 0–19–854002–7

May 1974, another one was held, in this very room, under the auspices of the World Wildlife Fund's 1001 Nature Trust, to discuss 'The Contribution of Zoos to the Conservation of Nature'.

These earlier meetings, each at the beginning of the last two decades, were highlights of the new and constantly recurring theme of zoos and conservation. Hardly any zoo gathering, whether international, regional, national or local, has taken place without reference to it, while zoo publications throughout the world, from scientific journals to children's magazines, have repeatedly turned to it.

If fine words and intentions were the measure of success, the last 20 years should have been a period of great achievement by zoos in their conservation role. The remarks which follow try to see if this was so.

Conservation is one of the great catchwords of our time. It has been freely used by zoos as the main reason for their policies and activities and often as a general justification for their existence. Cynical or uncharitable observers might say that it has sometimes also been used to cover up unsatisfactory standards.

Zoos claim to serve the cause of conservation in two ways: by helping to preserve those species of animals which are or may one day be in danger of extinction in the wild and by educating and encouraging public opinion to support the cause. The preservation of rare species is the role which attracts the most attention. It is also the easiest to use in putting over the zoo case. There is a dual aspect to this role, for breeding rare species helps to make them less rare but also reduces the need for zoos to acquire animals of those species from the wild, thus indirectly protecting wild stocks.

Thus captive breeding has become the major goal of zoos in these last 20 years, encouraged by the increasing knowledge of breeding biology and techniques, as one difficult species after another has been bred in captivity for the first time and the experience and know-how gained have been passed on throughout the zoo world. Two aspects in particular have helped this process; first, the series of world conferences on the Breeding of Endangered Species, starting in Jersey in 1972 and continued in London and San Diego in 1976 and 1979 respectively (the fourth to take place later in 1984 under the organization of the Rotterdam Zoo), and second the increasing support of zoo research groups such as the Institute of Zoology in London and the research departments of the National and the San Diego Zoos in the U.S.A. Learning how to breed new species, how to raise captive-born young successfully so that they in their turn also breed, and how to develop this process till it becomes continuous, are tasks to which zoo research has turned its skills more and more in these 20 years, and with increasing effect.

But there has been another powerful spur to captive breeding. The acquisition of animals from the wild has become much more difficult. Reasons for this were the end of the European empires overseas from which the great metropolitan zoos drew stocks, the new international political alignments which have closed some erstwhile sources of supply, and most important of all, the controls which have been imposed for health and conservation reasons. New quarantine barriers against the spread of animal diseases in the age of air transport, and conservation measures to protect dwindling wild populations, particularly since the 1973 Washington Convention on Trade in Endangered Species, have made the process of moving animals around the world far more complicated and costly, and in many cases impossible. Moreover, zoos, which have never been a major consumer of wild stocks, despite the claims of some to the contrary, have come to regard as almost a matter of honour the ending of any reliance on imports from the wild.

We must now look at the results of these influences.

The performance of zoos in breeding their animals over the last 20 years can be measured through the statistics of the *International zoo yearbook*. This unique publication, with the essential data which it provides every year in its reference sections, has been going since 1960. Zoo breeding facts are recorded in several sections, one group listing the numbers of mammals, birds, reptiles, amphibians and fishes bred in each zoo reporting to the *Yearbook*, the other the numbers of animals of rare and endangered species kept by these zoos, including the vital information as to how many of these were themselves born or hatched in captivity. The *Yearbook* does not list every zoo in the world but it covers most of any importance, whatever their size or status. With the exception of China, from which such information is not yet easily available, these zoos all provide details for the reference sections and although not every one can be relied upon to send in absolutely accurate information every year, the majority do so. The figures given in these sections can therefore be regarded as a fair reflection of general trends in the zoo world as a whole. The trends in the last two decades are illustrated in the Tables which follow, based on *Yearbook* information.

Table I. Animals bred in 20 major zoos[a]

	Mammals	Birds	Reptiles	Amphibians	Total	% of total stock
1964	1675	2032	194	23	3924	8.27
1977	4172	3760	913	252	9097	17.63
1982	4689	4149	1378	435	10651	22.13

[a] Amsterdam, Antwerp (including Plankendael), Barcelona, Basel, West Berlin, Chester, Lincoln Park Chicago, Dallas, Hannover, Leipzig, London, Melbourne, Paris (Jardin des Plantes and Vincennes), Prague, Pretoria, San Diego, Sydney, Tokyo (Ueno Park), Vienna, Washington.

Table I takes 20 selected major world zoos and gives the numbers of mammals, birds, reptiles and amphibians born or hatched in them in 1964,

1977 and in 1982, the latest year for which complete figures are available.

These figures show the all-round improvement in that time, undoubtedly due to better animal management and closer co-operation between zoos.

Table II. Percentages captive-born of rare animals in zoos

	Mammals %	Birds %	Reptiles %	Amphibians %	All animals %
1964	37.37	40.05	0.33	—	36.10
1981	76.32	59.66	52.79	42.52	71.01

Table II tells an even more important story. It shows, in respect of the years 1964 and 1981, for all zoos reporting to the *Yearbook*, the percentage of animals of rare or endangered species in those zoos which were themselves bred in captivity. The figures are taken from the *Yearbook's* 'Census of Rare Animals in Captivity'. This includes all the species kept in zoos which are listed in the IUCN *Red Data Book*, with the exception of some which are relatively common in zoos and breed freely, such as the wolf. But it also includes certain other species which, although not necessarily rare or endangered in the wild, are rare in zoos and of special interest.

In effect, the breeding record of zoos overall in respect of the rare animals in their collections is now twice as good as it was 20 years ago.

Table III. Percentages bred of rare species kept in zoos

	1964 Yearbook	Red data book	1981 Yearbook	Red data book
Mammals (%)	52	56	78	80
Birds (%)	43	50	44	58
Reptiles (%)	11	14	80	85
Amphibians (%)	—	—	50	33

Table III gives the proportion of rare species kept in zoos which have also been bred in them and shows that the improvement in the breeding of rare animals has not been in just a few 'easy' species, but in an increasing number of the rare species kept in zoos. For comparison, figures are given both for the *Yearbook* 'Census of Rare Animals in Captivity' and the IUCN *Red data book*.

Tables I, II and III show that zoos have been doing better in breeding all the species in their care, including the rare and endangered ones. The improvement shows up best in reptiles and amphibians, reflecting the catching-up process of technical advance and the greater resources which have been put into the management of these two classes. That birds show up less well than the others can be explained by the fact that a number of relatively easy breeding species of waterfowl and pheasants, some held in large numbers in private collections, were included in early *Yearbook* lists but are now omitted.

To put this progress in more imaginable form, the captive-born proportion of the stocks of some well-known zoo species at various times during the 20-year period is given in Table IV.

Table IV. Captive-born percentages of total zoo stocks of certain species

	1964/5		1974/5		1981/2	
	Total stock	Zoo-bred %	Total stock	Zoo-bred %	Total stock	Zoo-bred %
Orang-utan	349	13	620	39	655	59
Gorilla	232	4	429	17	482	34
Cheetah	187	nil	653	16	542	50
Black rhinoceros	124	13	159	24	150	43
Red-crowned crane (Manchurian crane)	70	19	53	36	119	57
Rothschild's mynah	100	19	595	53	720	95 +

But to round off these impressive statistics on a note of caution, it should be added that, of the 377 species listed in the *Yearbook's* 'Census of Rare Animals in Captivity' for 1981, there were still 113 whose zoo populations were composed entirely of wild-caught stock; more than half of these were birds and marsupials and many were kept only in very small numbers (sometimes only one) in a few zoos. But at the other and more satisfactory extreme, 75 species were represented by stocks which were entirely or almost entirely made up of zoo-bred animals. This number is increasing all the time as older, wild-caught animals in zoos die out, leaving an entirely captive-born population.

There is, therefore, good evidence of progress made by zoos over the last 20 years in breeding their animals and, in particular, those of rare and endangered species. This should, therefore, support the claim of a substantial contribution to wildlife conservation by:

(i)   increasing the captive stock of rare species, thus creating a reserve against decline or extinction in the wild, and

(ii)   reducing the need for zoos to seek further stocks from the wild.

But do the figures presented really justify this claim? One question to be answered is whether the improvement in breeding has not simply been a reflection of the zoo proliferation which took place in the 1960s and early 1970s. In 1964, 560 zoos reported to the *Yearbook* and this went up to a peak of 926 in 1972. The number has gone down since then and now there are about 800; but despite this decline in the last decade, the number of animals bred has continued to go up. In fact, only about 100 zoos are responsible for most of the breeding of rare and endangered species, so that the total number of zoos in existence at any time in the last two decades has not been an important factor.

The value of breeding success, and indeed the overall efforts of zoos to help wildlife conservation, are regularly denied by those who have never accepted and never will accept that zoos have any useful purpose. But some criticism is constructive. A notable example was the 1972 paper by Perry, Bridgwater & Horsemen which broadly asserted that, while captive breeding success up to that time had increased and was increasing, the results still did not indicate more than a minor contribution to conservation. The paper drew up some performance standards to test this contribution. A decade later, it is worthwhile applying these standards to the position in the early 1980s to see if the progress since then has been more effective. I believe it has.

Perry *et al.* (1972) based their survey on the 73 IUCN *Red data book* mammal species which reproduced in zoos at least once during the ten-year period 1962–71. From those 73 species they selected the 41 which had zoo populations of ten or more animals in either 1962 or 1965.

The authors then went on to choose eight out of these 41 species as being cases 'where zoo propagation has been sufficient to give reasonable assurance that a species can be permanently maintained without further acquisition from the wild'. They made this choice by using two arbitrary factors: a 1971 captive population of 100 or more, and a captive-born proportion of at least half; they commented 'While these factors alone could not guarantee long-term security, it is unlikely that anything else would'.

Using their methods, the progress made in the ten years since they did their survey is as follows:

(i)   The 41 endangered mammal species which in the mid-1960s satisfied the first requirement of a zoo population of ten or more had increased in number to 53 by 1971 and to 86 by 1982, more than double the figure nearly 20 years earlier. Moreover, while in the mid-1960s the 41 species represented 56 per cent of *Red data book* mammal species breeding in zoos, the 86 species of 1982 represented 83 per cent.

(ii)   The eight mammal species which qualified in 1971 under the second test (zoo populations of 100 or more with at least half captive-bred) had increased to 32 by 1982. In addition to these 32, there were 10 more which satisfied one criterion and were very near to doing so for the other.

Table V presents the main feature of these changes.

Table V. IUCN *Red data book* mammal species bred in zoos (species selected by criteria in 1972 survey by Perry *et al.*)

	Mid-1960s	1971	1982
Number of species with zoo population of 10 or more	41	53	86
Number of species with zoo population of 100 or more, half captive-bred	6	8[a]	32[a]

[a] The species involved are listed in Appendix I.

Perry *et al.* (1972) came to the conclusion that, although things had improved in the previous decade, i.e. the 1960s, 'Zoos have not become a significant resource in the preservation of rare or endangered animals'. Their view was that only a handful of species had achieved reasonably secure captive populations with potential for re-introduction. However, the four-fold improvement in the last decade must deserve a more positive commendation; certainly zoos are now a significant resource and the number of species with a potential for re-introduction is not inconsiderable.

The re-introduction of captive-bred animals into the wild is regarded as the ultimate conservation achievement for zoos, although by zoo detractors as the only one. The fact that there have not been many re-introductions from captive-bred stock in the last 20 years might therefore be held to show that zoos have achieved little. The best-known case is that of the Hawaiian goose but other birds including eagle owls and some pheasants have been re-introduced; the Arabian oryx is the most important mammal species to have followed the successful example of the European bison. That more species have not been re-introduced is not the fault of zoos but is due to the conditions, both political and ecological, in the wild. Zoos have produced, and keep in stock, enough animals of several species to start re-introduction schemes, but they cannot do anything if the receiving countries are not ready to do their bit.

Nevertheless, the number of rare species in zoos with self-sustaining populations is still relatively small. The problems to be solved to increase the numbers are financial, organizational, and political, rather than scientific. Zoos have learnt, remarkably quickly in retrospect, how to manage and breed most species, but this has created, paradoxically, the new problem of having to keep larger numbers of animals than are strictly necessary for exhibition, educational and scientific purposes.

Trying to cope with this problem led, in the 1960s and 1970s, to the establishment of 'satellites' or 'outstations' for some of the world's big zoos, on the London/Whipsnade pattern. San Diego, Paris, Antwerp, Washington, New York, Pretoria, Sydney, and Melbourne are some which have gone this way, using the new sites either as public zoos or as closed breeding and research centres. In every case, an essential requirement was that they should provide space for the keeping of larger groups of animals than would be possible at the headquarters zoo.

But the good progress made by zoos in their animal management and breeding work in the last 20 years is due as much to the better co-operation between them, both nationally and internationally, as to scientific and technical factors. The change in attitude which has produced this co-operation is a significant feature of the period.

There is no doubt that, 20 years ago, most zoos were reluctant to part with individual animals of high exhibition value to be sent elsewhere for breeding. Moreover surplus animals would tend to be sent to the highest bidder rather than to the place where the animals could contribute most to improving the captive breeding potential of the species. This selfish, some would say realistic attitude, was noted by the 1964 Symposium: 'Successful breeding on a wide scale will require close co-operation between zoos over exchanges and pooling of stock' (IUCN 1964: 13). Co-operation has greatly improved and has done so during a period when transferring animals from one country to another (or indeed within national boundaries) has become much more difficult.

Such co-operation has gradually transcended the rivalry which once existed; the 'biggest collection' syndrome gave way to breeding success as the measure of achievement; this has in its turn been replaced by a more sophisticated attitude which seeks communal rather than individual results. Thus it is no longer regarded as unsuccessful for one zoo not to breed some species if the proper course is to support another zoo in such breeding; the keeping of 'all male' herds is now accepted as an honourable and efficient way of looking after spare male animals for which space cannot be found in the zoos with breeding groups. Breeding success has therefore become a more co-operative, indeed a communal matter; total success comes from the concerted efforts of several zoos, each complementary to the others.

The strong development of the wild animal studbook system has been a major and a successful feature of these years. Inter-zoo co-operation has both ensured that this development took place and in turn been fashioned by it. It was something else which the 1964 Symposium called for (IUCN 1964: 13). Since then the number of studbooks has increased from eight to 60.

In 1966, the International Union for Conservation of Nature and Natural Resources and the International Union of Directors of Zoological Gardens both made recommendations about the future of wild animal studbooks which were to set the pattern for the following decade. In 1979, the International Union of Directors of Zoological Gardens held a Symposium in

Copenhagen, which recommended changes to studbook rules and called upon its members, representing the great majority of the world's leading zoos and those responsible for a large proportion of the captive populations of endangered species, to abide by them. Now the Studbook Keepers, backed more effectively by their employing institutions, have mostly introduced much firmer order into the management of the species for which they are responsible. Some complicated and expensive animal transfers across the world, such as tigers from East Germany to the U.S.A., and Przewalski's horses from Britain to Japan, have been carried out under their directions or approval. To be noted here is another contribution by the *International zoo yearbook*. The Editor is the Studbook Co-ordinator and the *Yearbook* is the publication through which zoos are kept informed about studbooks and kept in touch with the Keepers.

There are other examples of the new co-operation. At national or regional level several zoo organizations were established following the model of the AAZPA, the first of its kind and dating from 1924. In Britain, what is now called the National Zoo Federation of Great Britain and Ireland was formed in 1966 and similar associations have since been set up in most of the main zoo countries of the world.

The British Zoo Federation has taken very seriously its conservation role, and established early on a Conservation Committee. This year it made a appointment of a Conservation Co-ordinator, on the lines of a similar appointment made some years ago by AAZPA.

Close relationships have been established in special aspects of zoo management. In North America formal breeding plans for a number of species have been drawn up and in general accepted and applied by the zoos concerned. In Britain in 1977, zoos keeping great apes came together to form an Advisory Panel, which has subsequently produced breeding plans for gorillas, orang-utans and chimpanzees. In Britain also, in the last four years, the larger Society and Trust Zoos have set up a process of informal consultation over the management of the stocks of certain species, whose numbers within the British Isles are relatively small and cannot easily be increased except by captive breeding. Examples are the Californian sealion, black rhinoceros and some of the cranes. The process is expected to develop from co-operation in the management of the animals concerned to communal ownership of them. Such an arrangement, as far as is known ahead of any other elsewhere, did indeed come into effect at the beginning of 1983 when the Zoological Society of London and the Marwell Preservation Trust put their stocks of more than 20 species of ungulates into joint ownership and management.

While zoos and zoo organizations have been 'getting their co-operative act together', as it were, a welcome change has also come about in the attitude of other conservation interests towards zoos. This has taken the form of a gradual, if sometimes reluctant, recognition that zoos do have a part to play. The main international conservation body, the IUCN, set up in the mid-1960s a Zoo Liaison Group as part of its Survival Service Commission (now the Species Survival Commission). In 1978 this was replaced by the Captive Breeding Specialist Group, for which IUCN funds were made available. This Group has been working with the International Union of Directors of Zoological Gardens to provide what should become the zoo world's specialist technical advice body.

The relationship between the World Wildlife Fund and zoos has been, for zoos, something like the curate's egg. At national level it has been satisfactory, with zoos often taking part in WWF activities, and helping in fundraising. In Britain, in particular, there has also been reciprocal financial help in recent years with some grants and loans from the WWF for zoo work. The international picture has not been so favourable, since there was a time when the International Branch of WWF was not sympathetic to the idea of wildlife conservation through captive breeding; but this view has changed in the last decade.

In general, however, it can be said that whereas 20 years ago zoos were considered by most conservationists to have nothing to do with conservation, indeed to be inimical to it, they are now accepted as allies in the cause.

The other side of the zoo contribution to conservation is in influencing public opinion. The public's sympathy for the difficulties that animals like giant pandas or gorillas face in the wild, presented so regularly on television or in the press, is fostered and strengthened by its knowledge of these and other threatened animals from visits to zoos, for the old adage still prevails; there is no substitute for the real thing. Seeing a living animal is the best way to full appreciation of it and such a sight, at reasonably close quarters, is worth any number of television programmes, however live the pictures, however excellent the production, in applying the final touch which turns passive sympathy into active support for wildlife conservation. And a zoo is still the only place where the vast majority of people, and particularly that opinion-forming group which lives in the great conurbations of the northern hemisphere, will ever see most wild animals. Even some of those who live, as in Africa, close to the world's few remaining rich wildlife areas, may well have seen their first lion in the zoos of Europe and America and their first elephant in a travelling circus; and they will rarely have seen the wild animals of other continents except in zoos.

The general improvement in zoos over the last 20 years, not only in their breeding achievements but in the care of their animals, the presentation of their exhibits and the information they provide, has contributed to the positive influence which they have been able to exercise in spreading knowledge about animals and providing sympathetic explanations of the need for conservation. At the same time, most zoos have preached the gospel of conservation more formally and more effectively by the extension of their educational work. In 1964, there were only some 15 zoo staff appointed to deal specially with the subject of education; now there are well over 100. Modern zoo education programmes, both for school-children and for adult visitors, emphasize the conservation theme, and the tens of thousands of hours of lectures, addresses, and guided tours for millions of zoo visitors over the years have been a very considerable help to the conservation movement.

The cost of additional specialist staff, and of the other expenses of zoo conservation work, have been a financial burden on those zoos which have taken this responsibility seriously. The public approve and applaud this work, which they now expect of a reputable zoo; but they do not pay for it. They are attracted mainly by the entertainment and recreation which a zoo can offer, so that zoos must find the funds for conservation work and the science which supports it, either by charging the visitors more, which may drive them away, or from grants or public subsidies. At the 1964 Symposium (IUCN 1964) there was discussion as to how zoos could raise money for conservation; 20 years later, zoos may justifiably ask how the rest of the conservation movement can contribute funds for zoos.

Some criticize the amount of money which zoos have put towards their breeding programmes and other conservation work. The cost of keeping all the rare animals at present in the world's zoos is at least £10 000 000 a year; it is suggested that this amount would be better used in protecting wild habitats. But like most calls for alternative use of funds, there is a world of difference between the idea and its practical application. If all zoos gave up keeping rare animals and offered the money saved to habitat protection, the political and administrative barriers against its acceptance would be overwhelming, while the amount involved would be small in relation to the vast areas to be covered. The effect on zoos might be equally disastrous, for the public would neither thank them for their sacrifice nor flock to see their depleted and far less interesting collections of animals.

In the last 20 years, zoos have done a good and cost-effective job for wildlife conservation; they have become its friend and agent, its back-room boffin, its public relations officer in the cities and conurbations of the world. But more than this, they have shown that they can become and may well soon be the last refuge for many species.

References

IUCN (1964) *Symposium Zoos and Conservation.* (Report IUCN Publs (N.S.): Supp. Pap. No. 3.) IUCN, ICBP & IUDZG, London.
Perry, J., Bridgwater, D.D. & Horsemen, D.L. (1972). Captive propagation: a progress report. *Zoologica, N.Y.* 57: 109–17.

Appendix I. Number of mammal species with zoo population of 100 or more, half captive-bred (Table V)

1971		1982	
Siberian tiger	— *Panthera tigris altaica*	Brush-tailed bettong	— *Bettongia pencillata*
Przewalski's horse	— *Equus przewalskii*	Black lemur	— *Lemur macaco macaco*
Onager	— *Equus hemionus*		
Formosan sika	— *Cervus nippon taiouanus*	Mongoose lemur	— *Lemur mongoz*
		Cotton-top tamarin	— *Saguinus oedipus*
Père David's deer	— *Elaphurus davidianus*	Goldon lion tamarin	— *Leontopithecus rosalia*
Wisent	— *Bison bonasus*	Goeldi's monkey	— *Callimico goeldii*
Scimitar-horned oryx	— *Oryx dammah*	Lion-tailed macaque	— *Macaca silenus*
Addax	— *Addax nasomaculatus*	Barbary macaque	— *Macaca sylvanus*
		Orang-utan	— *Pongo pygmaeus*
		Maned wolf	— *Chrysocyon brachyurus*
		African hunting dog	— *Lycaon pictus*
		Ocelot	— *Felis pardalis*
		Asiatic lion	— *Felis leo persica*
		Leopard	— *Panthera pardus*
		Siberian tiger	— *Panthera tigris altaica*
		Sumatran tiger	— *Panthera tigris sumatrae*
		Snow leopard	— *Panthera uncia*
		Clouded leopard	— *Neofelis nebulosa*
		Przewalski's horse	— *Equus przewalskii*
		Onager	— *Equus hemionus*
		Grevy's zebra	— *Equus grevyi*
		Hartmann's mountain zebra	— *Equus zebra hartmannae*
		Pygmy hippopotamus	— *Choeropsis liberiensis*
		Barasingha	— *Cervus duvauceli*
		Formosan sika	— *Cervus nippon taiouanus*
		Gaur	— *Bos gaurus*
		Banteng	— *Bos javanicus*
		Lechwe waterbuck	— *Kobus leche*
		Scimitar-horned oryx	— *Oryx dammah*
		Arabian oryx	— *Oryx leucoryx*
		Addax	— *Addax nasomaculatus*
		Arabian dorcas gazelle	— *Gazella dorcas saudiya*
		Markhor	— *Capra falconeri*

Symp. zool. Soc. Lond. (1985) No. 54: 71–87

The genetic management of exotic animals

K. BENIRSCHKE

Director of Research
San Diego Zoo
PO Box 551
San Diego
California 92112 USA

Synopsis

Genetic management of zoo animals must encompass *all* captive species, as though no new animals are to come from the wild. This chapter reviews the paucity of practical information that exists to make intelligent choices for sound breeding strategies. With the use of several examples, the need for more basic genetic research is emphasized. The storage of genetic material (cells, gametes, DNA) is considered to be essential for future management as are directions from studbook keepers and computer pedigree programs. The dangers to genetic conservation, i.e. genetic variety, are principally introgression, founder effect, inbreeding, selection, and drift, which are reviewed individually with special examples given for each. New data on the complexity of the cytogenetics of several gazelle species of the subgenus *Nanger* are presented. It is suggested that *Gazella granti* be separated from the other two species as has been recommended by others on other evidence. Dama and Soemmering's gazelles on the other hand form a cytogenetic cline of considerable complexity.

Reasons for the need of genetic management

'Genetic variation is the essence of life' (Frankel 1970) and since there exists little doubt now among most zoo professionals that the availability of wild animals for exhibition is in serious jeopardy, the challenge to zoo professionals is to maintain this variation. The relentless destruction of wild habitat, incursions of man's activities into this habitat directly or by altering climate and water supplies, and poaching have led to the diminution of populations of many exotic species that have been the mainstay of exhibits in zoological parks. Restrictions we have imposed upon ourselves further decrease the availability of animals. These restrictions, such as laws of importation or exportation, are aimed at the protection of wild species in their native land. However, recent examples of the fate of animals such as the giant panda, California condor and clouded leopard show that the hope

ZOOLOGICAL SYMPOSIUM No. 54
ISBN 0–19–854002–7

for continued wild existence is by no means secure. Moreover, the pace of wild extinction has accelerated in the last decades. Yet, as Greig (1978) states so eloquently, 'Genetic conservation . . . is still regarded as an esoteric mystery divorced from applied ecology'.

Irrespective of one's opinion as to the wisdom of the existence of zoos and other captive animal populations, given their existence, it is incumbent upon the zoological parks to seek means by which best to protect the populations of animals now is captivity and to enhance their well-being. To create 'self-sustaining captive populations of exotics' has thus become the principal *modus operandi* for enlightened zoological societies. The successes with the Père David's deer, Przewalski's horse, Arabian oryx, and Hawaiian goose, to name a few, testifies to the feasibility of the approach if not its necessity. There are, however, many important decisions that now will have to be made by zoological communities who represent one group of concerned conservationists. Among these decisions is the proper genetic management of the captive stock.

Recommendations abound in numerous publications upon how to avoid genetic drift and inbreeding depression, and what should be the minimum size of a breeding population; moreover the deleterious results of inbreeding are already evident in zoos' breeding efforts. Aside from general dictates to increase by some usually arbitrary number the effective population size, and calls for 'genetic exchange', specific recommendations on the management of any given species have only been made for the Siberian tiger (Seal & Foose 1983). Only sporadically have serious efforts been made on behalf of the maintenance of an appropriate genetic composition of any species and then usually by the efforts of a few concerned individuals. Through these efforts species such as the lion-headed tamarin, Przewalski's horse and pygmy chimpanzee come close to being managed reasonably well.

This chapter will briefly review the current obstacles to genetic management of larger zoo animal populations and make some specific recommendations for possible future action.

There is no question that inbreeding is by and large harmful. This is not to say that it necessarily leads to extinction, but is does place the species at much greater risk. This has been vividly demonstrated recently by the death of a substantial number of cheetahs in Oregon from infectious feline peritonitis (Pfeifer *et al.* 1983). It is presumed that the particular virus variant was peculiarly adapted to this genetically impoverished species, whereas it caused insignificant disease in domestic cats. That cheetahs are genetically completely homogeneous comes as a great surprise to mammalogists and is still not formally explained (O'Brien, Wildt *et al.* 1983). Nevertheless, it makes understandable the poor semen quality (Wildt *et al.* 1983) and perhaps also the captive reproductive difficulties encountered with this species, although other aspects such as behavioral circumstances and palatine erosion from inappropriate food supplies (Fitch & Fagan 1983) may also play a role.

Close inbreeding is the cause of extinction of up to 90 per cent of mouse strains during the production of inbred lines of mice. It often follows severe temporary reductions in the size of the population (bottlenecks) in the evolution of many species, but when as in Syrian hamsters it is followed rapidly by outbreeding, then the deleterious effects can be minimized. The Mongolian horse, Père David's deer, and a few other well known species successfully passed through such a bottleneck and some genetic aspects of these species are understood (Ryder, Brisbin, Bowling & Wedemeyer 1981), but no exotic species is as well explored genetically as the cheetah (O'Brien, Roelke *et al.* 1985). What must be recognized is that a sizeable number of zoo animals (not exclusively mammals) at present find themselves at the threshold of a bottleneck, and that it will depend upon the wisdom of their guardians to bring them safely through this period of danger.

Selander (1976) has summarized evidence from other studies which suggest that periodic bottlenecking has reduced genetic variability for many island species or species inhabiting caves. Similarly, restriction of genetic variability because of small populations—the founder effect—is fundamental to the current situation in zoos. Since the 'maintenance of a species' gene pool is thought to provide the genetic plasticity that increases the chances of successfully surviving in varying environmental conditions' (Ryder 1983), care must be taken not to lose any of these genes, if possible. But as Ryder points out, 'the goal of preservation of genetic variation within a captive population over time is an elusive one'. How to minimize the loss is what should determine our strategy. The critical factors to be taken into consideration are introgression, founder effect, inbreeding, genetic drift and selection.

I shall very briefly deal with some aspects of these concepts that were not covered by Ryder's (1983) discussion of genetic considerations relating to birds.

Introgression

Introgression refers to the introduction of genes from one species into the population of another species. To identify and avoid it demands considerable knowledge about the genetic composition of the species. A notorious case of introgression is the hybridization of Przewalski's horses with the infamous domestic mare at Halle (Mohr 1959). It is now known that *E. przewalskii* with a chromosome number of $2n=66$ is significantly different from *E. caballus*, the domestic horse, with $2n=64$ (Benirschke, Malouf, Low & Heck 1965). A presumed fusion of two acrocentric pairs of autosomes has led to the new genotype of the domestic horse. While fertile hybridization is still possible (Short, Chandler, Jones & Allen 1974), the two species are sufficiently different chromosomally and morphologically that they must be regarded as distinct species. For instance, the uniform colour pattern of *E. przewalskii* differs from the numerous coat colours of the domestic horse: the Mongolian horse characteristically has a standing mane, not so the domestic horse, etc. Nine Przewalski's horses make up the founding population of the 'pure' line, while 12 altogether are the founders of all 500 *E. przewalskii* now in captivity. The distinction of *E. caballus* from *E. przewalskii* may not have been so precisely understood when this introgression occurred as it is now—certainly the difference in chromosome number was unknown—but the consequences of this single action in 1906 have plagued the management of the now captive-only population of *E. przewalskii* ever since. The genes from this Mongolian mare, *E. caballus*, may never be completely eliminated. While no value judgment is here intended, it is to be pointed out that the introgression that took place in 1906 was completely avoidable.

Given that knowledge, should we not be resolute now to prevent repetition of such errors with other species? The answer is very clear if preservation of wild gene pools is contemplated. For instance, hybridization of the two forms of ruffed lemurs (*Varecia v. variegatus* and *V. v. ruber*)—probably not regularly occurring in Madagascar—is an example of an obviously avoidable management error in current zoo practice. Black and white ruffed lemurs not only have the same chromosome number as red ruffed lemurs but the fertility of hybrids attest to their presumably only recent evolutionary separation. Nevertheless, since they are distinct in nature, there is no justification to allow their hybridization in captivity. Similar examples abound, for instance with Bengal × Siberian tiger crosses. Most often such crosses are undertaken because of a temporary or local dearth of appropriate mates rather than because of carefully thought-out plans.

At the very minimum it must be required that much more study should precede such an irrevocable step as introgression, and here I plead for the expansion of serious biological research in zoological gardens on and for endangered exotic species. For instance, cytogenetics has developed into a very sophisticated tool, mostly in the study of human disease. Its help should be universally employed also in the future management of captive exotics. We must simply learn the cytogenetic composition of our animals. With such tools at hand, the hybridization of orang-utans might have been avoided, or earlier stopped, had cytogenetic efforts existed more universally. The phenotype of adult Bornean orang-utans is very characteristic and distinct from that of Sumatrans, particularly in the males. This is not so in young animals and numerous hybrids have been produced for lack of knowledge of origin of the founding stock. Only too recently (Seuanez, Fletcher, Evans & Martin 1976) has it been ascertained that a pericentric

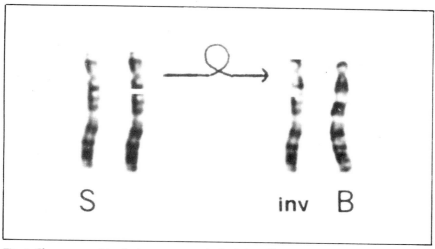

Fig. 1 Chromosome No. 2 of orang-utans. At far left is the Sumatran element with a centromere at level of horizontal line; in second left chromosome the area of presumed ancestral break leading to pericentric inversion with chromosomes of Bornean type (right) evolving. The direction of evolution is unknown. Both subspecies have 48 chromosomes.

inversion of chromosome No. 2 easily allows the determination of an animal's origin (Fig. 1). The population of captive orang-utans is now divided into Borneans, Sumatrans and hybrids (Jones 1980) and avoidance of future hybridization is clearly mandatory for, 'once a hybrid always a hybrid'. Would it not be sad if through further mixing—in this case introgression of subspecies—the distinctive orang-utan subspecific phenotypes were eliminated? Zoologists should also be ashamed to have placed owl monkeys from different parts of South America, whose phenotypic differences correlate with numerical chromosomal variation from $2n=46$ to $2n=56$ (!), together for breeding purposes. These chromosomal differences are easily ascertained and provide an interesting model of speciation (Ma 1981). Moreover, it is likely that hybridization among owl monkey subspecies— probably they should be accorded species denomination—is related to their poor reproductive performance in captivity (Hershkovitz 1983). Good evidence also exists for numerous chromosomal differences in spider monkeys (Kunkel, Heltne & Borgaonkar 1980) and can be assumed to characterize many other species. Science has become very sophisticated and tools have become available to aid zoo keepers to make proper management choices. Since we are the guardians of the few exotics left, it is incumbent upon us to employ these tools if the occasional call for closure of zoos is not to be taken more seriously as justifiable (Anon. 1984b).

Chromosome studies on gazelles

The gazelles of the subgenus *Nanger* highlight how little we know about some of our zoo animals. *Gazella dama*, *G. soemmeringi* and *G. granti* are three continuous forms from North Africa under severe pressure towards extinction. They are well known and favourite exhibit species. These phenotypically very distinct animals have been subdivided into numerous subspecies by colouration and horn form (Kingdon 1982). Often sharp opinions are expressed when the veracity of one 'authority' or another is questioned as to the identity of some specific animals. On the other hand, only a few precise phenotypic and skeletal studies have led to subspecific delineation and little biologic work has been done on these animals. Some forms (e.g. *G. d. mhorr*) are said to be extinct in the wild and recently doubt has even been expressed that the captive herd of mhorr gazelles from Spain represents true *G. d. mhorr* rather than another subspecies of dama gazelle (Eigener & Schliemann 1983).

Our interest has been a cytogenetic one. In a recent study of eight males and 20 females of *G. soemmeringi* from San Diego and Busch Gardens (Tampa, FL), we found the chromosome number to vary between 34 and 39. In addition to the numerical variation numerous structural differences exist among the chromosome sets that are the result of a Robertsonian system (Benirschke, Kumamoto *et al.*, 1984). A situation like this is found in no other 'good' species with the possible exception of the Appennine *Mus* forms (Gropp, Kolbus & Giers 1975). Cytogenetically an unusual feature of several antilopine species is their X/autosome 14 fusion (Effron, Bogart, Kumamoto & Benirschke 1976). In Soemmering's gazelles, a Y/17 compound chromosome, in addition to this X/14 fusion element, appears to be the normal feature. This new finding was reason to re-examine the sibling species *G. dama* and *G. granti*.

Gazella dama had been studied previously in four specimens (Effron *et al.* 1976), one male with $2n=39$, a female with $2n=38$, a male with $2n=40$ and a female with $2n=40$. In the latter animal the usual 18/11 translocation autosome was completely missing and in the male it was heterozygous. The X/14 fusion was present; the Y_1 was very small and Y_2 was the free autosome of No. 14 of the male. These animals had come from Chad and represent members of the large group of *G. d. ruficollis* which are now widely disseminated in zoos. Since then we have studied more animals of this subspecies and of *G. dama mhorr*.

G. dama ruficollis was found to have 39 elements in one male and 38 in two females. In contrast to the earlier study, however, this male clearly has the Y/17 translocation that also characterizes the Soemmering's gazelle (Fig. 2). The remainder of the chromosomes are also identical except that the 16/11 translocation is present in the heterozygous state.

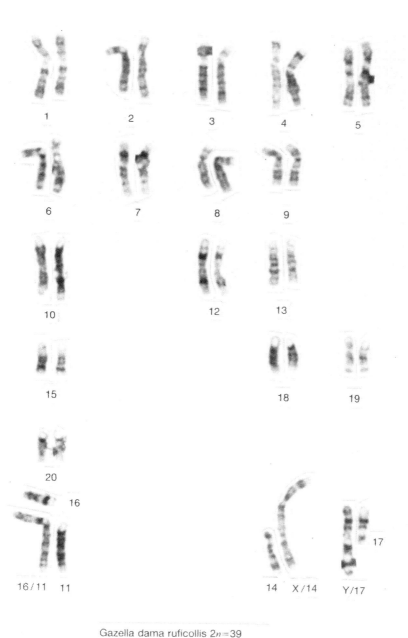

Gazella dama ruficollis 2n=39

Fig. 2 Karyotype of male *Gazella dama ruficollis* (Case 3197) from San Diego Zoo. The Giemsa banded chromosomes are arranged according to a unified nomenclature proposed by Benirschke, Kumamoto *et al.* (1984). Note that one No. 16/11 fusion product is heterozygous (bottom left) and that in addition to the X/14 translocation a Y/17 translocation exists.

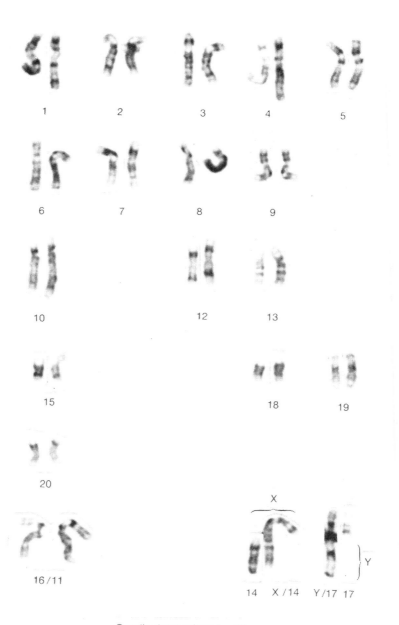

Gazella dama mhorr $2n = 38$

Fig. 3 Karyotype of male *Gazella dama mhorr* (Case 4782) from San Diego Zoo. This karyotype is essentially the same as in Fig. 2 except that No. 16/11 is homozygous and the chromosome number here is 38 instead of 39. The overall chromosomal content is identical.

The two male and one female *G. dama mhorr* studied came from the captive group in Almeria, Spain, a group now breeding at San Diego. These animals possess the 16/11 fusion chromosome, the X/14 translocation, and, as is true of the Soemmering's gazelle, a Y/17 translocation. Consequently one male has $2n=38$ (Fig. 3), but the other has $2n=39$ because of the heterozygous state of the 16/11 chromosomes found also in *G. d. ruficollis* (Fig. 2).

In the additional two male and one female *Gazella granti roosevelti* studied, males had $2n=31$, females $2n=30$. They were thus similar to the single male and female animals studied previously by Effron *et al.* (1976). The X/14 is composite but the Y_1 and Y_2 (No. 14) are small acrocentrics.

In summary, then, the situation in the subgenus *Nanger* is complex, particularly with *Gazella dama ruficollis*, *G. d. mhorr*, and *G. soemmeringi*. *Gazella granti* appears to be separated by sufficient chromosomal evolutionary distance to be no longer subject to the risk of introgression. This interpretation, of setting aside *G. granti* from the other *Nanger* forms, supports the notion of several older authors (review by Lange 1971), which was based on other criteria. Soemmering's and dama gazelles, however, present as a chromosomal cline. In view of the extensive heteromorphism of the autosomal fusion products, either there is an on-going process of speciation or there exist well-defined local subspecies that have inadvertently been put together in captive herds. Of greatest interest is the existence of the Y/17 fusion in all Soemmering's and mhorr gazelles, but in only some of the red-necked animals. Since all three *Nanger* forms, as well as some other gazelles, possess the X/14 composite chromosome, this feature seems to be an ancestral property, while the fusion of Y with an autosome would appear to be of more recent nature. It is possible that its addition to the chromosomal evolutionary process proves to be a hazard for normal cytokinesis in these animals. Only studies of larger numbers of animals of which the point of origin is precisely known will answer these questions. Cytogenetic study of male meiosis would be especially useful.

The point of this brief review of gazelles of the subgenus *Nanger* is that it emphasizes just how little is known of some of the most fundamental aspects of the biology of the exotics entrusted to us. When we consider the formation of self-sustaining populations of exotic animals as a future challenge for zoos, we must first and most importantly acquire knowledge of the species. Breeding gazelles without the benefit of chromosomal knowledge wastes scarce resources, and the very poor empirical success with reproduction of Soemmering's gazelles supports this contention. The acquisition of new knowledge is the most urgent task at this time in order to settle the question of the true cytogenetic identity of *G. soemmeringi* and its neighbouring species. Until this knowledge is acquired, the findings just detailed must tentatively be regarded as processes of hybridization and as examples of introgression.

Founder effect

The founder effect is imposed upon a small population by the restricted amount of genetic heterozygosity carried by a few founders. The fewer there are, the more dramatic the effect can be and rare alleles are brought to a captive population only by a large founder stock (more than 25), a rare situation for zoos. Nevertheless, a few animals can bring in a high percentage of the genetic variety carried by a population, providing the founders are not themselves closely related. Aside from a wide variety of adaptive genes, the heterozygous animal carries a number of lethal genes; lethal when represented in a double dose. The number of lethal genes is unknown for most species and presumably it is affected adversely by prior radiation exposure, perhaps even by chemical exposure. The smaller the founder population the more likely it is that through inbreeding heterozygous lethal genes become homozygous. An example of the effect of an abnormal gene introduced by one of a few founders is the autosomal dominant for pectus excavatum in black and white ruffed lemurs (Benirschke, Miller, Ippen & Heldstab, in press). Because of the small population size the (harmless) anomaly is now widespread in the population of captive lemurs. Its extent in the wild is unknown.

Past conferences and monographs also contain a variety of numbers as a suggested minimum effective population for long-term, self-sustaining captive stock to succeed. The numbers range from 50 to 500 animals; even higher numbers are cited to guarantee ultimate survival. The numbers are based on estimates derived from experiments with succinct genetic systems, e.g. fruit flies, and how valid they would be for most exotic species in zoos is unknown. In all candour, however, it must be admitted that it is difficult to maintain or achieve the higher numbers of effective breeding populations for most species at this time, perhaps at any time in the history of zoos. One may also ask whether it was at all useful to start with as small a population as the nine or 12 founding Przewalski's horses or the very small numbers available as founders for some species now under consideration. Answers hinge on a variety of factors, such as length of anticipated captive conservation, repatriation interests, environmental factors (e.g. virus infection in cheetahs) and other variables. A useful booklet to give directions has recently been issued by the AAZPA and should be consulted (Anon. 1984a). Shaffer (1981) has also succinctly reviewed these conditions and points out that the simplified genetic considerations for minimum numbers might be solidified by actual measurements of genetic heterozygosity, as well as by consideration of the breeding structure of the species to be conserved. Guesswork may be very misleading and this is exemplified by the homozygosity of cheetahs (no matter how large a population, the genetic variability would not increase) and the introgression that affects the founders of the current Soemmering's gazelle stock (the larger the number of animals, the greater the cytogenetic complexity). Thus, large numbers for founders will not alone be the answer unless more knowledge is gained about them. Moreover, it must be recognized that several species have successfully come through the bottleneck created by a small founder population. It is not the bottleneck that presents the problem, as Ryder (1983) remarks, but 'the events that follow the bottleneck that can most drastically affect the gene pool'. A valid criticism often made is 'why wait (with conservation) until the coefficient of inbreeding is already too large . . .' (Tangley 1982). The practical sequel to be drawn from such considerations is that the management of those zoo populations still represented by large numbers follow the same management schemes as those for endangered species.

For practical purposes in zoos it is important to enrol *all* available founders into the breeding program, irrespective of the social structure of the species. That is to say, if only two males and one female of a species were available both males should be allowed to breed alternately. Alternatively, semen of the unwilling males needs to be conserved even though the technology for artificial insemination is not yet sufficiently advanced in many exotics. Unless this suggestion is followed a large number of males of many species will die in zoos without having made their potentially very important genetic contribution. These are, in many cases, absolutely irretrievable genes that will not be available again in the future. Prompt attention to cryopreservation of semen of all exotics cannot be overemphasized and it is hoped that the complementary knowledge of female reproductive physiology will be acquired in time to make the semen useful.

Inbreeding

The third factor to be taken into consideration, inbreeding, is basically unavoidable in long-term propagation efforts. This being so, the quest is to reduce it as much as possible, and the sooner this aim is accepted and its consequences understood and applied in captive exotics, the fewer genes will be lost and presumably the more vigorous the population will remain. So well recognized are the ill effects of inbreeding that most religions, indeed governments, have forbidden the practice. For it has long been recognized that recessive genes with deleterious consequences become homozygous, and children of incest, for example (Baird & McGillivray 1982), have very frequently (43 per cent) severe anomalies that in some cases can also be precisely attributed to recessive genes, although more often the defects have a poorly defined pathogenesis. This is true also of ungulates in zoos where an increased perinatal mortality has been documented in inbred stock by Ralls, Brugger & Ballou (1979) and Ralls, Brugger & Glick (1980). In 15 of 16 species of a variety of ungulates with reasonable records these authors found the juvenile mortality of inbred animals to exceed significantly that of non-inbred stock. Because of the possibility that changing management practices influenced the results, the authors examined the large experience with 93 dorcas gazelle calves in greater detail. They were able to show not only that changing management (e.g. prophylactic neonatal penicillin administration) had no beneficial effect on greater survival of inbred animals, but also that sexual maturity of inbred females was markedly delayed with consequent reduced fecundity. Perinatal mortality for inbreds was 43 per cent as opposed to the 18 per cent of non-inbred animals. As is the case with human inbreeding, specific genetic diseases were not the identifiable major cause of perinatal deaths; rather the effects were attributed to a reduced overall vitality following the hypothesis of a multifactorial system with threshold. Nobody really doubts any longer that the practice of inbreeding is deleterious in the long run and, if not immediately harmful, that the *drift* also occurring with inbreeding will harm the population in the long run. Examples abound—witness the naked ruffed lemurs at the Institute of Zoology that resulted from father × daughter matings (Hearn, 1982: 17). So, why do it? Is it simply for reasons of complacency, from a lack of conviction or because immediate reprisal does not exist in our community as occurs in the case of human incest, or is it because of other obstacles that clearly could be overcome in well managed collections?

The topic of evolutionary changes that occur in small populations has been fairly assessed by Franklin (1980), who also has the following succinct prescriptions: 'One way to maintain effective population size is to ensure that each family contributes equally to the next generation by culling only within families. Another option, if management is sufficiently intense, is to employ mating schemes which lead to maximum avoidance of inbreeding. All such methods reduce the response to natural selection and postpone the elimination of particularly abnormal genotypes. Given a choice, however, it is perhaps best to sacrifice evolutionary change at the present, if by so doing one is conserving genetic variation for future evolutionary change. If a species is maintained in a number of small populations, not only is the danger of accidental extinction (for example, by disease) reduced, but an opportunity for local adaptation exists, which may increase the chance of ultimate survival. Genetic drift can be countered by allowing occasional migration'. An excellent example of such a practice is the recent exchange of three Przewalski's horses from the US stock with the relatively isolated gene pool that has been maintained in Askania Nova, Russia, from which three horses came to US institutions (Baker 1984). Several offspring have since been born in Russia and the USA and one can confidently expect that the 'new blood' will significantly invigorate both stocks. Such a practice has been recommended in the past, in order to aid genetic rehabilitation processes by breaking up small populations into several groups for very cogent reasons (Greig 1978).

As Ryder (1983) has pointed out we do not have the luxury to investigate possible sequelae of inbreeding but 'management decisions must be attended to immediately'. Fortunately, numerous computer programs and the central registry of ISIS and, regrettably less efficiently, the studbooks for endangered species, allow rapid identification of the best genetic fits of captive stock for breeding purposes. The management schemes for captive exotics must vary and are dependent on the nature of biologic behaviour of the species and the ultimate aims, e.g. captive propagation only or ultimate release into the wild. For instance, recommendations for Przewalski's horses are different to those for tigers as it would seem most improbable that reintroduction into Siberia of the latter species will be practical, while this is clearly a hope for Mongolian horses. But recommendations for both have been made. Thus, for horses, rehabilitation to semi-wild conditions in semi-reserves has not only been contemplated but is already in progress (Bouman-Heinsdijk 1982). The detailed Species Survival Plan (SSP) recently issued not only makes specific recommendations for creating an effective population sufficient to assure that loss of genetic variability be minimized, but also entails the collection of frozen gametes with development of embryo transfer techniques (Anon. 1984a). It is my opinion that effective breeding efforts must henceforth be undertaken for *all* zoo stock as though no new animals were coming. Only then will we be able to carry our heads respectably in contemporary society. We possess the necessary tools now, we need the political will (in-house) to carry through with the decisions.

Genetic drift

Drift, the loss of genetic variety, is an inevitable consequence of breeding small populations. It is enhanced by mutations and other events, less germane to the topic and amply covered by previous authors. To counter drift effectively it is suggested that populations be built up as rapidly as possible from founder stock. In mammals with low reproductive proclivity, typical of zoo exotics, only harvesting (and cryopreservation) of gametes can answer the emergency needs. In our own institution, for instance, we make the deliberate effort to preserve the semen of the severely endangered lion-tailed macaque males that have grown up inappropriately in various zoos, deprived of their social ability to copulate, with the belief that their potentially valuable genetic contribution would otherwise be lost. Clearly much research will have to take place before these techniques, which are so successful in domestic species such as cattle and sheep as well as the mouse, can become effective in exotic species. Such techniques also assure some protection against unforeseeable future cataclysmic events such as epidemics, fires, wars, etc.

Selection

Selection of course is contrary to the conservation of genetic variety since in most cases it is a subjective process. It is the means for domestication of animals, and value judgment can easily alter a small gene pool: witness the San Diego population of black and white ruffed lemurs. An autosomal dominant gene for pectus excavatum has clearly been identified and could readily be eliminated by 'selective' breeding (Benirschke, Miller *et al.*, in press). Since it seems only to be of cosmetic nature and since no real deleterious effects accompany the pectus, a decision not to eliminate this gene from the stock has tentatively been reached. Clearly, even this decision represents selection but that is the best we can do at present to maximize the genetic contribution of all members of a population.

One could also readily imagine that selection of more docile animals might occur in zoos, that a particular fancy, e.g. long or spiraled horns of some ungulates, thick or thin fleece and other locally advantageous characters might be selected for in zoos. The creation of subpopulations living in different parts of the world, as for instance in the case of Przewalski's horses, would work against such selective processes or at least minimize them. Furthermore, the greater acceptability now of wild animal parks with a more natural environment tends to retard some types of selection. Finally, the availability for the distant future, one would hope, of stored gametes from wild-caught founders will assure that ancestral genotypes created by natural selection remain available for possible 'curative' purposes.

Conclusions

Reviewing the needs of genetic management in zoos brings out several immediate goals. Foremost, in the author's opinion, must be the conduct of scientific research into the genetic composition of all exotic species. This includes immediately at least the establishment of karyotypes, the long-term conservation of cell strains, the methodical freezing of as wide a sample of gametes and tissue samples as possible, and, ideally, the preparation of DNA libraries of the most endangered species. How valuable stored tissue samples can be for modern molecular biologic questions can be shown by the example of the relationships of northern and southern subspecies of the white rhinoceros. When the question of evolutionary distance between these two forms was raised recently it was possible to make some reasonable estimate from the percentage of DNA fragment substitution in mitochondrial DNA because samples of liver from rhinoceroses had been preserved from autopsies in the past. Thus it was learned that black and white rhinoceros species diverged some 3.5 million years ago while northern and southern subspecies of *Ceratotherium simum* diverged two million years ago (George, Puentes & Ryder 1983). Since tissues of the most endangered species often become available only in zoological gardens, their conservation for the use of future scientists is mandatory. The biological techniques are developing so quickly and yet unpredictably that one can confidently assume that the availability of DNA in particular will ultimately find many uses, to answer diagnostic questions and also perhaps for cloning specific genes. It must be emphasized that *all* exotic species should be managed henceforth, not only those whose numbers are so low as to place them amongst the endangered. Zoo animals must be managed as though no new animals were coming. Not only would this bring experience, it would earn us much respect and we would learn more about our captive stock than ever before. Zoos must accept the responsibility for the biological study of exotics; they are the only places where such work can proceed. Because so little zoo research has been undertaken in the past, we know practically nothing about the biology of most exotic species, and if we are to succeed with the creation of self-sustaining populations, this dearth of knowledge will have to be repaired. What is true of the more frequently discussed mammals holds equally for reptiles and birds, if not more so, as even less is known.

In addition to the conduct of genetic research on exotics it will be essential that the captive animals are bred in a manner following the best established genetic principles to avoid inbreeding, drift, panmixia, and introgression. A number of SSP programs as written for the Siberian tiger are currently being developed. They will demand greater co-operation among zoos and also require additional research. Eventually they will be guided by the studbooks and computer programs written for that purpose. Most importantly, we must not condone deviation from such a resolution to maintain species by this best alternative to the selection of the wild—until the day that we know more.

Acknowledgement

Dedicated to Lord Solly Zuckerman at his 80th birthday.

References

Anonymous (1984a). *Species survival plan.* Am. Assoc. Zool. Parks & Aquariums, Oglebay Park, Wheeling, West Virginia.
Anonymous (1984b). The zoo at sunset—opinion. *BBC Wildlife* 3: 156–7.
Baird, P.A. & McGillivray, B. (1982). Children of incest. *J. Ped.* 101: 854–7.
Baker, M. (1984). Horse trading and behavioral research pay off. *Zoonooz* 57: 14–5.

Benirschke, K., Kumamoto, A.T., Olsen, J., Williams, M. & Oosterhuis, J. (1984). On the chromosomes of *Gazella soemmeringi* Cretzschmar, 1826. *Z. Säugetierk.* **49**: 368–73.

Benirschke, K., Malouf, N., Low, R.J. & Heck, H. (1965). Chromosome complement: Differences between *Equus caballus* and *Equus przewalskii* Poliakoff. *Science, N.Y.* **148**: 382–3.

Benirschke, K., Miller, C., Ippen, R. & Heldstab, A. (In press). The pathology of prosimians, especially lemurs. *Adv. Sci. comp. Med.* **29**.

Bouman-Heinsdijk, I. (1982). Semi-reserves for the Przewalski horse as an intermediary step between captivity and reintroduction into the wild and an international stallion exchange strategy to reduce inbreeding in captivity. In *Breeding Przewalski horses*: 221–9. Bouman, F., Bouman, I. & Groeneveld, A. (Eds). Fndtn. Preserv. Protect. Przewalski Horse, Rotterdam.

Effron, M. Bogart, M.H., Kumamoto, A.T. & Benirschke, K. (1976). Chromosome studies in the mammalian subfamily Antilopinae. *Genetica* **46**: 419–44.

Eigener, W. & Schliemann, H. (1983). Anmerkungen zu der irrtümlicherweise als Mhorr-Gazelle bezeichnete *Gazella dama* aus der spanischen Sahara. *Zool. Gart., Lpz* **53**: 313–6.

Fitch, H.M. & Fagan, D.A. (1983). Focal palatine erosion with dental malocclusion in captive cheetahs. *Zoo Biol.* **1**: 295–310.

Frankel, O.H. (1970). Variation–the essence of life. *Proc. Linn. Soc. N. S. W.* **95**: 158–69.

Franklin. I.R. (1980). Evolutionary change in small populations. In *Conservation biology*; 135–49. Soulé, M.E. & Wilcox, B.A. (Eds). Sinauer Associates, Sunderland, MA.

George, M.W., Puentes, L.A. & Ryder, O.A. (1983). Genetic differences between the subspecies of white rhinoceros. In *International studbook African rhinoceros*: 60–7. Kloes, H.G. & Frese, R. (Eds). Zoologischer Garten Berlin, Berlin.

Greig, J.C. (1978). Principles of genetic conservation in relation to wildlife management in Southern Africa. *S. Afr. J. Wildl. Res.* **9**: 57–78.

Gropp, A., Kolbus, V. & Giers, D. (1975). Systematic approach to the study of trisomy in the mouse. *Cytogenet. Cell Genet.* **14**: 42–62.

Hearn, J.P. (1982). Scientific report. Zoological Society of London. *J. Zool., Lond.* **197**: 1–123.

Hershkovitz. P. (1983). Two new species of night monkeys, genus *Aotus* (Cebidae, Platyrrhini): A preliminary report on *Aotus* taxonomy. *Am. J. Primatol.* **4**: 209–43.

Jones, M.L. (1980). *Studbook of the orang utan* Pongo pygmaeus. Zool. Soc. San Diego, California.

Kingdon, J. (1982). *East African mammals* **3** (D) (Bovids). Academic Press, New York.

Kunkel, L.M., Heltne, P.G. & Borgaonkar, D.S. (1980). Chromosomal variation and zoogeography in *Ateles*. *Int. J. Primatol.* **1**: 223–32.

Lange, J. (1971). Ein Beitrag zur systematischen Stellung der Spiegelgazellen (Genus *Gazella* Blainville, 1816 Subgenus *Nanger* Lataste, 1885). *Z. Säugetierk.* **36**: 1–18.

Ma, N.S.F. (1981). Chromosome evolution in the owl monkey, *Aotus*. *Am. J. phys. Anthrop.* **54**: 293–303.

Mohr, E. (1959). *Das Urwaldpferd* Equus przewalskii *Poliakoff 1881*. A. Ziemsen Verlag, Wittenberg.

O'Brien, S.J., Roelke, M.E., Marker, L., Newman, A., Winkler, C.W., Meltzer, D., Colly, L., Everman, J.F., Bush, M. & Wildt, D.E. (1985). Genetic basis for species vulnerability in the cheetah. *Science, Wash.* **227**: 1428–34.

O'Brien, S.J., Wildt, D.E., Goldman, D., Merril, C.R. & Bush, M. (1983). The cheetah is depauperate in genetic variation. *Science, Wash.* **221**: 459–62.

Pfeifer, M.L., Evermann, J.F., Roelke, M.E., Gallina, A.M., Ott, R.L. & McKeirnan, A.J. (1983). Feline infectious peritonitis in a captive cheetah. *J. Am. vet. med. Assoc.* **183**: 1317–9.

Ralls, K., Brugger, K. & Ballou, J. (1979). Inbreeding and juvenile mortality in small populations of ungulates. *Science, Wash.* **206**: 1101–3.

Ralls, K., Brugger, K. & Glick, A. (1980). Deleterious effects of inbreeding in a herd of captive Dorcas gazelle. *Int. Zoo Ybk.* **20**: 137–46.

Ryder, O.A. (1983). Genetic considerations in breeding threatened and endangered birds. In *Jean Delacour symposium*: 551–65. Schulman, G.L. (Ed.). International Foundation for the Conservation of Birds, North Hollywood, California.

Ryder, O.A., Brisbin, P.C., Bowling, A.T. & Wedemeyer, E.A. (1981). Monitoring gene variation in endangered species. In *Evolution today*: 417–24. Scudder, G.G.E. & Reveal, J.L. (Eds). Hunt Instit. Botan. Document. Carnegie-Mellon Univ., Pittsburgh.

Seal, U.S. & Foose, T. (1983). Species survival plan for Siberian tigers in North American zoos: a strategy for survival. *Proc. Am. Ass. Zoo Vets* **1983**: 33–40.

Selander, R.K. (1976). Genetic variation in natural populations. In *Molecular evolution*: 21–45. Ayala, F.J. (Ed.). Sinauer Associates, Sunderland, Massachusetts.

Seuanez, H., Fletcher, J., Evans, H.J. & Martin, D.E. (1976). A polymorphic structural rearrangement in the chromosomes of two populations of orangutans. *Cytogenet. Cell Genet.* **17**: 327–37.

Shaffer, M.L. (1981). Minimum population sizes for species conservation. *BioScience* **31**: 131–4.

Short, R.V., Chandler, A.C., Jones, R.C. & Allen, W.R. (1974). Meiosis in interspecific equine hybrids. *Cytogenet. Cell Genet.* **13**: 465–78.

Tangley, L. (1982). Captive propagation: will it succeed? *Science News* **121**: 266–8.

Wildt, D.E., Bush, M., Howard, J.G., O'Brien, S.J., Meltzer, D., van Dyk, A., Ebedes, H. & Brand, D.J. (1983). Unique seminal quality in the South African cheetah and a comparative evaluation in the domestic cat. *Biol. Reprod.* **29**: 1019–25.

Symp. zool. Soc. Lond (1985) No. 54: 89–101

The care of exotic animals

D. M. JONES

Institute of Zoology
The Zoological Society of London
Regent's Park
London NW1 4RY

Synopsis

Many animals now being managed in zoos and captive breeding centres are for various reasons virtually irreplaceable. This has resulted in a greatly increased demand for higher standards of husbandry and well organized and informed animal health services. During the last two decades our knowledge of the medical care of wild animals has improved dramatically and today over 300 veterinary surgeons, many of them supported by highly trained lay-staff and well equipped facilities, work full-time in zoos and wildlife parks throughout the world.

Our knowledge of animal behaviour, better housing and exhibit design, training programmes for personnel, specific nutritional needs, and the use of new anthelmintic drugs and of vaccines all contribute to reducing the incidence of clinical problems.

The use of new diagnostic tools in such fields as haematology, radiology, ultrasonics, and fibre-optics is now possible because continually improving methods of sedation and anaesthesia have enabled the clinician to be more specific in deciding on lines of treatment. Being able to control animals safely for relatively long periods has also brought about the development of more successful methods of intensive care.

Information from detailed pathological examination of carcases, now carried out at many more centres than was the case in the past, together with the clinical data accumulated from improved diagnostic techniques, is regularly published and exchanged, providing the wildlife veterinary clinician with a much more accurate basis on which to care for his stock.

The paper will provide an overview of the development and use of these advances.

Introduction

Until about 30 years ago it was possible to obtain almost any species of animal from the wild. Gifts from overseas governments, the products of private collecting trips and the activities of a wide range of animal dealers meant that stocks could be maintained in zoos without any need to make an effort to breed replacements. During the last three decades that situation has changed, and four main factors have combined to bring this about.

The first factor is that most of the world's nations are now party to legis-

ZOOLOGICAL SYMPOSIUM No. 54
ISBN 0–19–854002–7

lation which controls the export of animals from their own country and the importation of animals from other countries, particularly of those species which are in any way endangered. The second factor is that most developed countries apply strict control over the importation of animals in order to protect their domestic livestock from exotic disease. The third factor has been the severe reduction in the populations of many species, making those species difficult to find anyway, and the fourth factor is that public opinion and the opinion of responsible zoos has changed from indifference to strong, committed support of the concept of breeding their own replacement animals, concentrating in particular on those species which are now rare in the wild.

Thirty years ago, there were only a handful of full-time veterinary surgeons engaged in clinical work in zoological collections. Today there are over 300, most of them in America, Japan and the Eastern Block countries. In addition, a much larger number of veterinary surgeons are engaged for part of their time in this field and many of them are supported by colleagues from other medical and biological disciplines and, in some cases, by teams of experienced lay staff. During this same period there has also been a considerable increase in the number of veterinary surgeons and experienced practical zoologists taking part at a senior level in the administration of zoos. In the larger collections the facilities which have developed around such staff have also improved dramatically, especially where the organization has a long-term commitment to practical research.

Animals in the wild in most areas are not served by comprehensive veterinary facilities, largely because resources are lacking, and intervention is rarely practical. Some preventive veterinary care and the regular monitoring of wild populations, in particular of their disease status, has been of considerable value in preventing serious losses in a few cases. The main difficulty is that many of the great wildlife areas of the world are situated in some of the poorest countries where professional animal management is often regarded as an expensive luxury. For example, there is not a single full-time veterinary member of staff for the wildlife authorities of the Sudan, Kenya, Tanzania, Uganda or Zambia. Zimbabwe fares a little better, although with the changes there politically, the wildlife services have inevitably suffered. At the present time the South Africans and the Americans probably lead in this field, although the Russians and the Chinese also now have extensive veterinary services in their protected areas. The veterinary input into wildlife management in Europe is still relatively poor.

Preventive medicine

Wild animals are not easy to handle, and, despite improvements in our techniques for controlling them, regular intervention is neither practical, economic, nor often desirable from the point of view of the animals' welfare. Once a wild animal is already ill, immobilization to provide treatment in many cases often accelerates its decline. Much of the emphasis over the last 30 years has therefore been to improve the chances of that animal never needing interventive veterinary care.

Exhibit design

In the past there has been a tendency in many collections to design exhibits which are pleasing to the human onlooker, but not necessarily well adapted to the welfare of the animal. This view has been changing rapidly in recent years, although a compromise between the two needs is often difficult to reach. For example, injuries are still the most common cause of clinical problems and death in most species. These injuries often result directly from poor housing design, either directly, or indirectly in that friction between animals in the exhibits may be caused because the facilities are inadequate to keep them apart or out of sight of each other. In order to stimulate and educate the visitor about the animal he is looking at, there has been a tendency in the zoo world to produce new exhibits which attempt to emulate the animal's environment in the wild. The result may be aesthetically pleasing, but very often, in order to provide enough animals for the visitors to see them, the stocking rates are unnaturally high and the appearance of the 'habitat' is difficult to maintain in the pristine form. The risk of parasitic and bacterial disease increases and in many instances the animals are difficult to catch for movement or routine care. The designer and his advisers, therefore, have to please the zoologists and the non-professional visitor, so finding themselves very much in the front line of the preventive medical team.

Modern, 'habitat'-type exhibits usually display a number of species together. The curators and keepers then have the next problem, which is to introduce unfamiliar individuals of both the same and different species to one another. This has to be done carefully, and often takes a long time to achieve. There is now much more knowledge of animal behaviour and particularly of the way in which individuals of different species react to one another, which has helped this process.

Stockmanship

Probably the most important part of a sound preventive medical programme is to have well-informed, trained and experienced people. The zoo world rarely offers anyone the opportunity to make a fortune financially and, like most people concerned with animals, it has to recruit from a growing band of young people who have been interested in the natural world since childhood and whose enthusiasm can be built on through the experience and training given by long-established members of staff. Good stock-manship is an ancient craft, which does not change in its basic concepts, but whereas 30 years ago there was only the experience of older colleagues to draw on, there is now a considerable wealth of data collected together from many other sources, which today's keeper has to absorb if he is going to be on top of his job. In the UK, the Zoological Society of London runs its own formal courses for keepers and a zoo keeper's correspondence course has been launched by the National Extension College. Young recruits begin their careers with very different educational backgrounds and abilities. It is important to have these differences, because, in order to create an animal-keeping structure for the future, we need the less ambitious but dedicated practical person as well as the individual who can absorb and analyse new information and collate and report on it for the benefit of others. People are the mainstay of a preventive medical programme.

Nutrition

Until about 30 years ago there were considerable misconceptions about how to feed even the most easily-kept mammals. With the exception of a very few zoos the diets given were traditional, based on long-standing, unques-tioned practice. A high proportion of the clinical cases seen at that time were either directly caused by nutritional problems, or arose indirectly because animals were often in such poor condition. Monkeys were fed on fruit and vegetables, because it was assumed that that was what they ate in the wild, and flamingos were given shrimps, because shrimps and flamingos were both pink and it was assumed that flamingos must eat shrimps and other crustaceans in the wild in order to maintain their colour. The first moves in the right direction followed considerable improvements in the diets of dom-estic farm animals as research into their nutrition increased. A number of zoo managers then used this basic data to evaluate the diets being fed to cap-tive wild animals. A scientifically based commonsense approach to animal feeding, combined with an increasing amount of information coming from the study of the diets of these animals in the wild and in some zoos, had a marked effect on the incidence of clinical disease.

The majority of mammal species kept in captivity can be maintained ade-quately on diets which have primarily been designed for domestic farm stock, domestic pets and laboratory animals. In the last 10 years detailed pathological studies have also helped to refine these diets by revealing that some species seem to be particularly susceptible to fatty acid, vitamin and mineral deficiencies. For example, marine mammals are highly susceptible to deficiences of certain fatty acids, and Vitamin A, E, and B1. Macropods, camelids, and many antelope seem to require high dietary levels of Vitamin E and probably of selenium and copper, although this needs more research to elucidate the metabolic difficulties which take place. Now that we have a more accurate idea of the nutritional content of many plants eaten by animals in the wild, the provision of substitute foodstuffs of which detailed analyses are also available becomes much easier. This is not to say that nutrition is a closed subject in the zoo world. For a few mammals and for many birds and reptiles, a high proportion of which are 'specialist feeders', little is known of their diets or feeding biology in the wild. Although there is little chance that any of these animals require nutrients which are as yet unknown to science, there are good chances that many more will be shown to have special requirements for certain nutrients and there may be considerable seasonal differences in, for example, their requirements for energy and protein. Their reproductive physiology and growth may well necessitate changing the methods of feeding them in captivity from one period of the year to another for the animal's optimum welfare.

The current nutritional research work going on in zoos is concentrating on such factors as growth rates, reproductive success in relation to diet, qualitative and quantitative evaluation of milk, seasonal weight changes, trace element metabolism (particularly of copper, iron, and zinc), and a variety of studies on the metabolism of fatty acids and Vitamins A, D, and E. Research funding is difficult to obtain for wild animal nutrition without some immediate relevance to human or domestic animal welfare. Nutritional research frequently requires large numbers of animals under highly controlled situations to obtain the most accurate results and this is often not easy to provide alongside the needs of captive propagation, and exhibition to the paying visitor.

Applied pathology

Many collections are still reluctant to carry out detailed post-mortem examinations on animals dying in their care and some are also reluctant to publish the results, even when they do carry out such work. Pathology in many ways is the basis of good clinical medicine, especially in the zoo environment (Wallach & Boever 1983). Clinical care by its very nature is a highly subjective activity and frequently generates only a little factual information. Detailed pathology not only helps to identify immediate problems on which the clinician can act, but will also, especially when carried out over a long period of time, reveal patterns of disease in a collection and highlight particular susceptibilities of species and families of animals that are often not initially apparent. The rapid identification, for example of *Yersinia* or *Salmonella*, following a few sudden deaths, will lead to immediate action, which may well save the rest of the group. The diagnosis of a single case of bronchitis may go unnoticed, until it is found, perhaps, that during the previous five years a number of other similar cases have occurred in the same housing complex, which, on further enquiry, is then found to have defective heating or ventilation. In those centres where detailed pathology has been

carried out for many years one of the recent difficulties has been to analyse
and disseminate that information, and to make it readily available to those
less well-endowed collections, whose veterinary advisers would benefit from
such detailed background data. In the Zoological Society of London, as in a
number of other similar centres in Europe and the United States, considerable effort is now being expended to try to get this information onto a computer, so that it is available to all.

The pharmaceutical industry

As is the case for man and domestic animals, wild animals owe a considerable debt to the pharmaceutical industry where many commercial products
are important in preventive medical care. The early vaccines and anti-sera
produced for farm and pet animals were often unsuitable for use in non-
domestic species. They produced marked local reactions at the site of the
injection, or occasionally a serious anaphylactic shock response. Frequently
with living vaccines, the infectious agent in the vaccine, which was no longer
virulent to the species for which it was designed, did cause disease in closely-
related animals. The early vaccines for feline enteritis, for example, caused a
number of deaths in procyonids and viverrids and early clostridial vaccines
designed for sheep produced some serious reactions in deer and antelope.
Refinement in the manufacture of these products now means that, with very
few exceptions, they are safe for use in wild species and are extensively used
where it is practical to give them on a regular basis. Apart from the vaccines
for feline enteritis, others that are now regularly used include those for feline
respiratory viruses, vaccines against distemper, hepatitis, and leptospirosis
in small omnivores and carnivores, erysipelas in marine mammals, tetanus
and influenza in equids, and clostridia, mucosal disease and some respiratory tract viruses in ruminants.

Another area which has seen remarkable improvements in the last three
decades has been the production of anthelmintics. Generally speaking, providing animals are healthy and the stocking rate is reasonable, groups of
captive animals do not show undue clinical effects from endo-parasites.
There are, nevertheless, a number of species, notably amongst the ruminants
and some birds and reptiles, which seem to be particularly susceptible to
certain nematodes and these are often of species which are not normally
found in that host. In these situations some of the most modern anthelmintics are particularly useful. Where problems are known to exist, regular
monitoring of faecal samples at a minimum interval of six weeks is used to
help to evaluate the possible adult and larval worm burden. Nevertheless, it
must be remembered that any faecal egg or larval counts are only an indicator that nematodes in the gut are reproductively active. They do not
necessarily give an accurate indication of total numbers and of the possible
damage that they are doing. Such regular testing can only realize its full

potential if, from post-mortem examinations carried out on animals on those particular premises, the pathologist uses the opportunity to compare the egg and larval numbers found in faeces taken from the rectum, with the actual numbers of parasites seen throughout the intestinal tract. Once the clinician and pathologist are satisfied that they can assess the likely pathogenicity of the parasite in this way, the careful use of anthelmintics comes into its own. In situations where oral re-infection with the parasite is inevitable, anthelmintics should only be used while the animal hosts are establishing an ecological equilibrium with the parasite. In situations where re-infection can be avoided, particularly, for example, on hard yards, where faecal matter can be swept up daily, it is then feasible to eliminate the parasite altogether. If, nevertheless, those animals are then moved later to a situation where re-infection is likely, the clinician must remember that those animals are going to be very susceptible to the pathological effects of the parasite again. Some anthelmintics, notably the new injectible agent Ivermectin, are so effective in eliminating parasites that they have to be used with considerable care. There have been a number of instances in recent years where the total elimination of the parasite in a situation where it was possible to give Ivermectin regularly led to a much more severe infestation with those parasites at a later date.

The care of animals in the wild

Most of what has already been described is applicable to animals in captivity. The clinical care of wild animals, except where they are very valuable, is usually impractical and uneconomic, but a preventive medical programme should be an essential part of their management. Unfortunately, personnel with an extensive training in wildlife management are not available in many of the most important wildlife areas of the world, although game training schools have been running for some years in Tanzania and the Cameroons to serve African countries. A variety of courses are run in Europe and Russia, primarily for local needs. The specifically veterinary input into wild animal management is relatively limited, although in the more developed countries veterinarians have been involved, particularly in surveys of wildlife pathology, infectious disease, and aspects of nutrition, the latter especially where animals have been forced to the margins of their normal habitat, or where they have been moved to new areas. Detailed studies of wildlife pathology, although largely related to an economic interest in the inter-communication of disease between wild and domestic animals, has assisted in many cases with the better management of wild populations. Disease plays a much more important role in the regulation of natural populations than is often realized and frequently an increasing incidence of a particular disease problem may indicate that a population of animals is reaching its maximum sustainable level. In these circumstances, it may be necessary to reduce populations artificially by culling and in some cases, such as with bovine tuberculosis in badgers for example, elimination of whole populations around an infected area may be necessary in order to prevent the spread of disease to otherwise healthy groups of the same species. Vaccines, such as that for anthrax, have been used for the control of outbreaks of the disease in wild ruminants, but generally this type of preventive measure is not economical, except in the case of rare and endangered species.

Clinical surveillance

Handling, sedation and anaesthesia

Possibly the single most significant advance in the management of wild and captive animals during the last 30 years has been our ability to control and handle them. Not only are such techniques important for moving animals about, but almost all studies which have led to improvements in our medical care of such animals rely on being able to handle them safely. The development of both suitable drugs and 'delivery systems' to inject those drugs remotely took place largely in the 1960s and 1970s. As a result, there is now a bewildering range of weaponry, from blow pipes to rifles, pistols and crossbows all capable of firing metal alloy or plastic syringes each carrying volumes of 1 to 20 ml up to ranges of 50 m with reasonable accuracy. The principal drugs used are the narcotics etorphine and fentanyl, the sedative xylazine, and the sedatives of the promazine and butyrophenones series, and associated anaesthetics of the cyclohexamine series (Harthoorn 1976; Fowler 1978). Used singly, or in combination, there are very few animals which cannot now be safely controlled for periods of up to several hours. There have been relatively few developments in this field over the last 10 years, but now that we know a great deal more of the pharmacology of these substances and because more workers have extensive experience with them, it is possible to use the drugs in a far more refined way than was the case when they were first available. To the experienced eye, it is soon evident that considerable differences are seen in the reactions of different species to the drugs. This difference also occurs between individuals, but in a collection where the animals are well known, it is possible to decide on the exact doses to use for light sedation or for deep anaesthesia for each of those individuals. Now that sophisticated cardio-vascular and respiratory monitoring devices are more practical to use in the care of wild animals, clinicians have not been so reluctant to keep animals sedated or anaesthetized for periods of four or even six hours, so enabling more detailed examinations, and where necessary, the provision of intensive care to take place.

Partially as a result of these techniques, the study of wild and captive animals has led to the accumulation of a considerable data bank of normal physiological information, particularly relating to haematology and bio-chemistry. The so-called 'normal' parameters will vary slightly from one collection to another and it is important that each institution builds up its own background information, which can then be used as a basis for clinical diagnosis. Many institutions will not have in-house facilities to carry out what are detailed and fairly expensive tests, but in most cases zoos and wild-life organizations have been able to forge close links with human medical and domestic animal veterinary facilities who are often willing to carry out these tests in return for the comparative data which it gives them for some of their own studies. Until about 10 years ago most of this work centred on mammals, but in more recent years, with an increasing interest in birds, rep-tiles and amphibians (Marcus 1981; Cooper & Jackson 1981; Petrak 1982), and with the development of techniques to remove small blood sam-ples from such animals, it has been possible to establish data banks on these groups as well. Studies are in progress at the present time to try, for example, to determine whether changes in some of the different white blood cells may give a more accurate indicator to particular forms of disease and it has also been possible to show that some of the anaesthetic agents may have a fairly dramatic effect on the blood picture. These factors have to be taken into account when interpreting the clinical state of an animal. Monitoring of the circulating vitamin and trace element levels has also been regularly car-ried out, and, although such methods do not give such satisfactory data as those from tissues taken at a fresh post-mortem examination, they do enable us to watch carefully species which are known to be particularly susceptible, for example, to Vitamin A or E deficiencies, or to low dietary copper intake. Such techniques have also revealed that artificial carotenoids, the form of Vitamin A which we give in captivity to some animals, notably the marine animals, may not be the same form that they obtain in the wild; they may be less efficient at dealing metabolically with artificial carotenoids and, there-fore, more susceptible to what becomes, in effect, a Vitamin A deficiency.

Retrospective surveys

Over the last two to three decades, many of the major zoological collections have also carried out extensive retrospective serum antibody studies, par-ticularly on ruminants and carnivores, to try to establish which disease agents their animals have come into contact with. These surveys have often followed outbreaks of disease where the actual cause was never identified at the time, but where subsequent testing showed it to have been one of the major domestic animal diseases. Surveys, for example, for *Brucella abortus* antibodies, leptospirosis, bovine virus diarrhoea, bovine rhinotracheitis, foot and mouth disease, malignant catarrhal fever, and feline enteritis, have improved our information on how susceptible these animals are likely to be to infectious agents from domestic animals and whether they might then constitute a reservoir of these diseases. Fortunately, antibodies to some of the particularly worrying disease agents have never been found in non-domestic animals in the United Kingdom. The quarantine laws for ruminants coming into this country are very strict, and many such tests are carried out on every individual imported, even though they are usually born in known zoological centres in continental Europe.

Further aids to diagnosis

Following the rapid development of new diagnostic aids for the human medical field, some have quickly been taken up for veterinary application and the last decade has seen much more extensive use of radiography, ultrasonics, fibre-optics and cardiovascular and respiratory monitoring devices.

Radiographic techniques have been used in the zoo world for some time, but it was not until fairly recently, with considerable improvements in the quality of the films and screens which produced very high resolution pictures, that the full value of radiography was realized. The differentiation of many soft tissue changes is now possible. Using suitable radio-opaque substances infiltrated or injected into cavities and vessels, it is now possible, with experience, to detect fairly minor changes in the outlines of organs such as the bladder, the intestinal tract and the meningeal space of the brain and to evaluate the patency and wall thickness of blood vessels. Radio-opaque substances have also been extremely useful in studying the passage times of food, for example in reptiles, where intestinal movement and digestion is dependent on the body temperature and the metabolic rate of the animal. Such studies also reveal a great deal about the way in which the digestive tract physically 'handles' a food bolus.

Perhaps even more exciting than these advances has been the recent use of ultrasonic techniques for detecting changes in the density and shape of organs. Work carried out in the Institute of Zoology has now made it possible to detect even individual follicles on the ovaries of relatively small mammals and even smaller objects will probably be detectable in the near future. The value of this technique for sexing birds and reptiles is now being examined and could in time replace the surgical techniques now in common use.

A further major development in recent years has been the use of fibre-optics, both for looking at the normal anatomy of body cavities in animals and also for diagnostic purposes. Very fine fibre-optic telescopes of as little as 2 mm in diameter, connected to a powerful light source, can be used in relatively small species to examine most of the major organs. In larger animals this equipment can also be used to examine the joint cavities or nasal passages, for example, in considerable detail. Flexible fibre-optic columns can also be used for examining the upper and lower digestive tracts and the major bronchi and bronchioles. Where the telescopes are more than 5mm in diameter, it is possible to use instruments specially designed to be passed alongside the telescope in order to take tissue samples, or even to carry out minor surgery.

Improvements in micro-electronics have enabled us to use smaller, more portable and much more accurate instruments for the measurements of arterial and venous blood pressures in different parts of the body, cardiac output, changes in the partial pressures of blood gases, respiration rates, and tidal volumes. Body temperatures can also be recorded from different parts of the body, either through thermistors inserted into different cavities or tissues, or by implanting small temperature-sensitive transmitters, which give a continuous reading of the changes in those temperatures. Some of these parameters can now be recorded remotely on equipment attached temporarily to the animals, although there are still some problems in keeping such equipment functional on a free-moving, active animal for periods of longer than a few hours. In the Institute, such techniques are being used to look at the pharmaco-physiology of the commonly used sedative and anaesthetic agents in order to build up a much more accurate view of the effect that these drugs are having, particularly on large ruminants, and especially during the induction and recovery periods.

Intensive care and clinical treatment

The refinement of the techniques which allow the clinician to maintain an animal in a sedated or lightly anaesthetized state for long periods of time and to monitor its condition closely during that procedure, has meant that it is now possible to provide serious clinical cases with the type of intensive supportive therapy which a few years ago would have been impossible. Wild animals still remain a very high clinical risk when it comes to any form of intervention, although some species, notably ungulates, are very much more difficult to deal with in this respect than, for example, carnivores and primates. The intensive care of reptiles is also now feasible, although most birds still remain a considerable problem in this respect. All intensive care requires a high degree of art, as well as science. The procedures need considerable experience to operate effectively, and, despite all the high technology which is now available, the fundamental needs of warmth, darkness and silence are just as important as ever. Custom-built equipment, designed largely for domestic pets, is used extensively in most of the larger zoo veterinary departments. In the hospital at London there is an intensive care centre specially designed for birds. Human infant incubator units can be very useful for the neonatal care of mammals and for the care of the adults of smaller species. In recent years, intravenous feeding, along the lines of that used in human medicine, has become much more practical for patients with poor appetites or whose ability to digest food is for some reason impaired. This can be a very expensive procedure in larger animals, although the manufacturers of these products are often very helpful in subsidizing the cost. The female giant panda at London, which has been intravenously fed on over 150 occasions, has been maintained by this system over long periods of time and, thanks to many of the advances described above, providing her with such a facility no longer presents a significant problem. Even control of the infusion can now be electronically regulated, through a pump programmed to provide a fixed flow rate. Such a device will even provide information on the position of a fault in the equipment, should any part of the system not be working.

With these techniques of intensive care, and with an increasing amount of data on lactation and milk content in a wide range of mammals, caring for abandoned neonates is also a much more exact science than it was even 10 years ago. Much more work would probably have been done in this field, if it were not for the fact that hand-reared animals are often difficult to integrate into established groups and many collections are rightly reluctant to take animals away for artificial rearing unless they are of an endangered species.

Improvements in dental technology for humans have recently benefited wild animals. A number of centres now carry out a considerable amount of remedial dental work where this is appropriate. Some of the new acrylics and other dental plastics that have become available in recent years also make very hard and effective replacements for the reconstruction of fractured bills in birds. The many advances in human and pet animal orthopaedics can now often be applied to wild animals. Until about 10 years ago all the external supportive casts for fractured limbs were so heavy that, to provide the strength to support a limb fracture in a zebra for example, the cast had to be reinforced with steel bars. The total resultant weight was such as to make the animal almost immobile. Modern external splinting materials are so hard and light that apart from being highly supportive, most animals find them comfortable to wear, and are less likely to try to remove them.

Conclusion

During the 1950s and 1960s, veterinary involvement with wild animals was largely concerned with identifying the major existing disease problems, applying a commonsense approach to animal nutrition and establishing the basic methods of capturing and handling them.

During the last decade and a half, the number of veterinarians and supporting scientists involved in looking after wildlife has dramatically increased. This increase, together with considerable improvements in diagnostic technology, drugs and methods of clinical monitoring and treatment, has resulted in a situation where the standard of care of non-domestic animals equals, and in some fields has surpassed, that available for domestic species.

References

Cooper, J.E. & Jackson, O.F. (Eds) (1981). *Diseases of the Reptilia* 1 and 2. Academic Press, London.

Fowler, M.E. (1978). *Zoo and wild animal medicine.* W.B. Saunders, Philadelphia and London.

Harthoorn, A.M. (1976). *The chemical capture of animals: A guide to the chemical treatment of wild and captive animals.* Baillière Tindall, London.

Marcus, L.C. (1981). *Veterinary biology and medicine of captive amphibians and reptiles.* Lea & Febiger, Philadelphia.

Petrak, M.L. (1982). *Diseases of cage and aviary birds.* 2nd edn. Lea & Febiger, Philadelphia.

Wallach, J.D. & Boever, W.J. (1983). *Diseases of exotic animals.* W.B. Saunders, Eastbourne.

Symp. zool. Soc. Lond. (1985) No. 54: 103–110

The impact on conservation of animal disease

W. M. HENDERSON

*Yarnton Cottage
High Street
Streatley
Berkshire*

Synopsis

The major diseases of domesticated animals have been eradicated in the developed countries. The later realization of the importance of the diseases of wildlife was the consequence of the introduction of European agriculture into undeveloped countries. The indigenous flora and fauna of Africa had long been part of a stabilized ecology and disease was little threat to the wildlife populations. The disturbance of the habitat by the changes demanded for the large-scale production of farm livestock and for the cultivation of large areas of arable crops led to the emergence of diseases, some known, some new, most of serious consequence.

Three disease situations are discussed, each potentially prejudicial to conservation. These examples are:

(i)   Rinderpest in Africa. A 'new' disease to Africa introduced in the last century to which the native ruminants and swine were not adapted. Rinderpest can be eliminated by the immunization of cattle by vaccination.

(ii)   Foot-and-mouth disease in the southern African territories. Buffalo are healthy carriers of the unique FMD viruses in this region. The threat to cattle can be contained by a costly policy of game fencing and cattle vaccination.

(iii)   Trypanosomiasis. The tsetse fly and trypanosomes greatly impede rural development throughout Africa south of the Sahara. Many game are reservoirs of trypanosomes without suffering disease. For years the habitat of the game and the tsetse fly has been ineffectively attacked but new biotechnologies now make it more likely that trypanosomiasis will be conquered, which will pose a major threat to the conservation of wildlife.

The impact of disease on conservation is becoming paradoxical as wildlife would fare better if certain of the present ecological relationships could be allowed to persist and if there was less intent to remove all disease hazards for domesticated stock.

Introduction

The impact of disease on the well-being of flocks and herds is well known and much has been written and said about the disease handicaps to animal

ZOOLOGICAL SYMPOSIUM No. 54
ISBN 0–19–854002–7

production. The extension of these situations from the domesticated species to the wild species and *vice versa* has received less attention. Although outbreaks of disease in animals have been reasonably well documented over the centuries, especially in Europe, the principal focus of attention has always been the impact on the domesticated populations. Within the United Kingdom, as in most of the developed countries, there has been an embarrassing degree of success in reducing the losses caused by animal disease. For example, there is little curb on milk production to-day by reason of animal disease. The most significant factor which permitted the great expansion of dairy herds in this country was the almost complete elimination of bovine tuberculosis from the early 1960s, followed more recently by the success of the brucellosis control programme. A recurrent disaster used to be each of the frequent introductions of foot-and-mouth disease but these ceased 16 years ago. There are still the lesser problems of mastitis, respiratory infections, enteric infections, various causes of infertility and a variety of metabolic disorders but none rivalling in loss the devastating effects of the major animal plagues.

The study of the susceptibility of wildlife, the studies of the infections and infestations that they harbour and their place in the epidemiology of disease and in the ecology of their habitats is of relatively recent date. Much of the early progress in acquiring knowledge of these subjects was due to the members of the veterinary services of the colonial administrations of the first half of this century, especially those of the British, the French, the Belgians, and the Dutch.

There are a number of ways in which to present this subject of the impact on conservation of animal disease in that there are various aspects relevant to disease and various aspects relevant to conservation. Also, within the framework of the programme of the scientific symposia organized by this Society, consideration must be given to the topics and their discussion during the 1981 Symposium entitled 'Animal Disease in Relation to Animal Conservation'. Many specific diseases were described during that symposium and it is unnecessary again to provide a catalogue of those which would obviously prejudice the conservation of wildlife solely by the direct effects of their pathology. Such diseases are, of course, important but so also are droughts, political instability, the demands on land use by increasing human populations and insufficient attention to controlling man's cupidity. One must note, moreover, that virulent disease in wildlife is, so to say, an abnormal rather than a normal phenomenon. This was emphasized by Jones (1982) during the earlier Symposium in pointing out that disease in wild animals that have been well adapted to their habitat rarely constitutes a threat to that population. That happy state of affairs has been and continues to be progressively eroded by man's encroachment on the natural habitats.

Threats to conservation policies

This subtitle is another way of citing the conflict between conservation and human interest, or lack of interest. There are at least three disease situations, each different, that can be used to illustrate potential threats to conservation policies.

Rinderpest in Africa

Rinderpest is a virus disease of antiquity affecting domesticated and wild ruminants and swine. Its original focus is generally accepted as being Asia, from whence it came into Europe in the train of invading armies. The serious losses which it caused in western Europe during the 18th and 19th centuries led to the establishment of veterinary schools and to the creation of state veterinary services. It was eradicated from Great Britain in 1877 but it is pertinent to note that the most recent outbreak in Europe occurred in 1949 in the Zoological Gardens in Rome (Cilli, Mazaracchio & Roetti 1951). Most people are likely to associate rinderpest with Africa, which is correct, but it is less than 100 years since it became of any great importance. This story is well told by Mack (1970) and by Plowright (1982). A great epidemic began in 1889 in Somalia or Abyssinia associated with the importation of zebu cattle from India for the Italian troops there stationed. It spread by the traditional routes, northwards, westwards and southwards, travelling some 3 000 miles to the most southern territories of Africa by the end of 1896. Rinderpest is an acute disease of high mortality and millions of domesticated cattle died. With regard to the point already made by citing Jones (1982), this was not a disease to which, over centuries, the wildlife in Africa had had an opportunity to adapt. The mortality in wild ruminants during the pandemic was described as 'devastating'. It was estimated, for example, that 90 per cent of the buffalo in Kenya died and that the bongo were almost exterminated. The situation became stabilized by natural consequences and by animal health measures but it remained a disease of major concern, especially in the East African countries. Vaccination against rinderpest was pioneered by the late J. T. Edwards in India using passage of the virus in goats to reduce its virulence in cattle. This live virus vaccine was also used in Kenya, but neither goat passage, rabbit passage, nor chick-embryo passage in the hands of many workers produced sufficient attenuation for all breeds of cattle. Adaptation of the virus to cultures of bovine kidney cells by Plowright & Ferris (1959) led to the development of a safe vaccine capable of stimulating a prolonged immunity. The use of the vaccine in an international campaign in Africa between 1962 and 1968 led to the disappearance of rinderpest in all the major endemic areas.

In view of the persistence of rinderpest over many years in East Africa, where there is a close association with game, especially the migratory wildebeest, it was plausible to conclude that the domesticated stock became infected from wildlife sources. With the widespread use of the improved cell-culture vaccine, the disease was brought under control in farm live-stock. The great surprise, however, was that with the elimination of rinder-pest from the cattle population, it also disappeared from the game population. Plowright (1982), the most eminent authority on rinderpest, wrote, 'The only way to protect wildlife reliably and over the longer term in Africa is to eliminate rinderpest from cattle'. The protection of these two populations is thus achieved by the immunization of one of them. That seems to be good for conservation of wildlife—what is the threat? The suc-cess of the mass vaccination programme stimulated a complacent attitude. This, combined with increasing political disturbances and unrest through-out many countries of the Middle East and Africa, resulted in a failure to continue the vaccination programme. Although the vaccine stimulates a long immunity, non-vaccination means that the succeeding generations of young stock are without protection. The consequences of this first became clear in 1969 when a pandemic started in Afghanistan that progressed west to the Mediterranean. The prompt application of control measures reduced the seriousness of the situation (see Scott 1981). Since then, however, rin-derpest has asserted itself in Africa but it is difficult to obtain a comprehen-sive picture of today's situation. Nevertheless, there is little doubt that rinderpest has again been a problem in Abyssinia, Somalia, and in Sudan. Its subsequent appearance in Tanzania and Nigeria might be explained by less obvious spread through intermediately located countries.

The threat to conservation is that, by a failure to immunize cattle, a high mortality may ravage the susceptible populations of wildlife. Various assess-ments have been made about the relative susceptibility, always high, of the different species of wild ruminants and swine. The most vulnerable species are believed to be buffalo, warthog, eland, kudu, giraffe, bushbuck, bush-pig, sitatunga, Uganda kob, giant forest hog, bongo, and wildebeest (see Plowright 1982). This is an example of a threat to conservation which illus-trates human lack of interest.

Foot-and-mouth disease in southern African territories

Foot-and-mouth disease (FMD) is of greatest consequence in cattle, swine, and sheep although a number of species in these and other families are susceptible. The importance of susceptible wildlife in the epidemiology of the disease is variable and one factor of some significance would appear to be the densities of the populations. Although the very large concentrations of susceptible game in Africa cannot be discounted, there are many instances in which the presence of susceptible wildlife on a lesser scale is little or no complication to the control and eradication of the disease in cattle. This absence of a problem is confirmed by the results of successful eradication programmes in Europe and in Mexico where the susceptible deer and wild swine were not subjected to any action, with no detriment to the outcome of the campaigns. It may be of some slight passing interest to recall the author's part in confirming the spread of FMD in England by wildlife, in this case by the hedgehog (McLaughlan & Henderson 1947).

There is a special problem, however, if the disease is present in a particular species with no clinical signs of infection. This is true of the African buffalo. Long-term studies were conducted by the Animal Virus Research Institute, Pirbright, in collaboration with the Veterinary Services of the Ministry of Agriculture of Botswana (see Hedger, Condy & Falconer 1969). These projects became possible by the development of 'darting' of wild game. This made feasible the collection of biological samples for the isolation of virus from carrier animals and the detection of antibodies in verification of earlier infection with the possibility of repeated sampling over some years of marked animals. In the north of Botswana in the Chobe, where there are heavy concentrations of game in the area of the Savuti Channel, buffalo were found to be carriers of the foot-and-mouth disease virus types SAT 1, 2, and 3. There are important cattle raising areas in the north of Botswana and to preserve the health of these livestock a costly programme has had to be followed of cordon fencing, establishment of quarantine camps and inspection posts plus vaccination against foot-and-mouth disease, every six months in the Chobe and annually elsewhere. This, for periods of years, has been successful since it was commenced 20 years ago, but any failure is disastrous because of the impact on international trade. In 1977, for example, outbreaks of foot-and-mouth disease occurred in cattle in Ngamiland in the north-west of Botswana during the dry season when cattle and game were watering at the Taoghe river on the edge of the heavily populated game areas of the Okavango swamps. Of various game that were shot, kudu were found with lesions of the disease and virus was subsequently isolated from tongue tissue. The experience in the Kruger National Park, where, similarly, buffalo act as carriers, is that periodically foot-and-mouth disease spreads from buffalo to the kudu and the impala. It is thought likely that the spread of virus from the buffalo to cattle may occur through a kudu or other clinically susceptible game intermediary. There was considerable spread of the disease in Botswana during 1977, 1978, and again in 1980. Livestock producers in many areas could not move their cattle to the Botswana Meat Commission abattoir at Lobatse in the south of the country. The economy of Botswana depends to a great extent on the export of beef to African and EEC countries. Foot-and-mouth disease in the domesticated livestock results in an immediate embargo on importation by the recipient countries. From 1977, for a period of two to three years, extreme hardship was experienced in the north as the normal cash flow ceased on which the day-to-day commerce depended. A greater misfortune was the national loss of exports. This type of problem has two solutions. One is to continue an expensive vaccination, quarantine and inspection programme subject to the biological uncertainties of being successful, year after year, in maintaining adequate immunization against a notoriously labile virus. The second solution is to eliminate likely sources of infection such as cattle owned by squatters and carrier wildlife populations. The second solution will become more and more attractive in direct proportion to the pressures to preserve national balances of payments. This is an example of the pressure of human interest which could well result in the destruction of the wildlife which have so successfully attained the ideal host/pathogen relationship. Elimination of the buffalo has, in fact, been practised in parts of Zambia, but it is too soon to say whether this has succeeded in reducing the number of outbreaks of foot-and-mouth disease in cattle.

Trypanosomiasis

The trypanosomes are protozoal parasites found in the blood and tissues of many vertebrate hosts and transmitted by biting flies. Trypanosomiasis is a disease complex of man and domesticated livestock in Africa, Asia and South America. In Africa it is one of the major constraints of rural development and it is a serious disease of man. The African pathogenic trypanosomes are transmitted by the bite of infected tsetse flies. Many species of game are reservoir hosts of these trypanosomes. The most important species are *Trypanosoma brucei, T. vivax,* and *T. congolense*, causing nagana and sleeping sickness in animals and man respectively. The traditional method of attempted control of trypanosomiasis, with the principal objective of raising cattle, has been the destruction of the habitat of the tsetse fly by bush clearing. This procedure has been added to by the use of insecticides as they have become available. The observation, following the great pandemic of rinderpest, that the fly belts became reduced because of the absence of game initiated a policy of game destruction in southern Africa during the first half of this century. The availability of new drugs has added chemotherapy for use in cattle. None of these methods, however, has achieved the desired objectives at an acceptable cost. The advances being made in biochemistry, molecular biology and immunology are permitting strong research attacks to be made on exploiting the phenomenon of trypanotolerance and on conquering the complexities of the trypanosome's ability to escape the host defence mechanisms by a combination of antigenic variation and immunosuppression. Although trypanotolerance is interesting and important, the primary objective is to develop a vaccine. The outcome is by no means certain, but promising leads have been developed, sufficient to ensure the necessary backing for effective research programmes.

What are the consequences of success? The answer can be given by attempting to assess the potential for animal production in Africa, south of the Sahara. Large areas which could be used for raising domesticated ruminants are little used or are not being used for animal production. According to FAO data, the present cattle population is some 170 million, with as many, or more, sheep and goats. If trypanosomiasis could be kept under permanent control or eradicated, it is generally thought that these figures, especially for cattle, could be doubled or even tripled. This is no exaggeration as the assessment is based on an expansion of the cattle-raising regions without taking into account techniques, such as pasture improvement, for increasing animal production in a given area which, so far, are little exploited in Africa.

This objective of liberating very large tracts of land for domesticated animal production by the control of trypanosomiasis is not a simple example of local interest. It is much more an example of the inexorable pressure on land resources by the ever-increasing human populations.

General observations

In the space available it has been possible to present only three examples of diseases which are a threat to conservation of wildlife. Brief mention must be made of another pathogen, namely, the herpes viruses that infect wildlife and which are transmissible to cattle. The most important of these diseases is malignant catarrhal fever. Cattle become infected when mingling with wildebeest herds at the time of wildebeest calving (Plowright, Ferris & Scott 1960). Prevention is simple, by fencing to avoid shared grazing—which is, of course, impracticable for the large herds of the nomadic people of East Africa. Lumpy skin disease is also a herpes virus infection associated with wildlife and becoming widespread. The threat to wildlife is that with increased pressure on land use it will become too tempting to destroy animals which are especially a disease threat to man's flocks and herds. It is somewhat paradoxical that the conservation of wildlife would be better served if certain of the present ecological relationships could be allowed to continue and if there was less intent to remove all disease hazards for domesticated stock.

References

Cilli, V., Mazaracchio, V. & Roetti, C. (1951). L'episodio di peste bovina al Giardino Zoologico di Roma. Rc. Ist. sup. Sanità 14: 153–9. (French text in Bull Off. Int. Epiz. (1951) 35: 444–51.)

Hedger, R.S., Condy, J.B. & Falconer, J. (1969). The isolation of foot-and-mouth disease virus from African buffalo (Syncerus caffer). Vet. Rec. 84: 516–7.

Jones, D.M. (1982). Conservation in relation to animal disease in Africa and Asia. *Symp. zool. Soc. Lond.* No. 50: 271–85.

Mack, R. (1970). The great African cattle plague epidemic of the 1890's. *Trop. anim. Hlth Prod.* **2**: 210–9.

McLaughlan, J.D. & Henderson, W.M. (1947). The occurrence of foot-and-mouth disease in the hedgehog under natural conditions. *J. Hyg.* **45**: 474–9.

Plowright, W. (1982). The effects of rinderpest and rinderpest control on wildlife in Africa. *Symp. zool. Soc. Lond.* No. 50: 1–27.

Plowright, W. & Ferris, R.D. (1959). Studies with rinderpest virus in tissue culture. *J. comp. Path.* **69**: 152–72; 173–84.

Plowright, W., Ferris, R.D. & Scott, G.R. (1960). Blue wildebeest and the aetiological agent of bovine malignant catarrhal fever. *Nature, Lond.* **188**: 1167–9.

Scott, G.R. (1981). Rinderpest and peste des petits ruminants. In *Virus diseases of food animals* **2**: 401–32. Gibbs, E.P.J. (Ed.). Academic Press, London.

Symp. zool. Soc. Lond. (1985) No. 54: 111–119

Zoos of the future

ROGER J. WHEATER   *The Royal Zoological Society of Scotland*

Synopsis

Changes in approach towards the successful attainment of the roles of research, education, conservation and recreation will be the feature of the zoo in the future, rather than much physical change. It will be the rapidly changing situation in the wild which will have a profound effect on zoos' future development. The gulf that exists between conservationists concerned with the wild and those involved in captive breeding will be bridged to meet the challenge of the declining wild, in order that strategies may be developed to prevent the slide into extinction of some selected species.

The resources of the zoological collections will be directed towards the successful management of all captive animals. The development of workable species management plans will call for considerable scientific input. Implementation of such plans will require a change in attitude towards the financial value and ownership of animals and considerable discipline by participating organisations.

Such physical changes as do take place will relate mainly to the needs of animal husbandry in pursuit of the conservation role. One important addition to such a programme will be the creation of quarantine zones or national studs for exotic species. Such centres would develop and test new techniques and would provide the infrastructure to co-ordinate area programmes, and participate in international ones. All zoological collections, irrrespective of size or status, will be expected to play a role in species management.

Environmental education will be further developed to create an awareness in our communities of wild life and its conservation needs. Linking programmes with out-of-zoo educational resources will be developed locally as well as with out-reach programmes. The quality and importance of zoo-based programmes will result in their inclusion in the schools' curriculum. This will lead to an extension of teacher and volunteer training programmes.

The continued development of existing zoo roles will help to assure the future of some species whilst continuing to provide a dramatic recreational experience for the visitor.

Zoos of the future

The first question that has to be asked is 'Will zoos survive into the future?' I am enough of an optimist to believe that they will and enough of a realist to appreciate that it may be a rather close-run thing.

Accepting that zoos will survive, then what changes might we expect? In

ZOOLOGICAL SYMPOSIUM No. 54
ISBN 0–19–854002–7

a physical sense I do not believe that they will change very much in the course of the next 50 years. I doubt that they will get much larger as, generally speaking, land for such expansion and the financial resources necessary for such major development will in all probability not be available.

Physical changes in zoological collections

The physical changes that might be expected to take place may fall into two main areas. Firstly I suspect we will continue to spend relatively large sums in the development and construction of exhibits which are exciting and aesthetically pleasing to the human viewer and perhaps no more satisfactory for the animal occupants. I believe that as our response to species survival becomes more urgent, expenditure of this kind will be questioned and will lead to the second area of physical development which will be to provide exhibit areas which produce optimum conditions for the successful propagation of animals, even if this is at the expense of some aesthetic considerations. An example of this approach was the way in which the most urgent needs of the Arabian oryx, *Oryx leucoryx*, were provided for by way of fairly austere surroundings ideally suited to the task of producing more oryx (Boyle 1963).

I believe that the real changes which will be apparent in our zoos of the future will be in the roles which we play and the changes in management and husbandry necessary to fulfil these roles.

Concern for the future of species in the wild

Our concern for the future is a response to our awareness of the considerable dangers which now face so many species in the wild. I have had the good fortune to have spent nearly half my life with animals in the wild and as a result I am particularly sensitive to the increasing pressure to which wild habitats are now subjected. The decline of natural habitats, and therefore of the creatures which inhabit them, is patchy, but even in this patchiness one is able to see the truly terrifying pace at which catastrophic change is taking place.

I have seen in the space of some 25 years the population of African elephant, *Loxodonta africana*, in the Murchison Falls National Park in Uganda decline from over-population to almost total elimination. I can now reflect on how, in the early days of my stewardship of this great national park, I was conscious of unsatisfactory changes that were being wrought on the vegetation. Was it the fire which regularly swept unchecked through the area, often started in the surrounding lands, or was it the browsing of large numbers of elephant, which was destroying the woodland and preventing the regeneration of woody vegetation? The effect of this was to reduce the vegetational diversity of the Park, a diversity which we sought to retain in the interests of maintaining as wide a spectrum of animal species as possible. The evidence from scientific research (Buechner & Dawkins 1961) clearly indicated that it was indeed the elephant that was responsible and the large herds, particularly prevalent in the boundary areas of the Park, were animals which had been forced in by the human development which changed the use of land from elephant habitat to agriculture. These elephants finding sanctuary in the Park led to an increase in population which was more than the Park could sustain. Further study suggested this population of some 14 000 animals should be drastically reduced and a cull of 2 000 animals was recommended to Uganda National Parks in 1965. This was subsequently carried out (Laws, Parker & Johnstone 1975).

In 1980, following the war in Uganda, I was asked by the United Nations to examine the situation in national parks and reserves and to make recommendations as to the action that might be taken to conserve the animals which remained (Wheater 1981). I was informed that aerial counts indicated that the total elephant population in the Murchison Falls National Park now stood at 1408 animals (I. Douglas-Hamilton, pers. comm. (1980)), a reduction of over 11 000 animals. I. Douglas-Hamilton (pers. comm. (1980)) also recorded that rhinoceros, both black, *Diceros bicornis*. and white, *Ceratotherium simum cottoni*, were now absent from the Park and that there was little evidence of them elsewhere in the country: 'We must regretfully assume' he wrote, 'that Rhinos are virtually extinct.' In a space of eight years, elephants had gone from an excessive to a barely viable population. The good efforts of the World Wildlife Fund in translocating white rhinoceros from the west bank of the Nile, where they had been suffering from increasing human pressure, to the Murchison Falls Park (Savidge, 1964), where they had increased nearly threefold, had all been for nought. Law and order had gone from that land and with nothing to prevent it the larger animals had been nearly exterminated by poaching.

The Murchison Falls National Park might be described as a rather robust area in terms of size and terrain, and yet it had suffered. Imagine how fragile for instance are the Rift Valley Lakes of Kenya. Lake Nakuru, with its breathtaking population of flamingos and pelicans and over 400 other species of birds, could conceivably be destroyed in one moment of pollution, unable by its very nature to flush the impurities away and putting at risk the production of blue green algae, the crustacean *Lovenula*, and the fish *Tilapia grahamii* which provides sustenance for the magnificently varied bird life.

I would not want to suggest that all wild places will disappear in the immediate future. Many of these areas are thankfully supported by a tourist industry; and although the nature of the wilderness and sometimes the behaviour of the animals can change under the impact of tourism, it is hoped that the economic importance of these areas will ensure that they survive until such times as the indigenous populations recognize them as an important aspect of their own heritage and of considerable aesthetic value to the nation. The World Conservation Strategy has come at a critical time, because the development of national conservation strategies will help to emphasize wildlife as one of the nation's natural resources.

The reality of rapidly increasing human populations in many of the countries who currently have plentiful wildlife resources can frankly give us little confidence for the long-term future of so many fascinating creatures.

Co-operation between zoological collections

If we accept that we have an important conservation role to play in respect of maintaining options for species in the future, then how will that challenge be tackled in the zoo of the future? There are a number of fundamental changes in philosophy which are currently being discussed. I hope for instance that the zoo director of the future will not be concerned about the cost of animals, for they will have no monetary value, nor will the ownership of animals be a constraint, as they will be the common and shared property of all zoological collections. Breeding loans, an area in which the Zoological Society of London gave such a splendid lead, and the precursor of the Species Management concept, will be a thing of the past. Animal movements between collections will be based on the needs of the species, rather than those of the individual collection. The important committees of the future will be those involved in the development of species management programmes. The scientists, the veterinarians, the studbook keepers and the managers responsible for both wild and captive populations will make up these teams, with the task of ensuring that the member collections make the best possible use of the species for which the management team is responsible. Such strategies will be based on the total knowledge of the genetic profiles of the individual animals within the group, the demographic needs of the species and resources of space within individual collections.

Scientific techniques and research in aid of species management

Those involved in the species management programmes will have recourse to a number of techniques by then fully developed by supporting scientists. One of the contributing zoos has been described as the 'frozen zoo', providing sperm for artificial insemination, eggs and sperm for *in vitro* fertilization, cellular and genetic manipulation of eggs and embryos, and embryos for transplantation. Robert Bendiner (1981: 71), in examining the collective thoughts of a number of zoo directors, comments: 'If these procedures can in time be made to serve these ways the rewards will be great, even if one discounts the science fiction scenarios of a future in which creatures then long gone from earth will be created by combining sperm and egg from the deep freeze, or by cloning long stored genetic material'. My only comment on Bendiner's remarks is that often the science fiction of today becomes the reality of tomorrow. There are other techniques which would be featured in our efforts to maintain species, such as double clutching (nothing new in this), hormonal stimulation and perfected techniques of fetal examination leading to the development of safe methods of early termination of pregnancies which, if allowed to continue, could lead to the production of young physically unsatisfactory or of unrequired sex. This is very clinical, but it may be the only way in which to ensure the future of some species. I have used the word collection rather than zoos on a number of occasions because I believe that there will be an important part to be played in the future by the private collection working within the species management plan. The contribution made by such collections, particularly in respect of aviculture and herpetology, could be most significant. The success, for instance, of the World Pheasant Association shows what can be achieved by co-ordinating the efforts of a large number of small, often very small, collections having the advantage of a very special expertise concentrated on a few birds or species.

Another outcome of the co-ordinated species management concept will, I hope, be the development in various countries, or within quarantine zones, of stud farms for exotic species. In the United Kingdom there could be a national stud for exotic species with a responsibility for breeding particular endangered species, for the testing and development of the techniques already mentioned, and the provision of a centre for the administration of species management programmes. I hope it is not within the realms of science fiction to suggest that in the UK context, Her Majesty's Government might provide the financial support for such an undertaking by recognizing the contribution that such a centre would make in maintaining genetic diversity, which is one of the major responsibilities or commitments under the World Conservation Strategy (International Union for the Conservation of Nature and Natural Resources 1980).

The development of species management strategies

An important part of the co-ordination and planning of management programmes in our collections will be the need continually to overview the situation in the wild.

I make no apology for returning again to the question of the future of animals in the wild, for in my estimation what happens here, and the speed at which detrimental changes occur, will inevitably affect the role of zoos in maintaining species for the future. As the situation becomes critical with regard to some species in the wild, it is important that early decisions are made to bring into captivity those species that are at risk. Individual animals will be required from the wild from time to time to provide new genes for the managed captive group, and such requirements must be understood and met. Conversely, there should be no right for collections to take further animals from the wild if the existing captive resources are not being managed in a scientific and co-ordinated way. One of the present constraints upon this is that there is still a gulf between those responsible for animals in captivity and those responsible for them in the wild. I believe that as the zoos' role is better understood, so this unfortunate gulf between us will be narrowed and then bridged—for without understanding on both sides, the development of action-orientated strategies will prove most difficult.

There are those conservationists such as Norman Myers (1979) who, whilst recognizing the problems of the future, argue that breeding animals in captivity results in breeding animals for captivity. He argues also that captive propagation is in some areas very poor indeed. He cites, for instance, only a 10 per cent success in reptile breeding. I believe that our collections of the future will have addressed themselves to these problems and developed techniques which will ensure a very high rate of success. I can say this with some confidence in respect of reptiles, as in Edinburgh our breeding success has improved over the past few years from success with one or two species to 17 (Royal Zoological Society of Scotland, 1984). Myers (1979) also makes the point, very correctly, that it is much more costly to maintain populations of animals in captivity than in the wild, and suggests that the financial resources used to support animals in captivity should be diverted towards animals in the wild. This of course is too simplistic an approach, because it does not acknowledge that the resources that we have available to support our captive breeding efforts come in the main from visitors who come to our collections to see the animals for themselves.

Zoos and conservation education

There is, I believe, a second important input into conservation and this is through environmental education. The creation of an awareness, particularly in young people, of animal life and the difficulties animals now face in this modern world, is an important obligation that I hope all zoos in the future will have developed. The animal collection as a teaching resource is an important one, and fortunately, the experience of some larger collections can provide the foundation for the development of this resource in all zoos of the future. It is important to understand, however, that no collection is too small to make a valuable contribution to education. In the future the existing imaginative programmes which have been tested by time and experience will be further developed and modified.

Interlinking teaching resources

This applies particularly to the concept of linking various teaching resources. In Edinburgh we are using as part of our linked service the varied resources of the Royal Botanic Gardens, the Royal Scottish Museum, the Royal Commonwealth Institute, the Forestry Commission, the Scottish Wildlife Trust, and others. This has given much wider content to our educational work, and not only has greatly enhanced our programmes, but coincidentally has increased the educational output of a number of the participating organizations. This programme which we call 'Interlink' is gaining wider acceptance, particularly in the United States, and it is my hope that in the future every collection will have just such a programme. In addition to the educational value, it provides through its developmental and operational stages an increased understanding between the participants, which is most helpful towards the gulf-narrowing exercise which has been mentioned earlier.

The development of an environmental ethic

The creation of awareness in young people cannot be over-emphasized (Wheater 1979). I believe that the child who is sensitively introduced to the toad will like the toad and will therefore be more likely to show concern in the future for toads and toad habitat. The extension of this is to be concerned about the habitats of other creatures. The conservation of wildlife must surely depend on an informed and concerned public; to achieve this is one of the great challenges.

Further expansion of educational programmes will continue, and one of the most important requirements of this is that zoo education programmes attain a quality and importance in educational terms that ensures inclusion in the development of the curriculum. The attainment of this will depend on our ability and our enthusiasm to expand our programmes further. In the future much more will have to be provided by way of in-service training for teachers in environmental matters, and it is further hoped that such programmes might be made available to those involved in environmental education in the Third World. The implementation of out-reach programmes, taking the zoo's environmental teaching expertise to those who by reason of distance or other constraints are unable to use the zoo, is another important 'beyond-the-zoo-gate' area for development. In developing such programmes the Interlink concept, using local wildlife reserves, field study centres etc., could be most appropriate.

Zoo education must not be viewed only in a formal and structured sense; the visitors to our zoo of the future, as a result of excellent orientation at the start of the visit, good labels, good guidebooks and special programmes, must leave the zoo better informed and better satisfied by their day's recreation. Unless considerable financial resources are made available, a large part of the programmes for general zoo visitors will have to be met through the efforts of volunteers. It is my hope that every future zoo will have a volunteer service, because not only does it make much possible for the zoo; it also provides an outlet for those in the community who are interested in such work. Successful volunteer programmes are, in a sense, the reflection of the zoo's involvement with the community which it serves.

To conclude

These then are some of the contents, as I see them, of our zoo in the future: structurally probably little different, the needs of the animals perhaps better understood as a result of scientific research, and those needs met by design and other husbandry changes. The zoo of the future will be fuller of healthy young animals, as a result of our efforts in species management. This success will have been made possible by our national stud and through the co-ordination of species management programmes, both nationally and internationally. The other young animal which one would wish to see in numbers is the human one, in whom, if there is to be any future for wildlife, we must inculcate the awareness and understanding that we do have a responsibility for the other creatures of this planet and should not be selfishly concerned only with ourselves. It is hoped that through education such an awareness can be extended world-wide as it is only through an aware population that the future of the natural faunal reserves will be assured.

We all have a great responsibility. We must seek, in conjunction and consultation with our colleagues attempting to conserve species in the wild, to make the right decisions; not to dissipate our energies in disagreement, but together to attempt to save much of the wild and, at the same time, ensure that, should our best endeavours in this direction fail, we have a few, and it can only be a few, of this Earth's fascinating creatures in the ark of the zoological collection.

Bill Conway should have given this paper today and I would like to finish with something that Bill said a number of years ago. 'There is reason to hope should the great wildlife forest be lost, that the world may be grateful for even a few seeds, that is where captive propagation of wild animals should go from here.' (W. G. Conway, quoted in Bendiner 1981: 57).

This is the challenge for the future. I am confident that, despite the many difficulties which will beset them, our successors will rise to the challenge and succeed, for can we seriously contemplate a world without elephants, rhinoceros, Arabian oryx, or a multitude of other creatures large and small?

References

Bendiner, Robert (1981). *The fall of the wild, the rise of the zoo*. Elsevier-Dutton, New York.

Boyle, C.L. (1963). Operation Oryx. *Oryx* 7: 61.

Buechner, H.K. & Dawkins, H.C. (1961). Vegetation change induced by elephants and fire in Murchison Falls National Park, Uganda. *Ecology* 42: 752–66.

International Union for the Conservation of Nature and Natural Resources (1980). *World conservation strategy: Living resource conservation for sustainable development*. (In co-operation with the World Wildlife Fund and the United Nations Environment Programme.) IUCN, Gland, Switzerland.

Laws, R.M., Parker, I.S.C. & Johnstone, R.C.B. (1975). *Elephants and their habitats. The ecology of elephants in North Bunyoro*. Clarendon Press, Oxford.

Myers, N. (1979). *The sinking ark*. Pergamon Press, New York.

Royal Zoological Society of Scotland (1984). *Annual Report* **1983**: 81–2.

Savidge, J.M. (1964). *Second introduction of White rhino into Murchison Falls National Park Uganda*. (Mimeo.)

Wheater, R.J. (1979). Some aspects of the educational role of the Royal Zoological Society of Scotland. *Zool. Gart.* (N.F.) *Jena* **49**: 313–8.

Wheater, R.J. (1981). *Tourism rehabilitation programme. Uganda (UGA/80/008). Wildlife in Uganda Annex 1*. United Nations Development Programme, World Tourism Organisation, Madrid.

Conservation and comparative medicine

Symp. zool. Soc. Lond. (1985) No. 54: 123–135

Embryo manipulation and genetic engineering

C. POLGE

A.F.R.C. Institute of Animal Physiology
Animal Research Station
307 Huntingdon Road
Cambridge

Synopsis

Techniques for embryo transplantation which are being applied successfully in some of the large domestic species may provide new opportunities for breeding non-domesticated animals especially in relation to the conservation of genetic material by the preservation of embryos at very low temperatures. The provision of embryos from animals in captivity may be aided by the development of techniques for the maturation of oocytes *in vitro* and for *in vitro* fertilization. Other opportunities for the multiplication and conservation of rare species may also be provided by the development of methods for cellular and genetic manipulation of eggs and embryos. By the manipulation of embryonic cells it is possible to produce genetically identical twins and quadruplets from a single embryo and chimaeric animals from aggregated cells of two or more embryos and in some circumstances the principle of chimaerism may be used to overcome species barriers in embryo transplantation. Techniques for nuclear transplantation are being developed although the possibility of cloning mammals by transferring the nucleus from a somatic cell of an adult animal into an egg has not been realized. Nevertheless, gene transfer between species may become a practical possibility since transgenic mice have already been produced following the introduction of foreign cloned genes into the male pronucleus of a recently fertilized egg. All these methods extend the horizons for animal conservation.

Introduction

There is no doubt that the most effective means of animal conservation lies in the preservation of suitable environments in which the animals can continue to breed and maintain their species. But experience has shown that this may be very difficult and as disturbances and destruction of many natural habitats continue in a relentless fashion, zoos are called upon to play an increasingly important role in the provision of a refuge for at least some of the endangered species. Even in zoos, however, problems concerning the breeding and maintenance of populations of wild animals in captivity often arise and solutions to these problems can best be sought through a greater

ZOOLOGICAL SYMPOSIUM No. 54
ISBN 0-19-854002-7

understanding of reproductive processes and the development of new methods for the control or manipulation of animal breeding.

Two of the most important techniques for controlled breeding which have already been applied very successfully and quite extensively in some domestic species are artificial insemination and embryo transplantation and in recent years some progress has been made towards the use of these methods for breeding animals in zoos. Successful application in 'exotic' species still requires a lot of detailed study, but as the methods are developed they should provide a means for the more effective multiplication of some rare species. Hand-in-hand with these developments is the possibility of providing ancillary methods for animal conservation, especially by the establishment of 'banks' of sperm and embryos which can be maintained in the frozen state at very low temperatures for long periods of time. The spermatozoa of many different species have now been frozen and stored successfully in liquid nitrogen and although little is yet known about the potential fertilizing capacity of frozen spermatozoa other than in domestic animals, there is no doubt that the techniques should prove to be effective in many species. The eggs and embryos of a more limited number of species have also been frozen and stored at very low temperatures and produced viable young after thawing and transplantation to foster mothers. More research in this area should prove rewarding and recent progress is discussed in other chapters of this book. The concept of a 'frozen zoo' is not something to attract great public interest, but storage of gametes and embryos represents an important method of genome conservation which can be regarded as an insurance policy permitting the preservation and future reconstitution of unique genotypes. Research in experimental embryology, however, has been progressing very rapidly in recent years and there are now even more techniques on the horizon which may have great potential usefulness in artificial breeding and in animal conservation; these arise primarily from experiments on cellular and genetic manipulation of mammalian eggs and embryos (Willadsen & Polge 1980).

Oocyte maturation *in vitro*

The starting point for successful application of embryo transplantation in any species, and indeed for the opportunity to undertake further cellular or genetic manipulation of embryos, is the provision of an adequate number of eggs. In laboratory and domestic animals exogenous gonadotrophic hormones such as purified follicle stimulating hormone or pregnant mares' serum gonadotrophin have been used extensively to induce superovulation, but it has been found that ovarian responses to hormonal stimulation are always characterized by a great degree of variability. The relatively small, although significant, increase in the number of normal eggs that can be obtained for transplantation by these means appears to be governed by inherent ovarian restrictions which are related to the variable nature of the follicle populations which will respond to exogenous hormonal stimulation in different animals (for reviews, see Moor, Cahill & Stewart 1980; Moor, Kruip & Green 1984). In some species, such as cattle, in which non-surgical methods of embryo collection can be performed, the procedures for induction of superovulation and embryo recovery can be carried out repeatedly (Christie, Newcomb & Rowson 1979) thus providing relatively large numbers of embryos from individual animals over a period of time. However, problems of inducing superovulation and embryo recovery may be even greater in captive wild animals than in domestic animals, owing to physiological, environmental and nutritional factors, and there is therefore considerable interest in alternative methods that may be developed for 'tapping' the very large pool of immature oocytes which is present within the ovaries of all mammals.

If immature oocytes could be collected directly from ovaries and induced to undergo normal maturation during culture *in vitro*, then problems associated with ovarian stimulation might be circumvented and large numbers of eggs made available for fertilization, transplantation or further manipulation. Ever since the pioneering experiments of Chang (1955) and Edwards (1965) in which it was shown that a large proportion of oocytes liberated from immature follicles resumed meiosis and underwent spontaneous nuclear maturation during culture *in vitro*, the potential usefulness of this approach has been appreciated. Despite a large amount of experimentation, however, very few live young have, until recently, been produced from oocytes matured in this way when transplanted to inseminated recipients. It is now clear that the capacity for immature oocytes to acquire full competence for fertilization and normal embryonic development is dependent not only on the maturation of the nuclear components, but also on the maturation of the cytoplasm. The cytoplasmic changes involved, which include important changes in intracellular organelles and in protein synthesis, are normally induced by intraovarian signals mediated by hormones and directed by the follicular cells associated with the oocyte. The regulation of oocyte maturation has now been studied in great detail (Moor, Crosby & Osborn 1982; Moor & Osborn 1983). The importance of intrafollicular regulating mechanisms was first demonstrated conclusively in experiments in which intact follicles were cultured *in vitro* in media enriched with hormones. Under these conditions the oocytes within the follicles not only resumed meiosis but underwent cytoplasmic changes analogous to those observed during normal maturation *in vivo*. Moreover oocytes matured in this way displayed full competence to undergo fertilization and normal embryonic development leading to the birth of live young (Moor & Trounson 1977). These experiments have now been taken a step further and appropriate culture conditions have been developed in which sheep oocytes can be matured outside the follicle in such a way that they acquire full developmental competence (Staigmiller & Moor 1984). The important part of this procedure is that oocytes should be cultured with their cumulus and coronal cells intact and in a medium containing gonado-trophins and oestrogen. Supplementary follicle cells added to the medium enhance maturational ability and a non-static culture system ensures that the hormonal balance is appropriately maintained. This system, therefore, now provides a simple and reliable method of producing large numbers of fully matured oocytes for embryo manipulation and transfer. It seems prob-able that sheep oocytes obtained even from relatively small unstimulated follicles may be induced to undergo maturation in this way and appropriate modifications to the system may make it applicable to the maturation *in vitro* of oocytes of other species.

In vitro fertilization

The developmental potential of oocytes has generally been examined fol-lowing fertilization *in vivo* because it is only in a relatively few laboratory animals and in the human that satisfactory methods have so far been devised for the fertilization of oocytes *in vitro* (Wright & Bondioli 1981). Development of techniques for fertilization *in vitro* in other species would be highly desirable from the point of view of advances in animal breeding and for the production of embryos for further manipulation. Despite con-siderable investigations with oocytes of farm animals, there has been only one report of the birth of a calf from an *in vitro* fertilized bovine oocyte (Brackett *et al.* 1982). Recent experiments at the Animal Research Station, Cambridge, however, have now resulted in the birth of live young from both pig and sheep oocytes fertilized *in vitro*. In the pig, a medium based on that described by Pavlok (1981) was used to capacitate washed ejaculated boar spermatozoa during culture *in vitro*. When the spermatozoa were mixed with oocytes collected shortly after ovulation it was found that the most cri-tical requirement for penetration of the oocytes by spermatozoa was the temperature. Very few eggs were fertilized when cultured with spermatozoa at 37°C, whereas a high proportion (76 per cent) was fertilized when cul-tured at 39°C, the normal body temperature of the pig. Transfer of fertilized eggs following development to the two- or four-cell stage to recipient females resulted in the birth of 19 live young and, although the embryonic survival rate achieved was relatively low, the principles of the system for *in vitro* fertilization were clearly validated (W.T.K. Cheng & C. Polge, unpub-lished). A repeatable and reliable technique has now also been developed for the fertilization of sheep oocytes *in vitro* and moreover the oocytes used for these experiments were previously matured *in vitro* according to the methods of Staigmiller & Moor (1984). Ram spermatozoa were capacitated by a short incubation of the semen *in vitro*, but modifications to the pig system were required for fertilization. When fetal calf serum in the fertilization medium was replaced by sheep serum, sperm motility during culture at 39°C was well maintained and about 70 per cent of the oocytes were fertilized. Ten normal lambs have been born following transfer of oocytes fertilized *in vitro* to recipient ewes (W.T.K. Cheng, E.D. Wilson, C. Polge & R.M. Moor, unpublished). Further refinement of techniques for maturation and fertilization *in vitro* of oocytes of a wide variety of species will surely be made, thus extending the opportunities for embryo manipulation, preservation and transplantation.

Micromanipulation of embryos

Very significant advances have been made in the last two decades in the study of early mammalian development by the application of microsurgical techniques to early embryos; this has enabled the developmental potential and regulatory capacity of embryonic cells to be critically examined (Adamson & Gardner 1979). Until recently, however, the majority of such research has been confined to the mouse, principally because of the suitability of this species for laboratory work, the availability of inbred strains with genetic markers, the relatively cheap and easily accessible supply of eggs and embryos and, perhaps most importantly, the development of suitable culture media in which mouse embryos can be kept alive *in vitro* (Whittingham 1971). Mammalian embryos at early cleavage stages generally fail to survive *in vivo* if the zona pellucida is severely damaged or removed during microsurgery. Satisfactory culture media which will support early cleavage of embryos *in vitro* of the majority of species other than the mouse are still not available and this has imposed a severe restriction upon the extension of micromanipulative experiments to a wider variety of species. A major technical advance was made, however, by Willadsen (1979) when a method was developed for embedding embryos in agar following radical microsurgery. The agar coating effectively sealed any holes or defects in the zona pellucida and permitted the study of further development when the embryos were returned to the female genital tract. Embryos treated in this way were shown to be capable of development to the blastocyst stage at which time protection from the zona pellucida was no longer required and they could be removed from the agar and transplanted to recipient animals in which they could develop to term. By means of this procedure investigations involving the micromanipulation of cleaving embryos of a number of the large domestic species have now been carried out (Willadsen 1982).

Monozygotic twins have been produced in sheep by the separation of blastomeres from either two-, four-, or eight-celled embryos into two equal groups and the viability of such 'half' embryos appears to be equivalent to that of normal embryos (Willadsen 1980). Even embryos containing one quarter of the normal cell number, such as those derived from single cells from a four-celled embryo or two cells from an eight-celled embryo, appear to retain a high developmental potential and their viability is only slightly reduced as compared with normal embryos (Willadsen 1981). There is a limit, however, to how far it is possible to extend these procedures and it has been found that further reduction of cell number in cleaving embryos is not generally compatible with normal development. Although totipotency of early embryonic cells is probably retained at least until the eight-cell stage, very few live young have been produced from sheep embryos derived from a single cell from an eight-cell embryo (Willadsen 1981; Willadsen & Fehilly 1983). The reason for the restriction of developmental capacity in these circumstances appears to be that when the total cell number at the time of blastulation is very significantly reduced a functional inner cell mass is rarely produced. Nevertheless, the ability to produce identical twins or quadruplets from single embryos by micromanipulative procedures has practical significance not only for the provision of genetically identical animals for experimental purposes, but also for the more rapid multiplication of selected genotypes in circumstances where the supply of embryos for transplantation may be quite limited. The techniques have already been shown to be applicable not only in sheep but also in cattle, pigs, goats, and horses.

An even simpler procedure has more recently been developed for the production of identical twins by splitting embryos into half at the late morula or expanded blastocyst stage. When blastocysts are divided in such a way that each half contains inner cell mass and trophectoderm cells, both halves are capable of development to term. Since protection provided by the zona pellucida *in vivo* is no longer essential at this stage, the divided embryos can be returned directly to the reproductive tracts of recipients (Willadsen & Godke 1984; Williams, Elsden & Seidel 1984).

Chimaeras

Another very important technique in embryonic manipulation is the production of chimaeric embryos by the aggregation of embryonic cells from two or more embryos or by the injection of cells from one embryo into the blastocyst cavity of another. Following aggregation the cells will form a composite blastocyst and, provided the cells of each parent embryo are represented in the inner cell mass, a chimaeric animal can be produced. The frequency with which such composite embryos result in chimaeric animals is very high if the total number of cells at the time of aggregation is at least equal to the normal cell number (Fehilly, Willadsen & Tucker, 1984b). By contrast, and perhaps more interestingly, when chimaeric embryos are made to contain less than the normal cell number, the viability of such embryos is still relatively high but the animals produced are frequently not chimaeric. 'Quarter' embryos composed of single cells from each of two parent eight-celled embryos, for example, will form a composite blastocyst, but since the number of cells allocated to the inner cell mass is consequently reduced it seems that these may be derived from cells of only one of the initial parent embryos. Although cells from either of the parent embryos have a chance to give rise to the inner cell mass, sometimes the cells of one parent embryo predominate and identical animals are produced. Preferential selection of daughter cells from one of the embryos to form the inner cell mass may arise from slight asynchrony in development between the two parent embryos. Such preferential selection may also be directed by deliberately mixing one cell from an eight-celled embryo with one cell from a four-celled embryo and the animals produced then tend to be derived only from the blastomere from the eight-celled embryo. The largest number of identical lambs produced from a single eight-celled embryo by these means has been five (Willadsen & Fehilly 1983). These techniques, therefore, extend the opportunities for exploiting the totipotentiality of early embryonic cells.

Although chimaeric embryos can readily be produced from embryonic cells of the same species, they can also be produced from embryonic cells derived from two different species (Gardner & Johnson 1973) but such composite embryos do not generally develop to term unless the two species providing the embryos can also be hybridized (Rossant, Mauro & Croy 1982). By contrast, perhaps the most dramatic example of interspecies chimaerism has been the recent production of sheep–goat chimaeras by embryo manipulation (Fehilly, Willadsen & Tucker 1984a). These strange animals were produced by mixing cells from sheep and goat embryos and the composite blastocysts were then transplanted to either sheep or goat recipients which resulted in the birth of animals displaying many chimaeric characteristics including patches of sheep wool and goat hair in their coats. The most important feature of these experiments was the demonstration that embryos composed of cells from two different species that cannot normally be hybridized can sometimes survive to term. Offspring have never been produced from sheep embryos transplanted to goats or from goat embryos transplanted to sheep (Hancock & McGovern 1968). Nevertheless, through chimaerism the cells of one species can collaborate with and carry the cells of another incompatible species through embryonic and fetal development to birth. Does this, therefore, offer new opportunities for the rescue of endangered species? The use of embryo transplantation for the multiplication of rare species would normally only be effective if there were sufficient recipient female animals of the same species available to act as foster mothers. If there were only a few females of a rare species a situation might be envisaged whereby a closely related and more abundant species could be used to provide embryos for making chimaeras and to act as foster mothers. It would be hoped that in some of the chimaeric animals produced, cells from the endangered species would have entered the germ line and they could be used for breeding, but this would be a matter of chance. The experiments on sheep–goat chimaeras, however, have been carried further and it has been shown that a pure sheep fetus can survive to term in a goat and a pure goat fetus survive to term in a sheep. This was achieved by constructing chimaeric embryos in such a way that the cells of only one species gave rise to the fetus whereas the trophectoderm and placenta were derived mainly from cells of the other species which was also used as the recipient foster mother (Fehilly, Willadsen & Tucker 1984a). Further experiments to overcome incompatibilities between species in embryo transplantation would undoubtedly extend the possibilities for animal conservation.

The sheep–goat chimaeras are just one example of the way in which embryonic cells of different origin are able to collaborate in order to overcome incompatibilities in development. Chimaerism has also been used experimentally to rescue embryos of defective genotypes such as parthenogenetic embryos. Although parthenogenetic reproduction occurs naturally in some species, it does not do so in mammals. Parthenogenetic mouse embryos, for example, have the potential for quite extensive proliferation and differentiation, but their development is restricted and they do not survive to term. By contrast, if cells from a parthenogenetic embryo are mixed with cells from a normal fertilized embryo, the chimaeric embryos so formed are capable of normal development and offspring have been produced containing cells of both parthenogenetic and normal origin (Surani, Barton & Kaufman 1977). In some instances the parthenogenetic cells may even enter the germ line and give rise to normal eggs (Stevens 1978). Thus, embryo manipulation and chimaerism may again come to the rescue for the multiplication of rare genotypes.

Embryonic cells will proliferate and form teratocarcinomas when embryos are transferred to ectopic sites such as the testis. Teratocarcinoma cells retaining many pluripotential characteristics can be grown in culture and provide cells which in mice have also been used in the formation of chimaeras with normal embryos resulting in chimaeric animals. The teratocarcinoma cells may participate in the formation of many of the tissues and organs and occasionally in the formation of the germ line (Stewart & Mintz 1981), but this appears to be very rare because the karyotype of teratocarcinoma cells is generally abnormal. Recently, however, it has been shown to be possible to establish progressively growing cultures of pluripotential embryonic cells which have been isolated directly from in vitro cultures of mouse blastocysts (Evans & Kaufman 1981). These cells, unlike cells derived from teratocarcinomas, have a normal karyotype and should stand a far better chance of participating in the formation of the germ line when they are used in the production of chimaeras. If it becomes possible to establish cultures of normal pluripotential cells from a wide variety of species, then these would represent an important reservoir for genome conservation.

Towards cloning

Many of the microsurgical and manipulative techniques applied to embryos which have been described so far, such as the production of several identical animals from a single embryo or the formation of germ line chimaeras from a variety of embryonic cells, represent a form of cloning. The ultimate ambition in clonal reproduction, however, would be to produce an almost unlimited number of identical animals from a single adult animal. This would involve the transplantation of nuclei from adult cells into enucleated eggs coupled with the ability for the transferred nuclei to initiate full development of the eggs. The methods and success of nuclear transplantation in mammals have recently been surveyed by McLaren (1984). It is clear that the ultimate ambition of cloning from adult nuclei is still a dream and may remain so for a long time since it appears that nuclei in differentiated adult cells become irreversibly restricted in their potency. When transferred to enucleated eggs, nuclei from differentiated cells may induce some development, but no normal embryos have been produced. By contrast, some success has been achieved following transplantation of embryonic nuclei and the techniques for carrying out these procedures are being improved. One of the most successful methods for nuclear transfer, which inflicts least trauma to the eggs, involves sucking out a nucleus from a donor egg surrounded by a small piece of the egg plasma membrane into a micropipette. The fragment containing the nucleus is then inserted beneath the zona pellucida of a recipient egg into which it fuses with the assistance of Sendai virus (McGrath & Solter 1983). Experiments in mice involving the transplantation of pronuclei from recently fertilized eggs into enucleated fertilized or artificially activated eggs has resulted in the birth of live young. Interestingly, experiments in which haploid parthenogenetic eggs were used as recipients for male or female pronuclei showed that eggs which received a male pronucleus developed to term whereas those with two female pronuclei developed only poorly after implantation (Surani, Barton & Norris 1984). Thus the presence of both a male and a female pronucleus appears to be essential for full development. Experiments such as these clearly demonstrate the effectiveness of nuclear transplantation techniques. Experimental manipulation of the genome has already shed light on the reasons for the restricted developmental potential of parthenogenetic eggs. Unfortunately, however, there are no reliable reports of successful full term development following transplantation of more advanced embryonic nuclei into enucleated mouse eggs. It is possible that in some species other than the mouse the full potency of embryonic nuclei may be retained for somewhat longer during early development. Certainly it would be interesting if nuclei from pluripotential cell lines could ever be used successfully for nuclear transplantation and ultimately the aim will be to devise methods for 'reprogramming' the nuclei from differentiated adult tissues so that their totipotent status may be regained.

Gene injection

Nuclear transplantation is an important method for genetic manipulation, but a new era has now been opened up through developments in recombinant DNA technology and the possibility of introducing foreign cloned genes into the mammalian genome. Many recent studies have shown that a most effective method for the introduction of foreign DNA into the genome is by the microinjection of cloned genes directly into the pronuclei of eggs shortly after fertilization. The foreign genes may then become incorporated into the chromosomes during early development and following transplantation of the eggs produce so-called transgenic animals. In such animals the foreign genes may become stably integrated and in some instances expressed and transmitted through the germ line (Costantini & Lacy 1981; Wagner *et al.* 1981; Gordon & Ruddle 1981; Palmiter, Brinster *et al.* 1982). These techniques are still in their infancy and there is as yet much to be learned about the types of gene construct which will enable optimal integration into the genome and result in tissue-specific expression (Palmiter, Brinster *et al.* 1982; Palmiter, Chen & Brinster 1982), but much progress is being made and the methods are obviously a most powerful tool in the study of mammalian development and genetics. For the animal breeder new opportunities may be provided for the genetic manipulation of animals in such a way as to improve performance. But this technology would also seem to be extremely important from the point of view of genetic conservation of all animals. It is not too difficult to purify and store DNA of any species and zoos should be encouraged to make such a provision particularly from animals which are endangered. The many techniques which are now being developed for cellular and genetic manipulation of mammalian eggs and embryos and for genome preservation may thus provide a brighter future for animal conservation.

References

Adamson, E.D. & Gardner, R.L. (1979). Control of early development. *Br. med. Bull.* 35: 113–9.
Brackett, B.G., Bousquet, D., Boice, M.L., Donawick, W.J., Evans, J.F. &

Dressel, M.A. (1982). Normal development following *in vitro* fertilization in the cow. *Biol. Reprod.* **27**: 147–58.

Chang, M.C. (1955). The maturation of rabbit oocytes in culture and their maturation, activation, fertilization and subsequent development in the Fallopian tubes. *J. exp. Zool.* **128**: 379–99.

Christie, W.B., Newcomb, R. & Rowson, L.E.A. (1979). Ovulation rate and egg recovery in cattle treated repeatedly with pregnant mare serum gonadotrophin and prostaglandin. *Vet. Rec.* **104**: 281–3.

Costantini, F. & Lacy, E. (1981). Introduction of a rabbit β-globulin gene into the mouse germ line. *Nature, Lond.* **294**: 92–4.

Edwards, R.G. (1965). Maturation *in vitro* of mouse, sheep, cow, pig, rhesus monkey and human ovarian oocytes. *Nature, Lond.* **208**: 349–51.

Evans, M.J. & Kaufman, M.H. (1981). Establishment in culture of pluripotential cells from mouse embryos. *Nature, Lond.* **292**: 154–6.

Fehilly, C.B., Willadsen, S.M. & Tucker, E.M. (1984a). Interspecific chimaerism between sheep and goat. *Nature, Lond.* **307**: 634–6.

Fehilly, C.B., Willadsen, S.M. & Tucker, E.M. (1984b). Experimental chimaerism in sheep. *J. Reprod. Fert.* **70**: 347–51.

Gardner, R.L. & Johnson, M.H. (1973). Investigation of early mammalian development using interspecific chimaeras between rat and mouse. *Nature, Lond.* **246**: 86–9.

Gordon, J.W. & Ruddle, F.H. (1981). Integration and stable germ line transmission of genes injected into mouse pronuclei. *Science, Wash.* **214**: 1244–6.

Hancock, J.L. & McGovern, P.T. (1968). Transfer of goat and sheep hybrid eggs to sheep and reciprocal transfer of eggs between sheep and goats. *Res. vet. Sci.* **9**: 411.

McGrath, J. & Solter, D. (1983). Nuclear transplantation in the mouse embryo by microsurgery and cell fusion. *Science, Wash.* **220**: 1300–2.

McLaren, A. (1984). Methods and success of nuclear transplantation in mammals. *Nature, Lond.* **309**: 671–2.

Moor, R.M., Cahill, L.P. & Stewart, F. (1980). Ovarian stimulation or egg production as a limiting factor of egg transfer. *Proc. 9th Int. Congr. Anim. Reprod. Artif. Insem.* (Madrid) **1**: 43–58.

Moor, R.M., Crosby, I.M. & Osborn, J.C. (1982). Growth and maturation of mammalian oocytes. In *In vitro fertilization and embryo transfer*: 39–63. (Proceedings of Serono Clinical Colloquia on Reproduction No. 4.) Crosigniani, P.G. & Rubin, B.L. (Eds). Academic Press, London.

Moor, R.M., Kruip, Th.A.M. & Green, D. (1984). Intraovarian control of folliculogenesis: limits to superovulation? *Theriogenology* **21**: 103–6.

Moor, R.M. & Osborn, J.C. (1983). Somatic control of protein synthesis in mammalian oocytes during maturation. In *Molecular biology of egg maturation*: 178–96. (Ciba Foundation Symposium 98.) Porter, R. & Whelan, J. (Eds). Pitman Books, London.

Moor, R.M. & Trounson, A.O. (1977). Hormonal and follicular factors affecting maturation of sheep oocytes *in vitro* and their subsequent developmental capacity. *J. Reprod. Fert.* **49**: 101–9.

Palmiter, R.D., Brinster, R.L., Hammer, R.E., Trumbauer, M.E., Rosenfeld, M.G.,

Birnberg, N.C. & Evans, R.M. (1982). Dramatic growth of mice that develop from eggs microinjected with metallothionein-growth hormone fusion genes. *Nature, Lond.* **300**: 611–5.

Palmiter, R.D., Chen, H.Y. & Brinster, R.L. (1982). Differential regulation of metal-lothionein-thymidine kinase fusion genes in transgenic mice and their offspring. *Cell* **29**: 701–10.

Pavlok, A. (1981). Penetration of hamster and pig zona-free eggs by boar ejaculated spermatozoa preincubated *in vitro*. *Int. J. Fert.* **26**: 101–6.

Rossant, J., Mauro, V.M. & Croy, B.A. (1982). Importance of trophoblast genotype for survival of interspecific murine chimaeras. *J. Embryol. exp. Morph.* **69**: 141–9.

Staigmiller, R.B. & Moor, R.M. (1984). Effect of follicle cells on the maturation and developmental competence of ovine oocytes matured outside the follicle. *Gamete Res.* **9**: 221–9.

Stevens, L.C. (1978). Totipotent cells of parthenogenetic origin in a chimaeric mouse. *Nature, Lond.* **276**: 266–7.

Stewart, T.A. & Mintz, B. (1981). Successive generations of mice produced from an established culture line of euploid teratocarcinoma cells. *Proc. natn. Acad. Sci. USA* **78**: 6314–8.

Surani, M.A.H., Barton, S.C. & Kaufman, M.H. (1977). Development to term of chimaeras between diploid parthenogenetic and fertilized embryos. *Nature, Lond.* **270**: 601–3.

Surani, M.A.H., Barton, S.C. & Norris, M.L. (1984). Development of reconstituted mouse eggs suggests imprinting of the genome during gametogenesis. *Nature, Lond.* **308**: 548–50.

Wagner, T.E., Hoppe, P.C., Jollick, J.P., Scholl, D.R., Hodinka, R.L. & Gault, J.B. (1981). Microinjection of a rabbit β-globin gene into zygotes and its subsequent expression in adult mice and their offspring. *Proc. natn. Acad. Sci. USA* **78**: 6376–80.

Whittingham, D.G. (1971). Culture of mouse ova. *J. Reprod. Fert.* Suppl. **14**: 7–21.

Willadsen, S.M. (1979). A method for culture of micromanipulated sheep embryos and its use to produce monozygotic twins. *Nature, Lond.* **277**: 298–300.

Willadsen, S.M. (1980). The viability of early cleavage stages containing half the normal number of blastomeres in the sheep. *J. Reprod. Fert.* **59**: 357–62.

Willadsen, S.M. (1981). The developmental capacity of blastomeres from 4- and 8-cell sheep embryos. *J. Embryol. exp. Morph.* **65**: 165–72.

Willadsen, S.M. (1982). Micromanipulation of embryos of the large domestic species. In *Mammalian egg transfer*: 185–210. Adams, C.E. (Ed.). CRC Press, Florida.

Willadsen, S.M. & Fehilly, C.B. (1983). The developmental potential and regulatory capacity of blastomeres from two-, four- and eight-cell sheep embryos. In *Fertilization of the human egg* in vitro: 353–7. Beier, H.M. & Lindner, H.R. (Eds). Springer-Verlag, Berlin.

Willadsen, S.M. & Godke, R.A. (1984). A simple procedure for the production of identical sheep twins. *Vet. Rec.* **114**: 240–3.

Willadsen, S.M. & Polge, C. (1980). Embryo transplantation in the large domestic species: applications and perspectives in the light of recent experiments with eggs and embryos. *Jl. R. agric. Soc.* **141**: 115–26.

Williams, T.J., Elsden, R.P. & Seidel, G.E. Jr. (1984). Effect of embryo age and stage on pregnancy rates from demi-embryos. *Theriogenology* **21**: 276.

Wright, R.W. & Bondioli, K.R. (1981). Aspects of *in vitro* fertilization and embryo culture in domestic animals. *J. Anim. Sci.* **53**: 702–29.

Symp. zool. Soc. Lond. (1985) No. 54: 137–148

Storage of gametes and embryos

H. D. M. MOORE

MRC/AFRC Comparative Physiology Group
Institute of Zoology
The Zoological Society of London
Regent's Park
London NW1 4RY

Synopsis

There are essentially three main ways to store gametes and embryos: in culture medium at body temperature or just below (32–37°C) to mimic conditions *in vivo*; at cooler temperatures between 12 and 25°C in a medium containing a limited number of substrates to minimize the metabolic activity of the cells; or in solution containing cryopreservative (glycerol, DMSO) and at low temperatures substantially below freezing, usually at −196°C in liquid nitrogen. Only the latter procedure will ensure long-term (i.e. years) preservation but careful consideration should be given to which method will most practically meet what is needed. A vast array of protocols have been devised in order that gametes and embryos reach these storage states and can be returned to the body (or the culture dish) to undergo successful fertilization and embryonic development. In general, however, the ability of germ cells and perhaps to a lesser extent embryos to withstand these often unphysiological conditions and retain their viability and developmental potential depends on the cell type and the species.

The spermatozoon with its many surfaces and intracellular regions and a variety of metabolic requirements displays a remarkable and bewildering species diversity in its response to preservation which has confounded scientists in their attempts to elucidate the underlying mechanisms involved in sperm storage (i.e. cold shock, cryodamage). Most studies involve empirical procedures which can provide a satisfactory formula for preserving semen for one particular species. However, the task of finding the correct protocols for preserving semen for many exotic species seems formidable using this approach. A fundamental understanding of the nature of cell membranes during freezing and thawing will be essential if we are to cryopreserve viable gametes from the vast range of animals in captivity. To achieve this, studies are currently in progress to establish at the molecular level in isolated membrane the changes provoked by temperature variation.

The unfertilized oocyte in most mammalian species only remains viable for 12–24 h and is resistant to the sort of physiological manipulation which can be used to extend sperm viability for several days at ambient temperature. Cryopreservation has met with only limited success. By comparison, the embryo (particularly beyond the 4-cell stage) has a much greater propensity to survive both in culture and cryopreserving techniques. This difference is probably a combination of several factors including membrane biochemistry and metabolic requirements and the ability of the

ZOOLOGICAL SYMPOSIUM No. 54
ISBN 0–19–854002–7

embryo to recover and develop normally following injury or death of a substantial proportion of its tissue.

The purpose of storing gametes and embryos is to extend the useful life of these cells outside the body so that they can be manipulated for practical or experimental studies. Except for the possibility of using solely genetic material, this usually means that the functional capacity of gametes and embryos should be retained. To achieve this aim a number of associated protocols must be considered such as gamete collection (electroejaculation, induced ovulation), *in vivo* fertility assays, synchronized oestrus and embryo transfer. The role of gamete and embryo preservation in the conservation of exotic species will depend on finding the optimal conditions for all these procedures.

Introduction

As an example of the benefits to be derived from the preservation of spermatozoa and embryos, in the management of animals, we need look no further than domestic cattle. Since the initial findings on freezing of bull semen by Polge & Rowson (1952), there have been remarkable advances in the development and application of techniques, such that in many agriculturally developed countries nearly all cows are now artificially inseminated with frozen semen from genetically superior sires. The successful preservation and transfer of bovine embryos (see Polge 1978) has enabled an even greater exploitation of breeding and there is no doubt that cell microsurgery and genetic manipulations will extend the horizons even further (see Polge, this volume).

In the context of rare and endangered exotic species, the advantages of successful preservation of gametes and embryos are perhaps less spectacular but no less important. The storage of spermatozoa and embryos provides a much greater flexibility for finding ways (artificial insemination (AI), embryo transfer, *in vitro* fertilization) of enhancing the reproduction of the species and of individual animals which are refractory to natural breeding conditions or are subfertile. Furthermore, it enables genetic management of captive and semi-wild stocks to be made in a controlled and practical manner. Other considerations are in the transport throughout the world of genetic material, as spermatozoa and embryos, rather than animals. This lowers cost, eliminates unnecessary stress in animals, which incidentally may affect reproductive performance, and reduces the risk of disease transmission (Smith 1978). From an experimental viewpoint, semen or embryo preservation, whether under culture or freezing conditions, contributes directly or indirectly (by increasing the number of possible manipulations) to our understanding of gamete physiology, embryo development and genetics. Finally, where there is a critical threat of a species becoming extinct, preservation of genetic material of individual animals in the form of germ cells, embryos and somatic cells (for DNA transfer) will be increasingly necessary to ensure that an adequate genetic pool can be retained for future breeding programmes.

Although there is now a vast literature on semen and embryo storage, this is confined, with one or two exceptions (Watson 1978), to domestic livestock, laboratory animals, and man (see Brackett, Seidel & Seidel 1981). Semen from a number of exotic species has been frozen-thawed using a variety of methods (see Watson 1978). But the few inseminations that have been carried out to date do not afford any critical appraisal of sperm fertility. Indeed, the most notable and important feature of much of the research is the variation in the response of spermatozoa (and to a lesser extent embryos) of various animals to the methods of culture, cooling, and cryopreservation. This species specificity is reflected for instance in the much slower progress of the use of frozen semen for sheep and pig breeding due to the relatively poor conception rates following freezing and thawing. Such examples serve to emphasize the need to identify the fundamental mechanisms by which cells can be cryopreserved, and retain their viability and developmental potential, so that successful procedures can be quickly adapted from one species to another.

In this chapter, examples will be given of various methods of preservation of semen and embryos of exotic species, the work in domestic species having been amply reviewed (Foote 1975; Watson 1979). Most of the examples will be for mammals, although work has been carried out in other groups (Lake 1978).

Storage of semen

The purpose of storing gametes and embryos is to extend the useful life of these cells outside the body so that they can be manipulated for practical and experimental studies. Except for the possibility of using solely genetic material (i.e. gene transfer) this usually means that the functional capacity of gametes and embryos should be retained. Unlike domestic species, where agricultural economies and practical factors usually favour the use of cryopreserved semen and embryos, the protocols adopted for a particular exotic species (wild or captive) will depend on a number of separate criteria. For example, AI in one or a few captive individuals of a particular species may not warrant the research effort of developing suitable (but untested) cryopreservation methods, especially if semen collection can be synchronized with the time of ovulation (i.e. puma). Alternatively, when sedation prior to electroejaculation may pose a risk to the animal (i.e. gorilla) and well tried cryopreservation procedures are available in a closely related species, in this case man (Sherman, 1963), then maximum use should be made of each semen collection by long-term preservation. Clearly other factors, such as whether semen needs to be transported a long distance and the availability of ovulating females, will also influence the decision of which storage method should be adopted.

There are essentially three methods of storing semen:

(i)   *In culture.* By incubation *in vitro* in a milieu designed to mimic conditions *in vivo*, the fertilizing potential of the spermatozoon can be maintained for periods of hours or days depending on its inherent lifespan (see Yanagimachi 1981). The most successful techniques are those using media for *in vitro* fertilization which in general follow the methods for embryo culture first described by Brinster (1963), where small drops of culture medium are placed in a plastic petri dish and overlayered with mineral or silicone oil. The cultures are then incubated at 37°C in the presence or absence of 5% CO_2 in air. The composition of the culture medium is critical for maintaining sperm viability and although a variety of media have been produced (Rogers 1978) they are normally formulated from balanced salt solutions based on the ionic composition of blood plasma (usually human) and supplemented with energy substrates and protein (albumin or heat-treated serum). For *in vitro* fertilization, the most important parameters are ionic composition, energy source (usually glucose, lactate, and pyruvate), protein, and pH. The optimal combination of these factors varies for each species and may also differ if spermatozoa are merely going to be stored or need to be capacitated (see Yanagimachi 1981) as a preliminary to fertilization. For instance, the absence of Ca^{2+} from media will abrogate the sperm acrosome reaction and thus prevent fertilization, although sperm viability may be retained for several hours or days according to the species.

Such culture conditions are suited to spermatozoa which are inherently sensitive to the phenomenon of cold shock (Pace & Graham 1974) or for which effective long-term storage protocols have not been devised. Spermatozoa of felids provide a good example here. The fertility of semen from the domestic cat after freezing and thawing is poor (Sojka & Jennings 1973) while semen from large exotic cats collected by electroejaculation is generally of poor quality (low sperm motility, large proportion of abnormal sperm morphology) and has a low sperm concentration compared to most other mammalian groups. In seminal plasma, sperm motility is lost after 1–2 h, but washed spermatozoa placed in a modified Tyrode's solution (Biggers, Whitten & Whittingham 1971) with 20% heat-treated rabbit serum can be maintained for up to 16 h without a significant decrease in motility. This type of procedure was adopted for artificial insemination in the puma (*Felis concolor*) (Moore, Bonney & Jones, 1981) where it was necessary to store spermatozoa for several hours prior to transfer to females induced to ovulate with gonadotrophic hormones (Fig. 1).

(ii)   *Short-term storage.* The viability and fertilizing ability of spermatozoa of some mammals can be preserved for several days at room tempera-

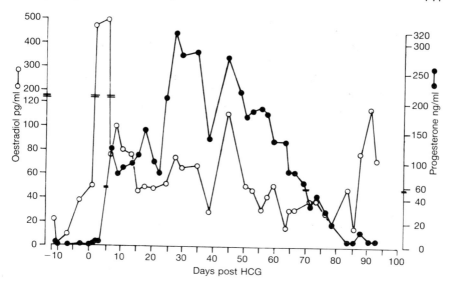

Fig. 1 Plasma concentrations of oestradiol and progesterone during induction of ovulation, insemination and pregnancy in the puma. Pregnant mare's serum gonadotrophin (1250 iu) was administered to the female in dioestrus and human chorionic gonadotrophin (1000 iu) 72 h later. This procedure induced follicular maturation and ovulation 30–40 h after the human chorionic gonadotrophin injection. Two inseminations of washed spermatozoa in media were carried out 20 and 40 h after human chorionic gonadotrophin. Plasma progesterone did not return to pre-ovulatory levels until immediately before parturition (day 95).

tures (15–25°C) with relatively simple diluents which normally only contain limited substrates and antibiotics. These media are often saturated with CO_2 (either by gassing or by chemical reaction) which acts to immobilize the cells reversibly, thereby reducing their metabolism. Such procedures were first used to maintain the fertility of bull semen for six to seven days (Van Denmark & Sharma 1957). Although in this species freezing methods are now more conventional, liquid preservation is still used extensively for the artificial insemination of boar spermatozoa which are susceptible to both cooling and freezing protocols (Moore 1975). For non-domestic animals, it can be anticipated that in a number of species (for example, ungulates), liquid preservation of semen by dilution would provide a suitable and practical alternative to freezing; however, few studies have been carried out. In the author's laboratory, spermatozoa from the giant panda (*Ailuropoda melanoleuca*) have been kept viable for up to five days in BWW medium saturated with CO_2 (Moore, Bush *et al.* 1984). Similarly blackbuck spermatozoa (*Antilope cervicapra*) maintained for two to three days at 15°C in a simple citrate buffered solution, have been used to impregnate females following artificial insemination (Holt, North *et al.*, in preparation).

(iii)   *Long-term preservation*. Since, with the correct application, the cellular integrity of the spermatozoon frozen in liquid nitrogen can be preserved for decades and possibly hundreds of years, deep frozen storage must be considered the method of choice *if* sperm fertilizing ability can be retained. Unfortunately this proviso is often disregarded and with many studies with exotic species (where animal numbers may be low) the assumption has been made that good post-thaw motility of spermatozoa *in vitro* can be equated with good sperm fertility. However, the paucity of pregnancies in wild species following AI with frozen semen perhaps testifies that at present freezing methods for most exotic species are inadequate (see Watson 1978; Moore 1984).

A wide range of cryoprotective diluents and freezing procedures have been employed, the majority again based on methods used for domestic species and man. In general, a cryoprotective compound, usually glycerol, at a concentration between 2 and 10% v/v is used in conjunction with a buffered solution containing protein in the form of skimmed milk or egg yolk. The proportion of these components depends on such species-specific factors as the threshold at which glycerol (or other cryoprotectants) will eventually exert a toxic effect on spermatozoa, and the beneficial contribution of proteins in minimizing membrane damage. Perhaps out of necessity, the development of preserving diluents has been largely empirical and hence there is little understanding of how these solutions may protect spermatozoa of one species while being detrimental to another. One might expect that spermatozoa of species related to domestic animals of which semen has been frozen successfully would also respond successfully to freezing. Certainly, there is good post-thaw viability of great-ape spermatozoa frozen according to methods developed for man and the author has obtained penetration of zona-free hamster oocytes (see p. 145) with frozen-thaw orang-utan spermatozoa (indicating a degree of functional competence). In contrast, buffalo semen shows poor survival in diluents devised for the bull (Bhattacharya 1974).

Storage of oocytes and embryos

After ovulation, the mammalian ovum maintains its ability to fertilize and undergo normal embryonic development for about 8–36 h depending on the species (hamster ± 12 h, human ± 36 h). In several laboratory and domestic species (mouse, cow, sheep, and pig), human, and non-human primates (marmoset, baboon, and rhesus monkey), embryonic development *in vitro* has been performed with the subsequent transfer of embryos to recipient females for establishment of pregnancy. Thus over two to three cell cleavages (i.e. 2–8 cell stages = 60–70 h) it is feasible to store embryos at 37°C and maintain their potential for development *if* a suitable recipient is available. This period *in vitro* is limited by the size of the returning blastocyst (which must be small enough to pass down transfer catheters) and by its inability to implant *in utero* if development proceeds too far. Short-term culture of embryos for several hours has been achieved in a number of exotic ungulates before transfer to their closely related domestic counterpart for continuation of development (i.e. gaur to Holstein cow; zebra to horse; Przewalski's horse to horse). However, the temporary inhibition of embryonic growth at ambient or body temperatures with maintenance of developmental capacity has not been achieved. Interestingly, delayed implantation in, for instance, the Bennett wallaby, is accompanied by embryonic homeostasis with the apparent cessation of cell division (at about 80 cells) for up to one year. The mechanism of this natural storage is unknown.

The long-term storage of oocytes by freezing has met with little success (except in rodents) probably owing to spindle disruption leading to disorganization of chromatin on the metaphase II plate. Fortunately mammalian embryos (particularly 4-cell to morula stage) are considerably more resilient to freezing and thawing protocols than gametes and those from a number of domestic species can be frozen and thawed, transferred and develop into normal young (see Leibo 1981). In exotic species, successful pregnancies have been established with frozen-thawed baboon (Pope, Pope & Beck 1984) and marmoset embryos (P.N. Summers, personal communication).

The tendency of embryos to survive freezing and thawing better than spermatozoa do may lie in their ability to recover after extensive cell damage given that some of the blastomeres remain intact. Furthermore, embryos can be frozen with the cryoprotectant dimethyl sulphoxide (DMSO) whereas this substance is toxic to spermatozoa.

Damage to cells during freezing and thawing

Since mammalian gametes (and those of birds) have evolved to function at or near warm body temperatures (31–42°C), protocols for cooling, freezing and thawing represent unphysiological processes which unless counteracted by cryoprotectants bring about the demise of the cell. Two areas can be considered; events occurring above freezing point and those below. At body or scrotal temperatures, sperm membranes, for example, function in a fluid state but on cooling pass through a phase transition to form crystalline domains (see Lucy 1977). Intramembrane protein, whose functions, such as ion transport, are essential for the viability of the cell, may aggregate in non-crystalline areas (Holt & North, 1984). On rewarming, these changes do not always reverse (especially on the tail) resulting in loss of sperm motility. During freezing, cells must accommodate dramatic changes to their intracellular contents initiated by the formation of ice (Mazur, Leibo *et al.* 1970).

This transition causes organelle damage by direct action of ice or indirectly by the increase in osmolarity as water is sequestered into crystalline formation. Clearly, several factors provoke cell damage during freezing and thawing and cryoprotectants exert their effect to minimize trauma.

The assessment of the functional competence of gametes

If gametes lose their fertilizing potential during storage (whether short- or long-term) then, unless sophisticated microinjection procedures are attempted, they no longer remain vectors of genetic information. Hence, the assessment of gamete fertility and embryo development following preservation is of critical importance. This is especially true for exotic species, for

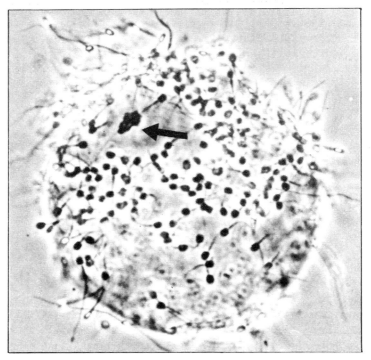

Fig. 2 A zona-free hamster oocyte incubated with giant panda spermatozoa (10^5/ml). Many spermatozoa were bound to the vitellus. A decondensing sperm head was also observed (arrowed) indicating sperm penetration. × 240. Lacmoid stain.

whereas insemination trials are a routine and practical proposition for laboratory and domestic livestock, this is rarely the case for captive wild animals. For endangered species only one breeding pair in a zoo may be present. The absence of reliable *in vitro* indicators of fertility is at present the most limiting factor in the development of gamete preservation for exotic species. Three areas show promise for the future:

(i) *Assays of functional competence.* In *vitro* fertilization procedures can now be carried out in most laboratory and domestic animals and man. The ability of, for instance, frozen-thawed spermatozoa to fertilize homologous ova *in vitro* may give a reasonable assessment of their fertilizing potential *in vivo*. The application of such a procedure to exotic species demands not only knowledge of ways of incubating spermatozoa so that they undergo essential prerequisites for fertilization such as capacitation and the acrosome reaction, but also a supply of homologous ova. The need for the latter can be partially circumvented by using zona-free hamster eggs (Yanagimachi, Yanagimachi & Rogers 1976). The hamster oolemma is particularly receptive to spermatozoa of other species and the presence after incubation of a decondensed sperm head within the vitellus gives an assessment of sperm fertilizing capacity. In the author's laboratory this technique has been used to measure sperm fertility in the yak, gorilla, orang-utan, chimpanzee, marmoset, and giant panda (Fig. 2).

(ii) *Quantitative measurements of sperm motility.* Recent evidence suggests that the fertility of human spermatozoa, at least, is most closely correlated with the mean sperm velocity of a sample (Holt, Moore, Parry & Hillier, 1984). If this association holds for other animals then it may provide a cross-species test of sperm function which does not involve a specific phenomenon like capacitation. Certainly, it can be used to assess freezing procedures quantitatively. In the giant panda, for example, spermatozoa after freezing and thawing were shown to travel at the same mean velocity as at collection, indicating that sperm propulsive power had not diminished (Moore, Bush *et al.* 1984).

(iii) *Cell markers.* Probes, such as monoclonal antibodies when conjugated to fluorescent dyes (or enzymes), offer a means of examining the integrity of various regions of the spermatozoon or embryo following preservation. Some of these antibodies are highly specific to a region of the cell, but exhibit a wide species cross-specificity. For example, the author's laboratory has produced a monoclonal antibody which binds to the acrosomal region of all eutherian mammals so far tested (Ellis, Hartman & Moore, 1985) and can be used as a marker of acrosomal integrity after freezing and thawing (Fig. 3).

Fig. 3 Hamster spermatozoa labelled with fluorescent monoclonal antibody recognizing surface determinants over the acrosome. This antibody cross-reacted with spermatozoa from all eutherians so far tested and can be used as a marker of acrosome integrity after freezing and thawing. × 650.

Conclusion

This chapter has emphasized the need for a practical rationale for storing gametes and embryos of exotic species. Although long-term storage of cells in liquid nitrogen should be the ultimate objective, this procedure is of little value if fertilizing potential or embryonic development is largely lost. Furthermore, associated techniques of electroejaculation, detection and induction of ovulation, embryo recovery, and insemination must be sufficiently reliable if preserved gametes and embryos are eventually to fulfil their function of passing on genetic information or becoming a new individual. Short-term storage (above freezing point) should be contemplated as an alternative as artificial breeding techniques are acquired. There is no doubt, however, that gamete and embryo preservation will in the future play an ever-increasing role in the conservation of all animals.

Acknowledgements

I should like to thank Terry Dennett for photography. The author's work is supported by grants from the MRC/AFRC, The Ford Foundation, and Elf-Acquitaine (UK) Ltd.

References

Bhattacharya, P. (1974). Reproduction. In *The husbandry and health of the domestic buffalo*: 105–58. Ross-Cockvill, W. (Ed.). FAO, Rome.

Biggers, J.D., Whitten, W.K. & Whittingham, D.G. (1971). The culture of mouse embryos *in vitro*. In *Methods in mammalian embryology*: 86–116. Daniel, J.C. (Ed.). Freeman, San Francisco.

Brackett, B.G., Seidel, G.E. & Seidel, S.M. (1981). *New technologies in animal breeding*. Brackett, B.G., Seidel, G.E. & Seidel, S.M. (Eds). Academic Press, New York.

Brinster, R.L. (1963). A method for *in vitro* cultivation of mouse ova from two cell to blastocyst. *Exp. Cell. Res.* **32**: 205–8.

Ellis, D.H., Hartman, T.D. & Moore, H.D.M. (1985). Maturation and function of the hamster spermatozoon probed with monoclonal antibodies. *J. reprod. Immunol.* **7**: 299–314.

Foote, R.H. (1975). Semen quality from the bull to the freezer: an assessment. *Theriogenology* **3**: 219–35.

Holt, W.V., Moore, H.D.M., Parry, A. & Hillier, S. (1984). A computerized technique for the measurement of sperm cell velocity: correlation of the results with *in vitro* fertilization assays. In *The male factor in human infertility*: 3–7. Rolland, R. (Ed.): Harrison, R.F., Bonnar, J. & Thompson, W. (General Congress Eds). MTP Press, Lancaster, Boston, The Hague, Dordrecht.

Holt, W.V. & North, R.D. (1984). Partially irreversible cold induced lipid phase-transitions in mammalian sperm plasma membrane domains; freeze fracture study. *J. exp. Zool.* **230**: 473–83.

Lake, P.E. (1978). The principles and practice of semen collection and preservation in birds. *Symp. zool. Soc. Lond.* No. **43**: 31–49.

Leibo, S.P. (1981). Preservation of ova and embryos by freezing. In *New technologies in animal breeding*: 127–40. Brackett, B.G., Seidel, G.E. & Seidel, S.M. (Eds). Academic Press, New York.

Lucy, J.A. (1977). Mechanisms of chemically induced cell fusion. In *Membrane fusion, cell surface reviews*: 268–304. Poste, V.G. & Nicolson, G.L. (Eds). North-Holland, Amsterdam.

Mazur, P., Leibo, S.P., Farrant, J., Chu, E.H.Y., Hanna, M.G. Jr. & Smith, L.H. (1970). Interactions of cooling rate, warming rate and protective additive on the survival of frozen mammalian cells. In *The frozen cell*: 69–88. Wolstenholme, G.E.W. & O'Connor, M. (Eds). J.A. Churchill, London.

Moore, H.D.M. (1975). *Some effects of seminal plasma proteins on the long term preservation of boar spermatozoa*. PhD. Thesis: University of Reading.

Moore, H.D.M. (1984). Artificial breeding in zoos. *Biologist* **31**: 90–2.

Moore, H.D.M., Bonney, R.C. & Jones, D.M. (1981). Successful induced ovulation and artificial insemination in the puma (*Felis concolor*). *Vet. Rec.* **108**: 282–3.

Moore, H.D.M., Bush, M., Celma, M., Garcia, A.L., Hartman, T.D., Hearn, J.P., Hodges, J.K., Jones, D.M., Knight, J.A., Monsalve, L. & Wildt, D.E. (1984). Artificial insemination in the Giant Panda (*Ailuropoda melanoleuca*). *J. Zool., Lond.* **203**: 269–78.

Pace, M.M. & Graham, E.F. (1974). Components in egg yolk which protect bovine spermatozoa during freezing. *J. Anim. Sci.* **39**: 1144–9.

Polge, C. (1978). Embryo transfer and embryo preservation. *Symp, zool. Soc. Lond.* No. 43: 303–16.

Polge, C. & Rowson, L.E.A. (1952). The fertilizing capacity of bull spermatozoa after freezing at −79°C. *Nature, Lond.* **169**: 626–7.

Pope, C.E., Pope, V.Z. & Beck, L.R. (1984). Live birth following cryopreservation and transfer of a baboon embryo. *Fert. Steril.* **42**: 143–5.

Rogers, B.J. (1978). Mammalian sperm capacitation and fertilization *in vitro*: A critique of methodology, *Gamete Res.* **1**: 165–223.

Sherman, J.K. (1963). Improved methods of preservation of human spermatozoa by freezing and freezing-drying. *Fert. Steril.* **14**: 49–64.

Smith, G.F. (1978). Disease control in semen transfer and artificial insemination. *Symp. zool. Soc. Lond.* No. 43: 329–38.

Sojka, N.J. & Jennings, L.L. (1973). Collection and storage of cat semen for artificial insemination. *Va J. Sci.* **24**: 166.

Van Denmark, N.L. & Sharma, U.D. (1957). Preliminary fertility results from the preservation of bovine semen at room temperatures. *J. Dairy Sci* **40**: 438–9.

Watson, P.F. (Ed.) (1978). *Artificial breeding of non-domestic animals*. (Symp. zool. Soc. Lond. No. 43). Academic Press, London.

Watson, P.F. (1979). The preservation of semen in mammals. In *Oxford reviews of reproductive biology* **1**: 283–350. Finn, C.A. (Ed.). Clarendon Press, Oxford.

Yanagimachi, R. (1981). Mechanisms of fertilization in mammals. In *Fertilization and embryonic development in vitro*: 81–182. Mastroianni, L. Jr. & Biggers, J.D. (Eds). Plenum Pub. Corp., New York.

Yanagimachi, R., Yanagimachi, H. & Rogers, B.J. (1976). The use of zona-free animal ova as a test system for the assessment of the fertilizing capacity of human spermatozoa. *Biol. Reprod.* **15**: 471–6.

Symp. zool. Soc. Lond. (1985) No. 54: 149–168

The endocrine control of reproduction

J. K. HODGES

MRC/AFRC Comparative Physiology
Research Group
Institute of Zoology
Zoological Society of London
Regent's Park
London NW1 4RY

Synopsis

The management of natural or artificial breeding of exotic mammals in captivity depends upon an understanding of the physiology of reproductive function.

Practical considerations dictate that studies on wild animals employ non-invasive procedures. Urinary hormone analysis provides the only feasible approach to longitudinal studies in most captive situations, but requires careful biochemical and physiological validation of hormone measurement for each species. Thus, chromatography and assessment of individual steroid metabolites are prerequisites for accurate and informative results from urinary hormone analysis. In addition, it is necessary that procedures for hormone assay be made as simple, versatile, and inexpensive as possible if endocrine studies are to find wide application in zoos and animal reserves. The development of direct assays for steroid conjugates, without hydrolysis and extraction, represents an important step in this direction and recent advances in non-isotopic assays using colorimetric or luminescent endpoints open up exciting possibilities for field application.

Primates, the giant panda, and ungulates are used to demonstrate the application of these methods with special reference to the detection of ovulation and pregnancy. Oestrone conjugates are highly informative in monitoring ovarian function in primates and the giant panda, but in ungulates, such as the blackbuck and okapi, the timing of ovulation is best achieved by monitoring the fall in pregnanediol-3α-glucuronide at the end of the preceding luteal phase. The pattern of pregnanediol-3α-glucuronide in the giant panda has provided the first clear indication that pregnancy is associated with a delay in implantation.

The ability to monitor reproductive function in exotic animals provides the basis for controlled studies designed to accelerate captive breeding by artificial means. By applying knowledge gained from laboratory and domestic animals it will be possible to increase reproductive output in exotic species through manipulating the natural control mechanisms in a variety of ways. Prostaglandin can be used to synchronize ovulation for timed mating and embryo transfer; melatonin may help to overcome the limitations of seasonal anovulation; LH-RH has similar potential but may also find wide application in the treatment of infertility in captive animals; and the use of exogenous gonadotrophins or passive immunization against steroids, by increasing ovulation rate, would facilitate the collection of larger numbers of embryos for long-term storage. Ultimately, however, the success of these techniques depends upon a

ZOOLOGICAL SYMPOSIUM No. 54
ISBN 0–19–854002–7

sound knowledge of basic physiology which can only be obtained through careful scientific investigation.

Introduction

Successful captive breeding of rare and endangered species, whether by natural or artificial methods, requires a clear understanding of reproductive physiology. Knowledge of the endocrine control of reproduction is particularly important since it is on the measurement of hormones that the detection and timing of key reproductive events is based. Thus, endocrine studies allow the assessment of reproductive status, precise timing of ovulation, early pregnancy diagnosis, and the prediction of parturition, as well as extending basic knowledge of the comparative aspects of mammalian reproductive physiology.

Faced with the diversity of species becoming endangered in the wild, the limited number of animals available for study, and the practical difficulties of working with wild animals, it is essential that any work designed to study the endocrine control of reproduction is based on methods that are versatile, practical, and reliable. Since non-invasive procedures are necessary when working with animals that are easily stressed, urinary hormone analysis at present provides the only feasible approach to long-term studies on most exotic species. This paper describes the development and application of endocrine techniques for assessing reproductive status in female mammals, with emphasis on the detection of ovulation and pregnancy. The prospects for manipulating the natural endocrine control of reproduction to accelerate captive breeding in exotic mammals are also considered.

Methodology

Sample collection

Practical considerations dictate that studies on wild animals employ non-invasive techniques. In domestic or laboratory animals the collection of blood samples poses few problems. However, since many exotic species are easily stressed, difficult to handle and also potentially dangerous, the repeated capture and restraint necessary for daily blood sampling is both undesirable and impractical. Thus, where the avoidance of stress and its associated effects on fertility is essential, urinary hormone analysis provides the only feasible approach to long-term studies either in captivity or in the wild (Hodges, Czekala & Lasley 1979; Hodges & Hearn 1983).

Although the collection of 24-hour urine samples is preferable in providing a complete picture of daily hormone excretion, the prolonged periods of isolation involved make this impractical for most animals. Urine samples are therefore collected overnight or as single voidings and in order to compensate for variations in fluid intake and output and for varying periods of collection, hormone concentrations are indexed by creatinine as determined by a simple microcolorimetric test (e.g. Taussky 1954; Brand 1981). Although there are certain limitations to the use of creatinine in this way (Hodges, in press), good correlations between hormone to creatinine index and 24 h excretion have been demonstrated for a number of species (Metcalf & Hunt 1976; Shideler & Lasley 1982; Hodges & Eastman 1984). Furthermore, the hormone profiles during the cycle and pregnancy obtained from studies incorporating creatinine measurements clearly indicate that the method is both practical and highly informative (see Hodges & Hearn (1983) for references).

Method validation

Since comparative studies in wild animals require multi-species application of assays, validation of hormone measurement in each species is essential for accurate and informative results. Species differences in the qualitative nature of the hormone metabolites excreted in urine is a particularly important factor to consider. Thus, chromatography and assessment of the relative abundance of individual metabolites in each species is needed to determine the most informative measurement for monitoring reproductive function. Table I illustrates the use of sequential enzyme hydrolysis in identifying the different types of oestrogen conjugates in the urine from two related species

Table I. Comparison of urinary oestrogen metabolites and hydrolysis efficiency in the common marmoset and cotton-top tamarin.

	Common marmoset		Cotton-top tamarin	
	Oestrone	Oestradiol	Oestrone	Oestradiol
	(μg/mgCr)		(μg/mgCr)	
Glucuronide fraction	0.58	1.16	9.47	1.11
Sulphate fraction	7.41	31.96	1.69	0.10
Residual[1]	1.94	18.29	0.47	6.04
Total[2]	9.50	48.90	11.40	6.41

[1] Oestrogen liberated by acid hydrolysis (Hodges & Eastman 1984) following sequential enzyme hydrolysis.
[2] Acid hydrolysis of a separte portion of urine, without prior enzyme hydrolysis. The values approximate the sum of glucuronide, sulphate and residual fractions determined separately.
   Urine samples are from the period of maximum oestrogen excretion during the cycle, i.e. mid luteal phase. Adapted from Hodges & Eastman (1984).

of South American primate and emphasizes the importance of the procedure in selecting the most appropriate hormone measurement for monitoring ovarian function (Hodges & Eastman 1984). Briefly, the results show that oestradiol sulphate appears to be the most abundant urinary oestrogen during the ovarian cycle of the common marmoset, whereas, in contrast, the cotton-top tamarin excretes oestrone glucuronide in greatest amounts. The implications of this observation for the accurate assessment of ovarian function in these particular species are obvious but the data also provide a note of caution for comparative studies of oestrogen excretion on a broader scale.

Simplification of assay methodology

In addition to accuracy and reliability, comparative studies on wild mammals require that methods for hormone analysis be made as simple and versatile as possible. This is particularly important if we are ever to consider the application of endocrine studies beyond the sophisticated research laboratory and into the smaller zoos and animal reserves or eventually into the field.

Direct assays for steroid conjugates

One area in which hormone measurement has been greatly simplified is in the development of direct, non-extraction assays for steroid conjugates. Since steroids are present in urine mainly in the form of conjugates such as glucuronides and sulphates, conventional assay of urinary steroids involves hydrolysis of the conjugates before determination. Direct immuno-assay of steroid conjugates, however, not only avoids the hydrolysis step but also eliminates the subsequent extraction and purification processes, both of which are expensive and laborious. The application of direct conjugate assays has already proved useful for monitoring ovarian function in women (e.g. Samarajeewa, Cooley & Kellie 1979; Baker, Jennison & Kellie 1979; Collins, Branch & Collins 1981) and there is now increasing interest in their potential use in exotic species. Since conjugated steroids predominate in urine, direct assays offer a much more practical and simple approach to routine urinary analysis than was previously available. Additionally, by avoiding the need for hydrolysis, a process which has been shown to be inefficient at cleaving certain conjugates (Shideler, Czekala, Kasman, Lindburg & Lasley 1983; Eastman, Makawiti, Collins & Hodges 1984; Table I), direct assays can provide greater resolution in measurement and thereby generate a more informative hormone profile (Shideler et al. 1983). It should be emphasized that the need for assessing the nature and relative abundance of individual conjugates present in urine is particularly relevant when monitoring reproductive function by direct, non-extraction assays.

Non-isotopic assays

Radioimmunoassay has been the predominant analytical technique in endocrinology over the last 12 years. More recently, however, the development of enzyme immunoassays for reproductive steroids offers an attractive alternative to conventional assays using radio isotopes (e.g. Joyce, Read & Riad-Fahmy 1977; Joyce, Wilson, Read & Riad-Fahmy 1978). The advantages of the enzyme assay are its low cost, ease of performance, and convenience, as well as its avoidance of the problems associated with the use and disposal of radioactive isotopes. Additionally, the end point of the assay, for example a colour change, is both easy to read and simple to quantify.

Many of the steroid enzyme immunoassays currently available are still performed in test tubes, although in the last few years rapid and sensitive solid phase assays using microtitre plates have also been described (e.g. progesterone: Sauer, Foulkes & Cookson 1981; Munro & Stabenfeldt 1984). An example of the use of a microtitre plate ELISA for progesterone in the marmoset monkey is shown in Fig. 1. The assay, modified from the method described by Boland, Foulkes, MacDonnell & Sauer (1985), measures progesterone directly in plasma without extraction and gives values which compare favourably with those obtained by the more laborious radioimmunoassay procedure (J. K. Hodges & D. Green, unpublished results). The assay, which is used for retrospective determination of ovulation in the marmoset, is performed in 2–3 h and produces results which can be read in less than one minute. When similar assays for the measurement of urinary

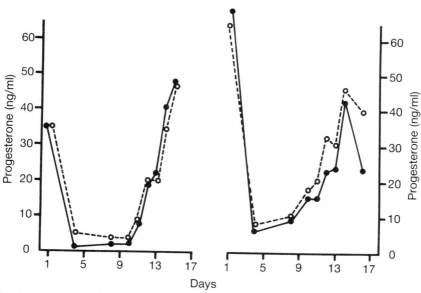

Fig. 1 Comparison of plasma progesterone levels during part of the ovarian cycle in two marmoset monkeys as determined by radioimmunoassay (●——●) and microtitre plate ELISA (○ – – – – ○). The profiles show the rapid fall in progesterone levels at the end of the luteal phase and the subsequent increase after ovulation. The day of ovulation is that preceding the day on which progesterone rises above 10 ng/ml.

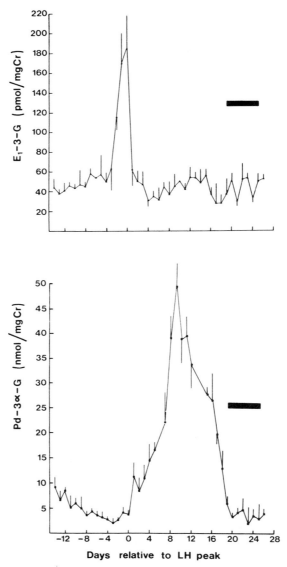

Fig. 2 Mean ± s.e.m. levels of oestrone-3-glucuronide (E_1-3-G) and pregnanediol-3α-glucuro-nide (Pd-3α-G) measured by direct non-extraction assay of urine samples collected throughout the menstrual cycle of the vervet monkey. The data are indexed by creatinine (Cr) and are normalized to the day of the LH peak. The solid bars indicate menses. From Makawiti, Hodges, Collins & Else (in prep.).

glucuronides become available within the next few years, the combination of practical, non-invasive sample collection with simple and rapid methods of hormone analysis should greatly extend the use of endocrine techniques for the study of exotic animals, not only in captivity but also in the field. The ultimate objective would be the development of a urinary dipstick test for ovulation and pregnancy which would require virtually no facilities to perform and which could be read by eye.

Applications to monitoring reproductive function

Primates

Many of the recent advantages in methodology for monitoring reproductive function in exotic species have stemmed from studies in primates. Initially, the application of urinary steroid analysis was based on the non-specific measurement of total immunoreactive oestrogens after hydrolysis and extraction (e.g. Martin, Seaton & Lusty 1975; Hodges, Czekala *et al.* 1979; Lasley, Hodges & Czekala 1980). More recently, the trend towards the simplification of assay methods has continued with the development and application of direct conjugate assays in a variety of exotic species (e.g. Shideler *et al.* 1983; Hodges, in press).

Figure 2 illustrates the pattern of excretion of urinary oestrone-3-glucuronide and pregnanediol-3α-glucuronide as determined by direct assay during the menstrual cycle of the vervet monkey (Makawiti, Hodges, Collins & Else, in prep.). The levels of oestrone-3-glucuronide, the major urinary oestrogen metabolite in this species, increase gradually throughout the follicular phase and show a rapid and marked rise beginning 4–5 days before ovulation. Levels of pregnanediol-3α-glucuronide increase within a day of ovulation and provide an adequate reflection of progesterone secretion throughout the luteal phase.

In certain primate species, including man (Branch, Collins, Kilpatrick & Collins 1980), measurement of oestrone conjugates may also provide information on implantation and early pregnancy. Figure 3 shows the levels of urinary oestrone-3-glucuronide during conception cycles in two baboons. The data points are normalized against the day of the LH peak and in each case clearly describe the rise in urinary oestrogen excretion which occurs prior to ovulation. Of particular interest, however, is the rapid and very marked increase in oestrogen excretion beginning 15–16 days after ovulation. The rise in oestrogen excretion at this time is specific to pregnancy cycles and is presumably related to the onset of chorionic gonadotrophin production which is detectable by 10–12 days of pregnancy. The significant point is that the measurement of oestrone glucuronide allows the detection of both ovulation and implantation by the same simple technique. Furthermore, Shideler *et al.* (1983) have recently reported similar findings in the

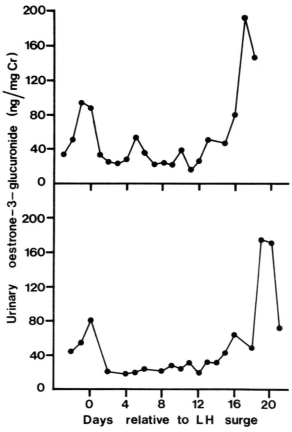

Fig. 3 Levels of urinary oestrone-3-glucuronide during conception cycles in two olive baboons. In each case the pre-ovulatory oestrogen rise is followed by a second marked increase in oestrogen excretion at about day 15 of pregnancy.

lion-tailed macaque and suggest that the approach is potentially applicable to a large number of other primate species. Their findings also demonstrate that the endocrine changes associated with ovulation and early pregnancy are better resolved by direct assay than after enzymatic hydrolysis and extraction.

As studies on animals in captivity continue to improve our knowledge of their basic physiology there is, at the same time, an increasing interest in the possibility of combining physiological measurements of reproductive activity with behavioural and ecological studies of animals in their natural habitat. Until recently, however, this has not been regarded as feasible, largely because of the assumed difficulties of sample collection in the wild. An

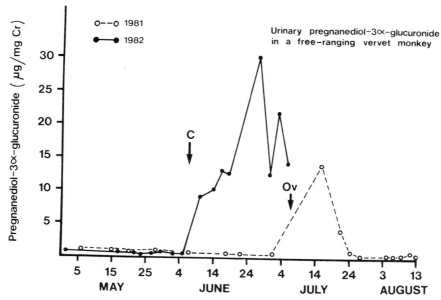

Fig. 4 The levels of pregnanediol-3α-glucuronide in urine samples collected from a vervet monkey in the wild. The data are from samples collected during 1981 (O – – O) and 1982 (●——●). Ov indicates approximate time of ovulation; C indicates date of conception. From Andelman, Else, Hearn & Hodges (1985).

example of the first application of sequential urinary hormone analysis for monitoring reproductive status in a free-ranging primate is shown in Fig. 4. The data are from a recent paper by Andelman, Else, Hearn & Hodges (1985) which reports the levels of urinary pregnanediol-3α-glucuronide in urine samples collected from female vervet monkeys in Amboseli National Park, Kenya. The example given here shows that in 1981, ovulation, as indicated by the increase in pregnanediol-3α-glucuronide excretion, first occurred in early July. The subsequent decline in levels indicates that conception did not occur and that there was no resumption of cyclic ovarian activity. In the following year, however, ovulation took place at the beginning of June and the sustained elevation in pregnanediol-3α-glucuronide shows that conception occurred. This was later confirmed by the birth of an infant in December giving an estimated date of conception (gestation length 160 days) of 5 June. Significantly, copulation in this female was poorly correlated with reproductive status, mating being observed before the onset of ovarian cyclicity and during pregnancy. Since, in many species of primate, monitoring reproductive status by behavioural observations alone can be unreliable and potentially misleading there are distinct advantages to obtaining physiological information of this kind. Thus, the ability to obtain

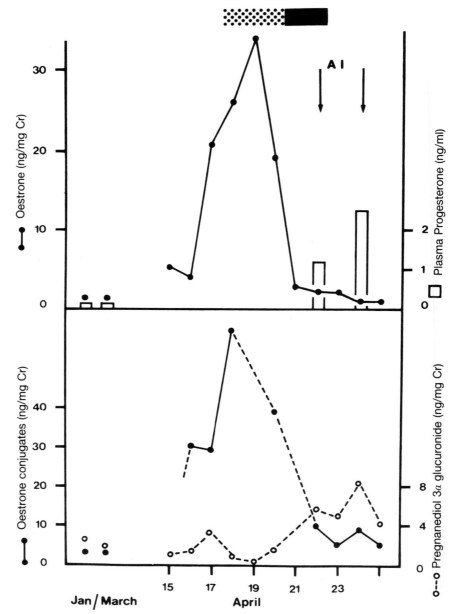

Fig. 5 Upper portion: Levels of urinary oestrone (●——●) and plasma progesterone (□) during anoestrus and around the time of behavioural oestrus in the London panda (1981). Lower portion: Levels of oestrone conjugate (●——●) and pregnanediol-3α-glucuronide ·(○ – – – – ○) measured by non-extraction assay over the same period. Dates of artificial insemination are shown. The stippled bar indicates pro-oestrus, the solid bar indicates oestrus.

useful hormonal data in free-ranging primates opens up exciting possibilities for combining physiology and ecology in field studies in the future.

Giant panda

Whilst studies in primates have led to the development of many of the available techniques for studying wild animals, the giant panda provides a good example of how their application can help to improve captive breeding. Since the panda is endangered in the wild and breeds poorly in captivity, its future survival may well depend upon the success of artificial methods of breeding. Practical and reliable methods for the detection of ovulation and pregnancy are therefore essential.

In captivity, the giant panda is thought to be seasonally monoestrous, exhibiting a short but variable period of oestrus between March and May (Anon. 1974; Kleiman 1983). The pattern of excretion of total immunoreactive oestrogens during behavioural oestrus in the Washington panda has been described (Bonney, Wood & Kleiman 1982) but more recently it has been shown that a clearer and more informative profile is obtained by the measurement of oestrone. Data obtained from the London panda in 1981 (Fig. 5) show that levels of urinary oestrone conjugates (measured after hydrolysis or directly) increased sharply during pro-oestrus and that maximum behavioural oestrus coincided with the period of declining oestrone excretion. That ovulation occurred at this time is supported by the rise in progesterone concentrations in plasma. Thus, measurement of conjugated oestrone provides a simple and practical method for detecting ovulation in the giant panda. In terms of predicting ovulation for the purpose of artificial insemination, probably the most useful approach is to monitor oestrogen excretion by daily assays for oestrone conjugates and to use the fall in oestrogen levels to schedule insemination.

The timing of ovulation in relation to the fall in oestrogen excretion is supported by the success of artificial insemination and subsequent pregnancy in the Madrid panda in 1982 (Hodges, Bevan et al. 1984; Moore, Bush et al. 1984) (Fig. 6). The pattern of pregnanediol-3α-glucuronide was useful in indicating pregnancy albeit at a relatively late stage of gestation and may also help in predicting the time of parturition. The significance of the late increase in pregnanediol-3α-glucuronide excretion (assumed to reflect increased progesterone secretion) is not entirely clear although it may indicate an increase in ovarian and/or placental activity coincident with implantation after an initial period of delay (Hodges, Bevan et al. 1984). The known variability in gestation length (115–178 days) and the extremely low birthweight in the panda (100 g : adult body weight 70 kg) would certainly be consistent with an extended period of delay and a relatively short post-implantation stage although direct evidence for this has yet to be obtained.

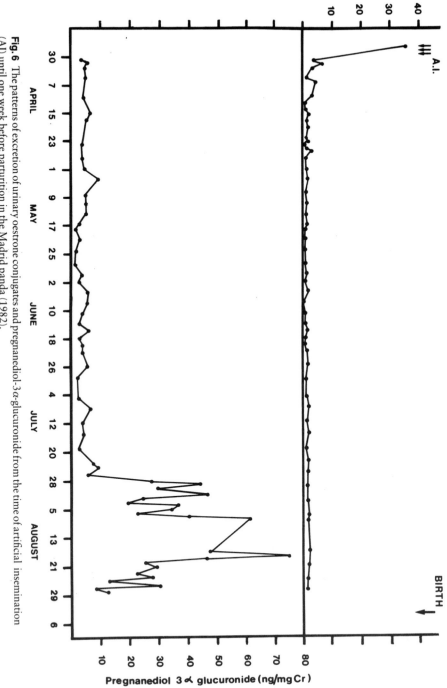

Fig. 6 The patterns of excretion of urinary oestrone conjugates and pregnanediol-3α-glucuronide from the time of artificial insemination (AI) until one week before parturition in the Madrid panda (1982).

Ungulates

In contrast to previous examples in which the measurement of urinary oestrogens is highly informative in monitoring pre-ovulatory events, it is of much more limited value in the case of many ungulates. The reasons are due partly to qualitative and quantitative differences in oestrogen excretion but also to the marked differences exhibited in the control of the oestrous cycle. Unlike many primates, for example, in which there is a relatively long period of follicular development after the end of the luteal phase, in most of the ungulates studied so far the follicular phase is compressed into a very brief period of a few days. Thus, the limited duration of the follicular phase and attendant increase in oestrogen excretion typical of the Artiodactyla (cattle and antelope) is insufficient to enable oestrogen evaluations to be used for prospective timing of ovulation. In these animals in which falling progesterone triggers the onset of oestrus and the final stages of follicular maturation, the prediction and detection of ovulation is best achieved by monitoring the rapid decline in progesterone or its metabolites at the end of the previous luteal phase. This is shown schematically in Fig. 7. Although there is little information on the excretion of progesterone metabolites in either domestic or exotic ungulates, the measurement of urinary pregnanediol-3α-glucuronide is effective in monitoring luteal function in a variety of species including the cow, okapi, bongo, oryx, and blackbuck (Loskutoff, Ott & Lasley 1982, 1983; Hodges & Hearn 1983). Thus, in these species, in which luteolysis precipitates the next ovulatory event, detection of declining levels of pregnanediol-3α-glucuronide is used to anticipate the time of ovulation. Successful artificial insemination and normal pregnancy in the black-

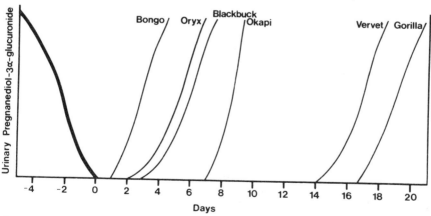

Fig. 7 Schematic representation of the approximate time interval between luteal regression and subsequent ovulation in four ungulate and two primate species as indicated by the patterns of excretion of urinary pregnanediol-3α-glucuronide. Modified from Loskutoff *et al.* (1983) to include author's unpublished data.

buck have recently been achieved by this approach (W.V. Holt, H.D.M. Moore & J.K. Hodges, unpublished results).

The pattern of excretion of pregnanediol-3α-glucuronide during successive oestrous cycles of the okapi is shown in Fig. 8. The cycle length of 15–16 days, similar to that described by Loskutoff *et al.* (1982), is composed of a 5–6 day follicular phase and a longer luteal phase of 10–12 days characterized by the excretion of high levels of pregnanediol-3α-glucuronide. Although the interval from luteal regression to the next increase in pregnanediol excretion is longer than that in the other species of ungulate shown in Fig. 7, oestrus and ovulation are still thought to occur within two days of the end of the previous luteal phase (Loskutoff *et al.* 1982). Thus, in many ungulates, the direct measurement of urinary metabolites of progesterone and not oestrogen represents the method of choice for monitoring ovarian function and predicting ovulation.

Artificial control of reproduction

The ability to monitor reproductive function in exotic animals provides the basis for controlled studies designed to accelerate captive breeding by artificial means. By applying knowledge gained from studies on laboratory and domestic animals it should be possible to increase reproductive output in

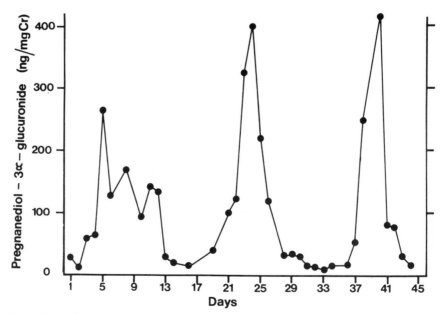

Fig. 8 The pattern of excretion of urinary pregnanediol-3α-glucuronide during three consecutive oestrous cycles in an okapi.

endangered species through manipulating the mechanisms by which fertility is regulated. Although little progress has been made so far, largely because of the lack of information on the basic reproductive physiology of most endangered species, there are a number of approaches which, if developed on a proper scientific basis, could have considerable potential to enhance captive breeding.

One such approach is the modification of the oestrous cycle to synchronize the time of ovulation. Here the objective is to predetermine the precise time of ovulation using pharmacological treatment to override the animal's endogenous reproductive rhythm. Since the accurate prediction and detection of ovulation is essential to the management of natural and artificial breeding there are many potential advantages to this type of approach. Based on the large volume of literature on domestic hoofstock and our growing knowledge of the reproductive physiology of their exotic counterparts, it is reasonable to anticipate that procedures to control the lifespan of the corpus luteum will provide an effective method for regulating the time of ovulation in many endangered ungulates. An example of the use of a synthetic luteolytic agent to terminate the luteal phase in the blackbuck is shown in

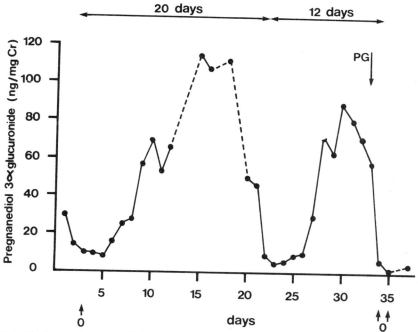

Fig. 9 The levels of pregnanediol-3α-glucuronide during two oestrous cycles in the blackbuck. An injection of synthetic prostaglandin (PG, arrow) shortened the length of the cycle from 20 to 12 days by inducing luteal regression and advancing the time of oestrus (O).

Fig. 9. A single injection of the prostaglandin analogue cloprostenol terminated corpus luteum function and, by abbreviating the luteal phase, advanced the time of oestrus and ovulation to within two days of the injection. In this way, it should eventually be possible to predetermine the time of ovulation for oocyte recovery and artificial insemination without the need for intensive endocrine monitoring. The precise timing of ovulation in relation to luteolysis would, however, need to be carefully determined for each species, before the method could be applied routinely. Treatment in two or more individuals at the same time would be of additional value in synchronizing ovulation for embryo transfer studies.

Other procedures for artificially modifying the control of reproduction in exotic species include induction of ovulation during seasonal anoestrus or in the treatment of infertility. Since many endangered species are seasonal breeders, research into their physiology and development of improved natural and artificial breeding is restricted to a limited time each year. It is now known that the timing of reproduction in seasonally breeding mammals such as sheep and deer is mediated by changes in the pattern of secretion of the pineal hormone melatonin (e.g. Lincoln & Short 1980) and that in these species an artificial increase in melatonin will result in early reproductive activity (Kennaway, Gilmore & Seamark 1982; Arendt, Symons, Laud & Pryde 1983; Bubenik 1983) Thus, administration of melatonin, by implant or by feeding, offers the potential for manipulating the onset of ovarian cyclicity (i.e. ovulation) in a variety of seasonally breeding exotic ungulates. The advantages of this type of approach are that melatonin is easy to administer (e.g. by addition to feed pellets in ruminants) and so can be used to induce the early onset of oestrus in a number of individuals at the same time. The major disadvantage is that little control over the precise timing of ovulation is likely to be achieved by the use of melatonin alone.

Perhaps the most exciting future possibility lies in the induction of ovulation by chronic administration of the hypothalamic decapeptide luteinizing hormone releasing hormone (LH-RH). Intermittent or pulsed delivery of synthetic LH-RH has been shown to induce ovulation within 2–3 days during seasonal and post-partum anoestrus in sheep (McLeod, Haresign & Lamming 1982) and cattle (Riley, Peters & Lamming 1981) as well as forming the basis for the treatment of certain types of anovulatory infertility in women (Leyendecker & Wildt 1983). During anoestrus in domestic animals, the response to LH-RH is rapid and the interval to ovulation relatively constant within species (or breed) and reproductive condition. With the development of simple delivery systems such as small subcutaneously placed osmotic pumps and the prospects for successful application using a continuous mode of delivery (McLeod et al. 1982; Wright, Clarke & Findlay 1983) the use of LH-RH becomes a practical proposition for the controlled induction of ovulation in a variety of exotic species. Thus, in wild animals, in which seasonal constraints on reproduction are common and the 'stress' of captivity all too often results in reproductive failure, there is enormous potential in the application of LH-RH treatment in the management of artificial breeding of endangered species in captivity. Work at the Zoological Society of San Diego and in our own laboratory is already under way to demonstrate the value of this approach.

LH-RH acts by stimulating the natural ovulation rate for the species in question. In many cases this is the most convenient form of ovulation induction since it avoids the complication of ovarian hyperstimulation and subsequent superfetation. Occasionally, however, it is desirable to induce superovulation whereby an animal which is normally monotocous can be stimulated to ovulate multiple oocytes in a single cycle. Once fertilization is achieved, either by natural mating or by artificial insemination, recovery of the embryos is necessary. Reliable procedures for superovulation would therefore be of considerable importance in facilitating the collection of large numbers of embryos for transfer to selected recipients either immediately or at a later date after storage in liquid nitrogen. As with previous methods mentioned in this section, techniques for superovulation have yet to be adequately tried and tested in exotic species but their current application in agriculture and clinical medicine provides a firm basis from which to start. Exogenous gonadotrophins such as PMSG and hMG have been widely used for inducing superovulation in domestic livestock (see Hunter (1980) for references) although the poor predictability of response with the former preparation may pose problems when dealing with the limited number of exotic animals normally available in captivity. More recently, passive immunization against gonadal steroids has been shown to result in a small increase in ovulation and conception rates in sheep (Scaramuzzi & Radford 1983) and further refinement of this and other immunological techniques may provide a more subtle approach to enhancing ovulation rate in rare and endangered species.

Acknowledgements

I am grateful to Mrs D. Bevan and Dr S.A.K. Eastman for their assistance in these studies; to Dr D. Makawiti, Dr W.V. Holt, Dr H.D.M. Moore, and Miss S. Andelman for permission to include unpublished material; and to the veterinary and keeper staffs of London, Washington, and Madrid Zoos and to the Institute of Primate Research, Nairobi, for the collection of urine samples. The work was supported by a programme grant from the MRC and AFRC and a core support grant from the ABRC.

References

Andelman, S., Else, J.G., Hearn, J.P. & Hodges, J.K. (1985). The non-invasive monitoring of reproductive events in wild vervet monkeys using pregnanediol-3α-glucuronide and its correlations with behavioural observations. *J. Zool., Lond.* **205**: 467–77.

Anon. (1974). On the breeding of the giant panda and the development of its cub. *Acta zool. sin.* **20**: 139–47.

Arendt, J., Symons, A.M., Laud, C.A. & Pryde, S.J. (1983). Melatonin can induce early onset of the breeding season in ewes. *J. Endocr.* **97**: 397–400.

Baker, T.S., Jennison, K.M. & Kellie, A.E. (1979). The direct radioimmunoassay of oestrogen in human female urine. *Biochem. J.* **177**: 729–38.

Boland, M.P., Foulkes, J.A., MacDonnell, H.F. & Sauer, M.J. (1985). Plasma progesterone concentrations in superovulated heifers determined by enzyme immunoassay and radioimmunoassay. *Br. vet. J.* **141**: 409–15.

Bonney, R.C., Wood, D.J. & Kleiman, D.G. (1982). Endocrine correlates of behavioural oestrus in the female giant panda (*Ailuropoda melanoleuca*) and associated hormonal changes in the male. *J. Reprod. Fert.* **64**: 209–15.

Branch, C.M., Collins, P.O., Kilpatrick, M.J. & Collins, W.P. (1980). The effect of conception on the concentration of urinary oestrone-3-glucuronide, LH/LCG and pregnanediol-3 alpha-glucuronide. *Acta endocr.* **93**: 228–33.

Brand, H.M. (1981). Urinary oestrogen excretion in the female cotton-topped tamarin (*Saguinus oedipus oedipus*) *J. Reprod. Fert.* **62**: 467–73.

Bubenik, G.A. (1983). Shift of seasonal cycle in white-tailed deer by oral administration of melatonin. *J. exp. Zool.* **225**: 155–6.

Collins, W.P., Branch, C.M. & Collins, P.O. (1981). Ovulation prediction and detection by the measurement of steroid glucuronides. In *Research on fertility and sterility*: 19–33. Cortes-Prieto, J., Campos da Paz, A. & Neves-e-Castro, M. (Eds). MTP Press, Lancaster.

Eastman, S.A.K., Makawiti, D.M., Collins, W.P. & Hodges, J.K. (1984). Pattern of excretion of urinary steroid metabolites during the ovarian cycle and pregnancy in the marmoset monkey. *J. Endocr.* **102**: 19–26.

Hodges, J.K. (In press). Methods for the prediction and detection of ovulation in exotic mammals based on urinary hormone analysis. In *Immunoassays in veterinary practice*. Bolton, T.A. & Morris, B. (Eds). Ellis Horwood, Chichester.

Hodges, J.K., Bevan, D.J., Celma, M., Hearn, J.P., Jones, D.M., Kleiman, D.G., Knight, J.A. & Moore, H.D.M. (1984). Aspects of the reproductive endocrinology of the female Giant Panda (*Ailuropoda melanoleuca*) in captivity with special reference to the detection of ovulation and pregnancy. *J. Zool., Lond.* **203**: 253–68.

Hodges, J.K., Czekala, N.M. & Lasley, B.L. (1979). Estrogen and luteinizing hormone secretion in diverse primate species from simplified urinary analysis. *J. med. Primatol.* **8**: 349–64.

Hodges, J.K. & Eastman, S.A.K. (1984). Monitoring ovarian function in marmosets and tamarins by the measurement of urinary estrogen metabolites. *Am. J. Primatol.* **6**: 187–97.

Hodges, J.K. & Hearn, J.P. (1983). The prediction and detection of ovulation: applications to comparative medicine and conservation. In *Ovulation: Methods for its prediction and detection*: 103–22. Jeffcoate, S.L. (Ed.). J. Wiley & Sons, London.

Hunter, R.F. (1980). *Physiology and technology of reproduction in female domestic animals*. Academic Press, London.

Joyce, B.G., Read, G.F. & Riad-Fahmy, D. (1977). Enzyme immunoassay for progesterone and oestradiol. A study of the factors influencing sensitivity. In *Radioimmunoassay and related procedures in medicine* 1: 289–95. International Atomic Energy Agency (Eds). Int. Atomic Energy Agency, Vienna.

Joyce, B.G., Wilson, D.W., Read, G.F. & Riad-Fahmy, D. (1978). An improved enzyme immunoassay for progesterone in human plasma. *Clin. Chem.* 24: 2099–102.

Kennaway, D.J., Gilmore, T.A. & Seamark, R.F. (1982). Effect of melatonin feeding on serum prolactin and gonadotrophin levels and the onset of seasonal estrous cyclicity in sheep. *Endocrinology* 110: 1766–72.

Kleiman, D.G. (1983). Ethology and reproduction of captive Giant Pandas (*Ailuropoda melanoleuca*). *Z. Tierpsychol.* 62: 1–46.

Lasley, B.L., Hodges, J.K. & Czekala, N.M. (1980). Monitoring the female reproductive cycle of great apes and other primate species by determination of oestrogen and LH in small volumes of urine. *J. Reprod. Fert.* Suppl. 28: 121–9.

Leyendecker, G. & Wildt, L. (1983). Induction of ovulation with chronic intermittent (pulsatile) administration of Gn-RH in women with hypothalamic amenorrhoea. *J. Reprod. Fert.* 69: 397–409.

Lincoln, G.A. & Short, R.V. (1980). Seasonal breeding: Nature's contraceptive. *Rec. Prog. Horm. Res.* 36: 1–52.

Loskutoff, N.M., Ott, J.E. & Lasley, B.L. (1982). Urinary steroid evaluations to monitor ovarian function in exotic ungulates 1. Pregnanediol-3-glucuronide immunoreactivity in the Okapi (*Okapia johnstoni*). *Zoo Biol.* 1: 45–54.

Loskutoff, N.M., Ott, J.E. & Lasley, B.L. (1983). Strategies for assessing ovarian function in exotic species. *J. Zoo Anim. Med.* 14: 3–12.

Makawiti, D., Hodges, J.K., Collins, W.P. & Else, J.G. (In prep.) *Measurement of urinary steroid glucuronides as a practical method for assessing ovarian function and pregnancy in the vervet monkey.*

Martin, R.D., Seaton, B. & Lusty, J.A. (1975). Application of urinary hormone determination in the management of gorillas. *Rep. Jersey Wildl. Preserv. Trust* 12: 61–70.

McLeod, B.J., Haresign, W. & Lamming, G.E. (1982). The induction of ovulation and luteal function in seasonally anoestrous ewes treated with small-dose multiple injections of Gn-RH. *J. Reprod. Fert.* 65: 215–21.

Metcalf, M.G. & Hunt, E.G. (1976). Calculation of estrogen excretion rates from urinary estrogen to creatinine ratios. *Clin. Biochem.* 9: 75–7.

Moore, H.D.M., Bush, M., Celma, M., Garcia, A.L., Hartman, T.D., Hearn, J.P., Hodges, J.K., Jones, D.M., Knight, J.A., Monsalve, L. & Wildt, D.E. (1984). Artificial insemination in the Giant panda (*Ailuropoda melanoleuca*). *J. Zool., Lond.* 203: 269–78.

Munro, C. & Stabenfeldt, G. (1984). Development of a microtitre plate enzyme immunoassay for the determination of progesterone. *J. Endocr.* 101: 41–9.

Riley, G.M., Peters. A.R. & Lamming, G.E. (1981). Induction of pulsatile LH release, FSH release and ovulation in post partum beef cows by repeated small doses of Gn-RH. *J. Reprod. Fert.* **63**: 559–65.

Samarajeewa, P., Cooley, G. & Kellie, A.E. (1979). The radioimmunoassay of pregnanediol-3α-glucuronide. *J. Steroid Biochem.* **11**: 1165–71.

Sauer, M.J., Foulkes, J.A. & Cookson, A.D. (1981). Direct enzyme immunoassay of progesterone in bovine milk. *Steroids* **38**: 45–53.

Scaramuzzi, R.J. & Radford, H.M. (1983). Factors regulating ovulation rate in the ewe. *J. Reprod. Fert.* **69**: 353–67.

Shideler, S.E., Czekala, N.M., Kasman, L.H., Lindburg, D.G. & Lasley, B.L. (1983). Monitoring ovulation and implantation in the lion-tailed macaque (*Macaca silenus*) through urinary estrone conjugate evaluations. *Biol. Reprod.* **29**: 905–11.

Shideler, S.E. & Lasley, B.L. (1982). A comparison of primate ovarian cycles. *Am. J. Primatol.* **1** (Suppl.): 171–80.

Taussky, H.H. (1954). A microcolorimetric determination of creatinine in urine by the Jaffe reaction. *J. biol. Chem.* **208**: 853–61.

Wright, P.J., Clarke, I.J. & Findlay, J.K. (1983). The induction of fertile oestrus in seasonally anoestrous ewes using a continuous low dose administration of gonadotrophin releasing hormone. *Aust. vet. J.* **60**: 254–5.

Symp. zool. Soc. Lond. (1985) No. 54: 169–181

Early embryonic development and the conservation of mammals

JOHN P. HEARN

MRC/AFRC Comparative Physiology
Research Group
Institute of Zoology
Zoological Society of London
Regent's Park
London NW1 4RY

Synopsis

The period from fertilization to implantation and the establishment of pregnancy is critical to the survival of any species. Estimates of early embryonic loss at this time range between 30 and 60% for the human and for several domesticated species. There is little known of the dialogue that must be initiated quickly to ensure attachment to and invasion of the endometrium by the embryo. Until recently the embryo was thought to be a passive partner in this process. New evidence suggests that the embryo transmits signals to the mother during and even before attachment and implantation. Study of the events that determine early development and differentiation of the embryo *in vivo* and *in vitro* helps to clarify the components of their dialogue and to advance our knowledge of the morphological, endocrine and immunological factors involved. The results may assist in improved reproductive efficiency, better methods for short- and long-term storage of embryos, new early pregnancy tests and, perhaps, novel approaches to the treatment of infertility or to the regulation of fertility in animals and man.

In searching for an animal analogue that approximates early pregnancy in women, the non-human primates are among the few candidates. Yet, for reasons of ethics and availability, we know little about the first four weeks of pregnancy in these species. The embryo enters the uterus three or four days after fertilization, hatches from the zona pellucida and attaches to the endometrium approximately on Day 7 in humans, Day 9 in rhesus monkeys and baboons and Day 12 in marmoset monkeys. In the past two years, marmoset embryos were grown in culture to Day 30 after fertilization and shown to differentiate well when allowed to attach to a layer of fibroblast cells. The morphology of attachment was studied *in vivo* and *in vitro*. The first clear signal from the embryo was the secretion of chorionic gonadotrophin (CG), detected immediately after attachment *in vitro*. Exposure of embryos to anti-CG sera inhibited early pregnancy and appeared directly to affect embryos in culture. Pre-implantation embryonic signals are currently being examined. There is considerable variation between primate species in the morphology of implantation although the endocrinology is similar. Data from other species exhibiting embryonic

ZOOLOGICAL SYMPOSIUM No. 54
ISBN 0–19–854002–7

diapause show that embryos may be stored for long periods at body temperature. The ability of primate embryos to undergo short-term delayed implantation has yet to be determined.

Introduction

Implantation, the process by which an embryo attaches to the mother's womb, is a critical event in the survival of any mammal. Many embryos are lost at this time. The morphological and endocrine factors that control implantation have been studied in detail in laboratory animals. Far less is known about implantation in primates, including the human, other than that the mechanism in primates differs from mechanisms in other animals (Short 1969). The primate embryo appears to take an active role in implantation, especially in secreting proteins, such as chorionic gonadotrophin, that extend the life of the corpus luteum (Knobil 1973; Ross 1979). The local effects of chorionic gonadotrophin on implantation and the functions of other proteins that may signal the initiation of pregnancy to the mother are not clear. Yet it is clear that within a few days of fertilization a physiological dialogue must be established between embryo and mother for pregnancy to proceed.

In this paper, some recent findings from primate embryos studied *in vivo* and *in vitro* are examined in the context of the ways in which such knowledge may contribute to the improvement of reproductive efficiency of rare primates. In addition, reference is made to ways in which new practical advances may assist in the artificial acceleration of animal reproduction. Finally, the needs for a greater fundamental understanding of primate implantation in order to develop new methods of fertility control in the human primate are noted.

There are several ironies in the shared physiological systems that control reproduction in primates. On the one hand, greater knowledge of early embryonic development and implantation is assisting in the treatment of human infertility, bringing hope to many individuals who suffer from sterility. On the other, the great success of human populations that have overcome all the natural checks to numbers faced by species that are in balance with the environment has forced many animal species, including primates, to a threatened or endangered status through the destruction of their natural habitats. While knowledge of early embryonic development has helped to improve the treatment of human infertility, the major advances in the last five years achieved for the human have yet to be translated into routine, practical methods for accelerating the breeding of non-human primates. In addition, these advances have yet to define limiting factors in the development of the embryo from fertilization to implantation that would provide hope for effective, new methods for human fertility control.

Conservation and human fertility

Undoubtedly the main problems to be faced over the next 50 years by those committed to achieving a balance between human and animal survival will continue to be related to expanding human populations. There is in some circles an impression that, with the advent of the oral contraceptives and the stabilizing of populations in many developed countries to less than 1 per cent growth per annum, the problem is being solved. Indeed, in several European countries there is concern that populations are falling; and incentives are being introduced to encourage increased childbirth. This complacency cannot be sustained as the moderate prediction for human population as a whole, prepared by the World Bank, an excerpt of which is shown in Table I, indicates that the world's population will almost double within the next 50 years and will not stabilize until the end of the 21st century (McNamara 1984). It follows that the increase will be mainly in developing countries, the very areas that are the homelands of most surviving large animal species. It is unacceptable for developed countries to criticize, since as their societies grew much of their own wildlife was wiped out. Yet it is crucial that we now face the facts, consider animals in captivity and in the wild as one stock to be managed as a whole, and learn more about the limiting factors of animal survival in genetics, nutrition, disease and reproduction to attempt to redress the balance.

Table I. Projections for the human population in developing and developed countries between 1980 and 2100 (population in millions, World Bank estimates and projections 1984).

Year	1980	2000	2025	2050	2100	Total fertility rate 1982
Developing countries	3298	4884	6941	8400	9463	4.2
Developed countries	1137	1263	1357	1380	1407	1.9
Total (world)	4435	6147	8298	9780	10870	3.6

Biological overproduction and loss

In all animal species, the numbers of gametes and embryos produced are far in excess of those required to guarantee replacement. This is well recognized in lower vertebrates, but it is also true for primates. Taking the human as an example, the average human male produces about 40 000 sperm per hour throughout reproductive life. An average human ejaculate will contain well over 50 million sperm. A sperm count of under four million is thought to indicate infertility, although successful conceptions have occurred when the male partner has a sperm count of one million.

The human female is born with approximately two million oocytes in her ovaries. In the normal course of events with one egg being shed each menstrual cycle from sexual maturity to menopause, only about 370 of these oocytes will be ovulated and the remainder will be lost in the process of atresia. Of the oocytes ovulated, 2–10 may result in young that survive to maturity. The *Guinness book of records* notes 32 and 22 as the maximum number of children produced by mothers (for Brazil and England respectively) in this century.

The period between fertilization and established clinical pregnancy is also subject to loss, with some estimates suggesting that as many as 60 % of fertilized embryos are voided (Boué, Boué & Lazar, 1975; Short 1979). These figures are difficult to validate but one may accept that about half the numbers of embryos formed do not survive to complete implantation. Among domesticated animals, a similar figure may be arrived at in cattle, although rodents appear to have a far greater embryonic survival.

A reason for presenting these estimates is to make the point that a high proportion of gamete and embryonic production is subject to natural wastage. Many of these cells or embryos could be 'rescued' or stored with the application of new methods of preservation and storage. The work of Polge and his colleagues (see p. 123) and others has had a major impact in applying such methods to agricultural animal production. The work of Edwards (1980), Trounson & Mohr (1983), and others is helping to transform our approaches to the treatment of human infertility. Increasingly, similar methods are being developed to assist in the acceleration of reproduction of exotic species (see the chapters by Moore, p. 137, and Hodges p. 149) and will be more successful when we have a deeper fundamental knowledge of the factors controlling the development of gametes and embryos.

It must be recognized, however, that techniques developed for one species do not immediately translate to practical methods for others. Species variations in the structure, biochemical constituents, and physiological requirements of gametes and embryos mean that it is necessary to take the time to study the basic requirements in detail before the chances of success can be improved and practical methods achieved.

In vitro fertilization, embryo storage and transfer

This section presents the status of current research on *in vitro* fertilization in mammals, including non-human primates, but excluding the human. Its purpose is a brief summary of the field, giving a few key references and identifying the problems at hand.

The history of *in vitro* fertilization dates back to 1890, with the outstanding contributions of Walter Heape at Cambridge. A great deal of work in the first half of this century was clouded by a lack of definition between fertilization and induced egg activation. With the discovery by Austin (1951) and Chang (1951) of sperm capacitation, the next phase was characterized by some success, especially in the rabbit, because the time of ovulation in relation to coitus was known in that species. In 1969 Edwards, Bavister & Steptoe reported the first successful *in vitro* fertilization in humans. Since that time *in vitro* capacitation of sperm has been achieved in several species and *in vitro* fertilization in a range of mammals including non-human primates. However, successful births from these externally fertilized embryos are still a very small proportion of the numbers transferred to synchronized females.

In vitro fertilization

Although Chang reported the first successful *in vitro* fertilization in the rabbit in 1959 and there are records of similar success in 11 species to date (Table II), the only unequivocal births resulting from these procedures are in the rabbit (Chang 1959), mouse (Whittingham 1968), rat (Toyoda & Chang 1974), and human (Steptoe & Edwards 1978). There was, in addition, a preliminary report of a cow pregnant after *in vitro* fertilization at the University of Pennsylvania (Brackett *et al.* 1982).

Table II. *In vitro* fertilization in mammals.

Species	Stage of development	First reports
Laboratory rodents		
Rabbit	Live births	Chang (1959)
Mouse	Live births	Whittingham (1968)
Rat	Live births	Toyoda & Chang (1974)
Hamster	2 cell	Whittingham & Bavister (1974)
Domesticated animals		
Cow	One live birth	Brackett, Bousquet, Boice, Donawick, Evans & Dressel (1982)
Sheep	—	Polge (1985 — this volume p. 123)
Pig	—	Polge (1985 — this volume p. 123)
Primates		
Squirrel monkey	2 cell	Dukelow (1983)
Marmoset monkey	4 cell	C. Harlow & J.P. Hearn (unpublished)
Baboon	6 cell	Kraemer (1973)
Human	Live births	Steptoe & Edwards (1978)

It is difficult to compare the 'success rate' of *in vitro* fertilization in a range of animals studied by different investigators using different methods.

However, it is clear that the procedure is relatively successful in rabbits, rats, and mice but that not enough is known from other species to allow routine experimental usage. Rates of success claimed for fertilization range from 5–70 %, but these figures are not related to numbers of live young; if they were, the rates would be considerably lower. Even in the rat and mouse, considerable loss is experienced through unsuccessful fertilization and poor viability after transfer.

There is an enormous literature on superovulation, the process of increasing the number of follicles maturing in the ovary by injecting exogenous gonadotrophins. There are suggestions from several workers (e.g. Dukelow & Kueh 1975) that superovulation is less efficient than working with ova that have been allowed to mature naturally in the ovary. There are also suggestions that stimulation with exogenous gonadotrophin may increase the incidence of chromosomally abnormal embryos (human: Boué & Boué 1973; rabbit: Fujimoto, Pahlavan & Dukelow 1974; mouse: Tagaki & Sasaki 1976). In addition, some authors have claimed that incubation of ova with excess sperm, particularly if the ova are ageing, may lead to polyspermy (E.J.C. Polge pers. comm).

The problems to be clarified remain as follows:

1. Precise recognition of the time of ovulation.
2. Maturation of the ovum *in vitro*, simulating the *in vivo* requirements for fertilization.
3. Capacitation of sperm.
4. *In vitro* culture of the embryo until the optimum time for transfer to the mother.

Ironically, apart perhaps from the rat and mouse, knowledge of the above stages is better advanced in the human than in animals. The work carried out by A.O. Trounson over the past five years in Melbourne has focused on simplified, practical methods to ensure adequate completion of each of the above stages with a resulting improvement in success rates. A similar approach by R.G. Edwards is yielding improved clinical results.

A lot of the data has yet to appear in press but there is no doubt that the 'animal models' are lagging behind. This is especially true for the non-human primates. The problems of dealing with the large, Old World species such as the rhesus monkey, producing one ovum a month and with only a five-month annual breeding season, have precluded rapid progress. In recent years more attention has been given to the smaller, faster breeding New World species such as the squirrel monkey (Dukelow 1983) and the common marmoset (Hearn 1980, 1983), but although they breed throughout the year and the marmoset produces two to three ova at each ovulation, progress has yet to match that obtained in the human.

Embryo storage

The procedure of embryo storage may be divided into short term (*in vitro* culture) or long term (freezing). The natural systems of *in vivo* embryo storage, such as embryonic diapause or delayed implantation, are not dealt with in this discussion.

In vitro culture of embryos

There is an extensive literature on the growth and development of naturally fertilized embryos placed in culture (for an introduction, see Whittingham 1979) from which, in the context of this paper, it is possible to make a few points.

1. Apart from the mouse, the post-implantation survival of cultured embryos is severely reduced after more than 48 h *in vitro* and still reflects our lack of knowledge of the embryonic requirements for pre-implantation development (Whittingham 1979).

2. Most of the work carried to a successful conclusion (i.e. live young) has entailed embryos kept for less than one day in culture. Recent reports from Melbourne and Cambridge indicate that a longer period may be advisable when dealing with human embryos fertilized *in vitro*.

3. In studies of primates, comparing the rates of pre-implantation embryonic development *in vivo* and *in vitro*, the rate is retarded after about 24 h *in vitro*. For example, Kreitman & Hodgen (1981) recovered 14 embryos from rhesus or cynomolgus monkeys and showed retarded cleavage rates, at whatever stage the embryo was collected, achieving only one to three cleavages *in vitro*. Hearn (1983) recovered 120 embryos from marmoset monkeys, finding little difficulty in growing them *in vitro* but showing a 24 h retardation in development after four to eight days in culture.

4. Embryos collected near to the time of implantation will continue to grow in culture and may 'implant' on the culture dish. In such studies, embryonic growth has continued *in vitro* to attachment in baboons (Pope, Pope & Beck 1981), to formation of the egg cylinder in marmoset monkeys (Hearn & Gems, in prep.) and to the 12-somite stage in mice (Hsu 1979). Studies of this nature may answer questions of embryonic differentiation, but are not compatible with survival of the embryo, since transfer to the mother cannot be carried out after the blastocyst has hatched from the zona pellucida.

Freezing of embryos

The first successful attempts to store embryos by freezing were by Whittingham, Leibo & Mazur (1972) and Wilmut (1972). Embryos of cattle, sheep, goat, rabbit, and rat have since been successfully frozen, thawed and developed to normal young after transfer to synchronized foster mothers.

Many systems of freezing and thawing have been used, with several cryo-protectants developed to prevent the formation of intracellular ice. The success rate in live births from frozen embryos varies between species and between laboratories, but may be as high as 70–80 % in the mouse.

Kasai, Iritani & Chang (1979) investigated the freezing of rat ovarian oocytes, which were then thawed and cultured with capacitated sperm. They found that successful *in vitro* fertilization occurred in more oocytes if they were allowed to mature before freezing, but there were considerable numbers of penetrated oocytes with abnormalities.

Theoretically there is no limit to the time that frozen embryos may be stored and the technique allows controlled investigations of genetic drift, preservation of rare strains, and transfer of embryos between geographical locations and may assist the treatment of infertility.

As yet there are few reports of successful births after freezing and thawing primate embryos. Preliminary studies with 10–15 human embryos in Melbourne resulted in two live births (A.O. Trounson, pers. comm.) and while ten marmoset embryos have recently been successfully frozen and thawed, six resuming apparently normal growth, they were not transferred to synchronized females. However, they appeared morphologically normal and, in the three examined cytogenetically, there was no evidence of chromosomal damage (J. Dibban, L. Wilson, S. Gems & J.P. Hearn, unpublished).

Embryo transfer

The technique of embryo transfer has long been a routine matter both in laboratory animals and in domesticated animals. The practice is now widespread in farm animals with many commercial firms involved. The easiest and most successful transfer technique usually involves working with embryos at morula and blastocyst stages. The technique is now frequently applied in conjunction with frozen embryos at these stages. In addition, the techniques of superovulation and synchronization of oestrus, relatively easy to control in cattle, sheep, pigs, etc., further simplify the methodology required. Success rates, in live births, are frequently reported to be in excess of 80% (Betteridge 1977).

Most embryo transfers to the oviducts are performed via laparotomy or laparoscopy, but non-surgical transfers of embryos at later stages of development may easily be performed via the cervix in animals where the cervix is straight.

In most laboratory and domesticated animals, the main requirement for successful embryo transfer is adequate synchronization of the donor and recipient. The embryo, according to its stage of development, is placed in the oviduct or uterus of the recipient. In rodents, with a short oestrous cycle, synchronization is critical as even a few hours asynchrony may lead to destruction of the embryo. In cattle, pigs, and sheep, although two to eight cell embryos will survive to term when placed in the uterus, survival is significantly higher when they are transferred to the oviduct.

Initial results suggest that synchronization between donor and recipient is less important in primates, perhaps because of the long luteal phase in primate species. Rhesus monkey embryos of from one to eight cells developed to term after transfer to the contralateral oviduct or to the uterus of the same female (Marston, Penn & Sivelle 1977). There is a report of one successful embryo transfer in the baboon (Kraemer, Moore & Kramen 1977). Recently, Summers & Wennink (1984) have achieved over 70% success with live births from embryo transfers in marmosets and studies with frozen embryos are encouraging, with two live births to date. Once again, the state of play in non-human primates lags behind that in the human, where non-surgical embryo transfer via the cervix is becoming routine. In the first successful human embryo transfer after *in vitro* fertilization (Steptoe & Edwards 1978), an eight-cell embryo developed to term after being placed in the uterus of the mother. Since that time several hundred human embryos have been transferred (Trounson, Leeton, Wood, Webb & Wood 1981; Edwards 1981).

Embryo manipulation

While a discussion of the manipulation of pre-implantation embryos is not within the scope of this paper, advances in such techniques currently being applied to animals deserve note. Studies in sheep, pigs, and goats at the AFRC Institute of Animal Physiology, Cambridge (see pp. 123–35), show the feasibility of separating early embryos into their constituent blastomeres, each of which retains the potency to develop into an entire individual. It may also be possible to produce viable young of interspecies crosses by forming chimaeras. Research on experimental chimaeras in embryos from rodents has proceeded for many years at the MRC Mammalian Development Unit and other centres (McLaren 1984). The results of these studies provide important advances in our understanding of the factors controlling mammalian development. In the immediate future, the same methods will allow for specific gene association, the possibilities of genetic surgery and the improvement of genetic stock (e.g. resistance to disease, growth rates).

With current advances in cell biology, immunology, and genetics, the development of new and improved stocks by genetic manipulation, long an actuality in the field of plant breeding, may extend to animals. Undoubtedly some of these advances will promise advantages to medical science, for example in the treatment of inherited diseases.

Early embryonic messages

A greater knowledge is required of the signals that pass between embryo and mother during the period from fertilization to implantation and the establishment of pregnancy. Over this period embryonic loss, in primates and domesticated species that have been studied to date, is in the region of 50%. The causes of loss are not fully understood but clearly a dialogue has to be established quickly for pregnancy to proceed. The identity and the function of signals between embryo and mother differ according to the species. Definition of these questions should lead to the development of new early pregnancy tests, ways of monitoring embryonic progress and, perhaps, therapeutic approaches designed either to reduce or to increase the rate of embryonic loss for purposes of overcoming fertility or improving contragestational and contraceptive methods.

In domesticated farm animals, oestrogens and/or proteins that are secreted by the embryo before implantation are thought to be necessary for prolonging the life span of the corpus luteum (Heap, Staples, Flint, Maule Walker & Allen 1983). In addition, an early pregnancy factor has been described by Morton, Rolfe, Clunie, Anderson & Morrison (1977) and by Morton, Morton & Ellendorff (1983) in several species including the mouse, pig, and human. This factor can be detected within the first two days after fertilization, but its role is uncertain. Recently, O'Neill (1985) reported a platelet-activating factor, possibly produced by the early embryo during the pre-implantation period, that is measurable in peripheral circulation and that may provide a new way of monitoring the viability of the pre-implantation embryo. The physiological function of this factor in the establishment of pregnancy has yet to be determined.

In the primate, the first clear message from the embryo to the mother is chorionic gonadotrophin, appearing in the peripheral circulation two to three days after invasion of trophoblast commences. It is likely that this hormone may be produced by the blastocyst at the time of embryo attachment and perhaps just before the blastocyst comes in contact with the wall of the uterus (Hearn, Gems, Hodges & Wennink 1984). Although the role of chorionic gonadotrophin in rescuing the corpus luteum of primates has been assumed for many years, it is possible that this hormone has an additional local function at the implantation site.

Conclusions

1. In the rat, mouse, and rabbit, *in vitro* fertilization, embryo storage, manipulation and transfer, have become a routine procedure, with a high survival rate of embryos transferred to recipient females.

2. In domesticated animals such as the cow, sheep, and pig, *in vitro* ferti-

lization is still at an early stage of development. Storage, manipulation, and transfer of naturally fertilized embryos are now becoming routine, with widespread agricultural and commercial exploitation.

3. In non-human primates, *in vitro* fertilization has yet to produce live young at birth. Embryo storage and transfer methods are receiving attention and considerable work is being initiated in the USA and UK in order to develop primates as experimental animals for such studies.

4. There is little evidence as yet of any abnormalities induced in developing embryos by the procedures associated with *in vitro* fertilization, storage, culture, and transfer of embryos. However, the work carried out in laboratory and domesticated animals has focused on the production of live young, not in analysing the reasons why many embryos do not survive to term.

5. While studies of abnormalities in embryos after *in vitro* fertilization have been minimal, there is no indication as yet in the species where such procedures are successful (i.e. laboratory rodents and humans) that there is an unusual incidence of abnormality at birth.

6. A great deal of progress has been made in the past five years in developing procedures to overcome infertility in humans. Translation of similar methods to assist in the conservation of rare mammals still requires a greater fundamental understanding of early embryonic development and implantation in these species.

References

Austin, C.R. (1951). Observations on the penetration of the sperm into the mammalian egg. *Aust. J. scient. Res. Ser. B* 4: 581–96.

Betteridge, K.J. (1977). Embryo transfer in farm animals. *Monogr. Can. Dep. Agric.* No. 16: 1–92.

Boué, J.G. & Boué, A. (1973). Increased frequency of chromosomal anomalies in abortions after induced ovulation. *Lancet* 1973 (i): 697–8.

Boué, J., Boué, A. & Lazar, P. (1975). Retrospective and prospective epidemiological studies of 1500 karyotyped spontaneous human abortions. *Teratology, Philadelphia* 12: 11–26.

Brackett, B.G., Bousquet, D., Boice, M.L., Donawick, W.J., Evans, J.F. & Dressel, M.A. (1982). Normal development following *in vitro* fertilization in the cow. *Biology Reprod.* 27: 147–58.

Chang, M.C. (1951). Fertilizing capacity of spermatozoa deposited in the fallopian tubes. *Nature, Lond.* 168: 697–8.

Chang, M.C. (1959). Fertilization of rabbit ova *in vitro*. *Nature, Lond.* 184: 466–7.

Dukelow, W.R. (1983). The squirrel monkey. In *Reproduction in New World primates*: 149–80. Hearn, J.P. (Ed.) MTP Press, Lancaster.

Dukelow, W.R. & Kueh, T.J. (1975). *In vitro* fertilisation of non human primates. In *La fecondation*: 67–80. Thibault, C. (Ed.). Masson, Paris.

Edwards, R.G. (1980). *Conception in the human female*. Academic Press, London.

Edwards, R.G. (1981). Test tube babies 1981. *Nature, Lond.* **293**: 253–8.

Edwards, R.G., Bavister, B.D. & Steptoe, P.C. (1969). Early stages of fertilisation *in vitro* of human oocytes matured *in vitro*. *Nature, Lond.* **221**: 632.

Fujimoto, S., Pahlavan, N. & Dukelow, W.R. (1974). Chromosome abnormalities in rabbit preimplantation blastocysts induced by superovulation. *J. Reprod. Fert.* **40**: 177–81.

Heap, R.B., Staples, L.D., Flint, A.P.F., Maule Walker, F.M. & Allen, W.R. (1983). Synthetic capabilities of the preimplantation conceptus and maternal responses to pregnancy. In *Fertilisation of the human egg in vitro—Biological basis and clinical implications*: 387–411. Beier, H.M. & Lindner, H. (Eds). Springer-Verlag, Berlin.

Heape, W. (1890). Preliminary note on the transplantation and growth of mammalian ova within a uterine foster mother. *Proc. R. Soc.* **48**: 457–8.

Hearn, J.P. (1980). Endocrinology and timing of implantation in the marmoset monkey, *Callithrix jacchus*. *Prog. reprod. Biol.* **7**: 262–9.

Hearn, J.P. (1983). The marmoset monkey. In *Reproduction in New World primates*: 181–215. Hearn, J.P. (Ed.). MTP Press, Lancaster.

Hearn, J.P., Gems, S., Hodges, J.K. & Wennink, C.J. (1984). The role of chorionic gonadotrophin during embryonic attachment and implantation *in vivo* and *in vitro*. *Programme and Abstracts of Papers: Society for the Study of Fertility, Annual Conference* **1984**: 48. (Abstract).

Hsu, Y.C. (1979). *In vitro* development of individually cultured whole mouse embryos from blastocysts to early somite stage. *Devl Biol.* **68**: 453–69.

Kasai, M., Iritani, A. & Chang, M.C. (1979). Fertilisation *in vitro* of rat ovarian oocytes after freezing and thawing. *Biology Reprod.* **21**: 839–44.

Knobil, E. (1973). On the regulation of the primate corpus luteum. *Biology Reprod.* **8**: 246–58.

Kraemer, D.C. (1973). Cited in Dukelow & Kueh (1975).

Kraemer, D.C., Moore, G.T. & Kramen, M.A. (1977). Baboon infant produced by embryo transfer. *Science, N.Y.* **192**: 1246–7.

Kreitman, O. & Hodgen, G.D. (1981). Retarded cleavage rates of preimplantation monkey embryos *in vitro*. *J. Am. Med. Ass.* **246**: 627–8.

Marston, J.H., Penn, R. & Sivelle, P.C. (1977). Successful autotransfer of tubal eggs in the rhesus monkey, *Macaca mulatta*. *J. Reprod. Fert.* **49**: 175–6.

McLaren, A. (1984). Chimaeras and sexual differentiation. In *Chimaeras in developmental biology*: 381–99. Le Douarin, N. & McLaren, A. (Eds). Academic Press, London.

McNamara, R.S. (1984). *The population problem: time bomb or myth*. World Bank, Washington DC.

Morton, H., Morton., D.J. & Ellendorff, F. (1983). The appearance and characteristics of early pregnancy factor in the pig. *J. Reprod. Fert.* **69**: 437–66.

Morton, H., Rolfe, B., Clunie, G.J.A., Anderson, M.J. & Morrison, J. (1977). An early pregnancy factor detected in human serum by the rosette inhibition test. *Lancet* **1977** (i): 394–7.

O'Neill, C. (1985). Examination of the causes of early pregnancy associated thrombocytopenia in mice. *J. Reprod. Fert.* **73**: 567–77.

Pope, V.Z., Pope, C.E. & Beck, L.R. (1981). Gonadotrophin production by baboon embryo *in vitro*. *Biology Reprod.* **25**: 104–5 (Abstract No. 99).

Ross, G.T. (1979). Human chorionic gonadotrophin and maternal recognition of pregnancy. In *Maternal recognition of pregnancy* (Ciba Symposium No. 64): 191–208. Excerpta Medica, Amsterdam.

Short, R.V. (1969). Implantation and the maternal recognition of pregnancy. In *Foetal anatomy* (Ciba Symposium No. 23): 2–26. Churchill, London.

Short, R.V. (1979). When a conception fails to become a pregnancy. In *Maternal recognition of pregnancy* (Ciba Symposium No. 64): 377–95. Excerpta Medica, Amsterdam.

Steptoe, P.C. & Edwards, R.G. (1978). Birth after the reimplantation of a human embryo. *Lancet* **1978**(ii): 366.

Summers, P.M. & Wennink, C.J. (1984). Embryo transfer in the common marmoset monkey (*Callithrix jacchus*). *Proc. 10th Int. Congr. Anim. Reprod. artif. Insem.* **2**: 245A.

Tagaki, N. & Sasaki, M. (1976). Digynic triploidy after superovulation in mice. *Nature, Lond.* **264**: 278–81.

Toyoda, Y. & Chang, M.C. (1974). Fertilisation of rat eggs *in vitro* by epididymal spermatozoa and the development of eggs following transfer. *J. Reprod. Fert.* **36**: 9–22.

Trounson, A.O., Leeton, J.F., Wood, C., Webb, J. & Wood, J. (1981). Pregnancies in humans by fertilisation *in vitro* and embryo transfer in the controlled ovulatory cycle. *Science, N.Y.* **212**: 681–2.

Trounson, A. & Mohr, R. (1983). Human pregnancy following cryopreservation, thawing and transfer of an 8-cell embryo. *Nature, Lond.* **305**: 707.

Whittingham, D.G. (1968). Fertilisation of mouse eggs *in vitro*. *Nature, Lond.* **220**: 592–3.

Whittingham, D.G. (1979). *In vitro* fertilisation, embryo transfer and storage. *Br. med. Bull.* **35**: 105–11.

Whittingham, D.G. & Bavister, B.D. (1974). Development of hamster eggs fertilised *in vivo* or *in vitro*. *J. Reprod. Fert.* **38**: 489–92.

Whittingham, D.G. Leibo, S.P. & Mazur, P. (1972). Survival of mouse embryos frozen to −196°C and −269°C. *Science, N.Y.* **178**: 411–4.

Wilmut, I. (1972). Effect of cooling rate, warming rate, protective agent and stage of development on survival of mouse embryos during freezing and thawing. *Life Sci.* **11**: 1071–9.

Symp. zool. Soc. Lond. (1985) No. 54: 183–207

Lactation and neonatal survival of mammals

A. S. I. LOUDON

MRC/AFRC Comparative Physiology Research Group
Institute of Zoology
Zoological Society of London
Regent's Park
London NW1 4RY

Synopsis

In both wild and captive populations of mammals, postnatal mortality can be high and frequently exceeds all other age-specific mortality rates. The high postnatal mortality rates suffered by many captive mammal populations are an extension of a phenomenon seen in many wild populations. In captive populations, however, postnatal mortality is commonly associated with a failure of the mother to establish a normal lactation. Thus, a successful captive breeding programme must have the twin aims of ensuring that the nutritional management and husbandry of the female is appropriate for the high energy demands of lactation and that adequate knowledge is available for a successful artificial rearing programme should this become necessary. Improvements in neonatal survival rates of captive populations of endangered species have in the past and will in the future make one of the biggest single contributions to the success of most captive breeding programmes.

In one group of mammals (the ungulates) considerable advances have been made in recent years in our understanding of lactational physiology and neonatal requirements for growth. The metabolizable energy (ME) requirements for maintenance of domesticated ungulates (sheep, cattle, goats, and horses) and wild ungulates such as deer lie between 100 and 140 kcals/kg$^{0.75}$/day, and rise to 140–170kcals/kg$^{0.75}$/day in late pregnancy and to 240–270 kcals/kg$^{0.75}$/day at peak lactation. Thus, while late gestation commonly results in an increased energy requirement of 40 per cent, peak lactation may require a 150 per cent increase. The offspring of all mammals are especially vulnerable at this stage of lactation and the peak in neonatal mortality usually occurs at a time of maximal energy requirements.

Introduction

The preservation of captive populations of rare and endangered species depends upon the application of principles of demographic and genetic management as well as upon a more complete understanding of reproductive physiology and nutrition. The low reproductive output of some captive breeding programmes has many causes, some of which are discussed elsewhere in this symposium. One of the most serious and least researched

ZOOLOGICAL SYMPOSIUM No. 54
ISBN 0–19–854002–7

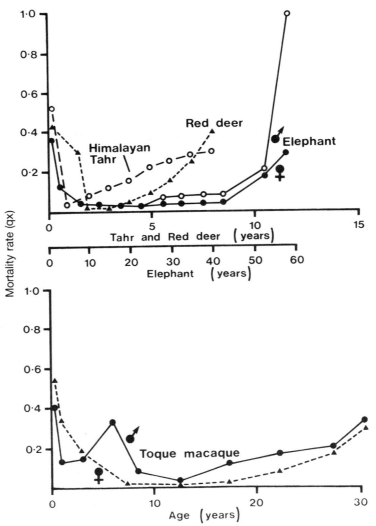

Fig. 1 Mortality rates for four species of mammal based on demographic studies of wild populations (sources of data are quoted in the text).

problems in these programmes is neonatal mortality. Mortality during the period when offspring are dependent upon maternal nutritional support is frequently so high that it may thwart all attempts to produce viable and expanding populations of captive endangered mammals. In this paper, the neonatal mortality of some captive and wild mammal populations is considered and these data are discussed in relation to the maternal energy costs of lactation.

Mortality patterns of wild mammals

Mortality patterns have been described for a number of species, including man. One of the earliest attempts at calculating mortality rates for man was made by John Graunt in 1667 (cited in Caughley 1977). Over the next 200 years the scope and complexity of human life-table analysis was increased so that by the end of the 19th century the science of human demography was established. By comparison, our understanding of the demography of other mammals is very poor. Indeed, no species of wild mammal has been properly described and essential data on birth and mortality rates are generally unavailable. In consequence, research workers on wild mammals tend, when they refer to demography, to consider patterns or trends, rather than precise rates (Caughley 1976).

Mortality data for four mammals, the Himalayan tahr, the red deer, the elephant, and a primate, the toque macaque, are shown in Fig. 1 (from Caughley 1970a, 1971; Laws, Parker & Johnstone 1975; Dittus 1975). These data are all based on studies of wild populations and are presented as qx curves, that is the proportion of animals alive at age x which are dead the following year. Neonatal mortality (qx at zero) is high in all four species, drops steeply in early life and then rises steadily with increasing age. It can be seen that all four species conform to the classic U-shaped mammalian mortality pattern described by Caughley (1976, 1977); indeed, such a pattern is robust enough to describe the mortality of most mammals, regardless of body size, habitat or life expectancy.

In general, the rate of juvenile mortality decreases sharply from birth. For instance, in deer the greatest proportion of the juvenile mortality occurs in the first three weeks of life. Three-week-old red deer calves have a mortality rate some three to five times lower than one-week-old calves (Lowe 1969; Clutton-Brock, Guinness & Albon 1982). In one study of 81 white-tailed deer fawns, the death rate was 0.67 in the first month and 0.15 in the second; in these two months, 53 fawns died (Cook, White, Trainer & Glazener 1971). Such trends are not confined to ungulates. In Dittus' study (1975) of the toque macaque, 21 and 45% of young male and female macaques died in the first six months; the figures for the second six months were 18 and 8% for males and females respectively. In Jeanne Altmann's study of yellow baboons (Altmann 1980), the mortality rate of infants was four times higher in the first than in the second month, while over the first and second years of life, 11 out of 49 and six out of 37 infants died respectively.

Amongst the seasonally breeding mammals, a number of authors have shown that neonatal survival is related to a complex interaction of factors, including weight at birth, date of birth, maternal body condition, size, and social status. For instance, in red deer, neonatal mortality is closely correlated with calf birth weight which is in turn associated with female body size and age, young and lightweight females producing calves with an above-average expectation of death (Blaxter & Hamilton 1980; Clutton-Brock *et al.* 1982). Studies on other seasonally breeding mammals such as reindeer, Soay sheep, and elephant seals support the conclusion that relative birth date and weight at birth are important determinants of neonatal mortality rate (Leader-Williams 1980; Jewell, Milner & Morton-Boyd, 1974; Reiter, Stinson & LeBoeuf 1978).

There are, clearly, substantial differences between mammals in the absolute time course of mortality rates. In many ungulates of below 200 kg adult weight qx is low at 2–3 years (see Fig. 1); at this age mortality rates of elephant and toque macaques are still high. Caughley (1966) observed that the lowest mortality rates occur at puberty, and that this trend is not confined to ungulates but applies equally to mice and men. Juvenile mortality can thus be set apart from adult mortality on statistical and physiological grounds, the pivotal point occurring at puberty. There is ample evidence that this trend applies equally within a species. For instance, in sexually dimorphic species where males grow faster than females and take longer to reach adult body weight, neonatal mortality rates of males are correspondingly higher (e.g. red deer, Clutton-Brock *et al.* 1982; white-tailed deer, Dapson, Ramsey, Smith & Urbston 1979).

Table I summarizes some of the published data on neonatal mortality

Table I. Neonatal mortality rates for some wild mammal populations.

Species	Mortality (%)		Period		Details and source
Toque macaque	21(♂)	45(♀)	0–6	months	Dittus (1975)
(*Macaca sinica*)	18(♂)	8(♀)	6–12	months	
Yellow baboon	8		0–1	month	Altmann (1980)
(*Papio cynocephalus*)	2		1–2	months	
	28		0–1	year	
	25		1–2	years	
Red deer	18		0–6	months	Guinness, Albon & Clutton-Brock (1978)
(*Cervus elaphus*)					
	11		6–12	months	Scotland
	41		0–12	months	Caughley (1971)
	30		12–24	months	New Zealand

Species	Mortality (%)	Period		Details and source
Roe deer	31($\male$) 34($\female$)	0–1	year	Loudon (1978)
(*Capreolus capreolus*)	20($\male$) 14($\female$)	1–2	years	S. England
Moose	66	0–39	days	Hauge & Keith (1981)
(*Alces alces*)	27	40–280	days	Alberta, Canada
Reindeer	15–29	0–6	months	Leader-Williams (1980)
(*Rangifer tarandus*)				S. Georgia
Caribou	58	0–2	months	Fuller & Keith (1981)
(*R. tarandus*)	15	Adult mean		Woodland caribou
White-tailed deer	35–43($\female$)	0–6	months	Mundinger (1981)
(*Odocoileus*	53–58($\male$)			
virginianus)	67	0–1	month	Cook *et al.* (1971)
	15	1–2	months	
	10	0–6	months	Heavy fawns
	68	0–6	months	Light fawns. Verme (1977)
Himalayan tahr	53	0–1	year	Stable population
(*Hemitragus jemlahicus*)	37	0–1	year	Expanding population. Caughley (1976)
Domestic sheep	16	0–1	year	Hickey (1960, 1963)
(*Ovis aries*)	4	1–2	years	N. Island, New Zealand
Elephant	36	0–1	year	Laws *et al.* (1975)
(*Loxodonta africana*)	12	1–2	years	
	4	2–3	years	
Red kangaroo	16	42–196 days of pouchlife		Frith & Sharman (1964)
(*Macropus rufus*)	15	PPE–weaning, good season		
	83	PPE–weaning, drought		
Eastern grey kangaroo	1.8	113–280 days of pouchlife		Poole (1973)
(*M. giganteus*)	50	Birth—weaning		Kirkpatrick (1975) and
	100	All births in drought		Kirkpatrick & McEvoy (1966) Quoted in Russell (1982)
Eastern barred bandicoot (*Perameles gunnii*)	39	Birth–PPE		Heinsohn (1966)
Ringtail possum (*Pseudocheirus peregrinus*)	68	PPE–reproductive maturity		Thomson & Owen (1964)
Mountain brushtail possum	48	Birth–PPE		How (1976)
(*Trichosurus caninus*)	62	Birth–1 year		

PPE, permanent pouch exit.

rates in mammals. The material is heavily biased towards ungulates, particularly deer, and no publications are available which describe the detailed demography of a carnivore. Amongst the ungulates described in Table I, mortality rate for the first year is high (at least 50% in some studies) and invariably falls with increasing age. The postnatal mortality patterns of one group of mammals, the marsupials, differ from those presented above. Because marsupials are born in an under-developed state and impose relatively little burden on the mother, mortality rates are often very low during much of pouch life (e.g. eastern grey kangaroo in Table I). Maximal milk yield probably occurs at or near to permanent pouch exit (PPE) (Findlay & Renfree 1984), and it is at this stage that marsupial young show the highest absolute postnatal growth rates (Russell 1982). Pouch exit may be considered the physiological equivalent of birth in a eutherian (Russell 1982), and it is at this stage of development (and not during early pouch life) that young marsupials suffer the highest mortality rates. It is for this reason that amongst the seasonally breeding marsupials births are so timed as to ensure that the subsequent pouch exit occurs at the optimal time of year.

In wild populations, the intrinsic rate of increase (Caughley & Birch 1971) is a result of the interaction of birth and mortality rate. In most studies of wild mammals, variation in the intrinsic rate of increase is primarily due to changes in mortality rate, rather than changes in the fecundity or survivorship of breeding females. Thus, in Caughley's study of the eruption of the Himalayan tahr from an original release point in New Zealand, changes in the rate of population increase were primarily related to variation in neonatal mortality rates rather than changes in female fecundity (Caughley, 1970a, b). A more recent example comes from a long-term study of the reproduction of breeding red deer on the Isle of Rhum, Scotland. In this study, 75.1% of the variance in reproductive success of breeding red deer hinds was attributable to calf neonatal mortality with differences in fecundity between individuals accounting for only 20.7% of the residual variance (Clutton-Brock *et al.* 1982). The message from these studies makes it clear that variation in neonatal mortality may be the most significant factor influencing both the reproductive success of individuals and the rate of increase of populations. With this in mind, it is worth looking at some of the figures for zoo-based populations.

The performance of captive-bred populations

Limitations of database

Data on the breeding records of all major zoos are now summarized annually in the *International zoo yearbook* (IZY), published by the Zoological Society of London, which provides the most comprehensive data base on the reproductive performance of captive populations. In all, statistics on over

700 mammalian species are provided. ISIS (International Species Inventory System) provides a more detailed computer-based analysis of certain species, but data are confined to a limited number of major zoological collections. All zoos which provide data for the IZY are requested to list the total number of each species held in captivity, the number captive-bred, the numbers and sex of those born in captivity, and finally the number of young born which subsequently died. Although 'neonatal' mortality has been arbitrarily set as deaths that occur within the first month, regardless of species, many zoos simply record all deaths of young animals born within the year as neonatal mortality. Thus, there is no clear indication of the time covered by neonatal deaths for any species. An additional complication is that while the sex of young born is usually recorded, the sex of young dying is usually not indicated so that it is impossible to examine the data for possible sex differences in mortality rate. For a total of 57 rare or endangered species of particular conservation interest, detailed studbooks are maintained. From these studbooks it is possible to gather a more detailed and comprehensive data set and analyse mortality rates by age and sex at death, although no studbook currently provides records on abortions, premature births or fetal mortality.

The more than 700 species of mammal covered by the IZY records include common and rare species and range from records of isolated individuals or pairs to several hundred animals in one collection. The following analysis has been restricted to three criteria: (1) those mammals for which an average of 20 or more individuals have been maintained in captivity for the three-year period 1978–80; (2) those mammals listed in CITES (Convention to control International Trade in Endangered Species of Fauna and Flora) Appendix A as being endangered; and (3) mammalian orders which are well represented in captivity (five or more species) and which have a reasonably comprehensive set of breeding records so that comparisons between orders can be made. On these criteria, four orders (primates, artiodactyls, perissodactyls and carnivores) and a total of 52 species have been selected for analysis.

Neonatal mortality of captive-bred populations

Data on the breeding performance of the 52 species selected are set out in Table II. All four orders have a remarkably high proportion of captive-bred adults in the population, particularly primates and artiodactyls. Birth rate and neonatal mortality are highly variable and direct comparison between orders is complicated by obvious biological differences in interbirth interval, generation length and maturation and growth rate. Amongst the primates, several species have low reproductive rates and high neonatal mortality rates and the mongoose lemur, crested gibbon and red uakari have poor

Table II. Some population statistics on the captive breeding success and neonatal mortality rate of primates, ungulates and carnivores, over the period 1978–80. For selection criteria see text. Symbol after mortality rate indicates that over this period captive populations are either expanding (+), declining (−) or stable (s). n.d. = no data available.

	Mean number in captivity	% bred in captivity	Mean number of births in captivity	Birth rate (%) No. born No. in captivity	Neonatal mortality rate (%)
PRIMATES					
Cheirogaleus medius (fat-tailed dwarf lemur)	30	78	9.3	30.0	18 +
Lemur coronatus (crowned lemur)	19	79	2.0	10.5	0 +
Lemur fulvus (brown lemur)	348	83	39.7	11.2	24 −
Lemur macaco (black lemur)	247	69	33.3	13.4	26 −
Lemur mongoz (mongoose lemur)	142	60	2.3	1.6	57 s
Lemur variegatus (ruffed lemur)	156	82	17.4	11.2	23 +
Microcebus murinus (lesser mouse lemur)	66	55	22.7	34.3	21 s
Callimico goeldii (Goeldi's marmoset)	97	58	32.7	33.7	15 +
Leontopithecus rosalia (golden lion tamarin)	171	85	65.7	38.4	42 +
Saguinus oedipus (cotton-top tamarin)	440	50	163.6	37.2	43 +
Cacajao rubicundus (red uakari)	23	32	0.7	3.0	n.d. −
Macaca silenus (lion-tailed macaque)	309	69	34.0	11.0	23 s
Pygathrix nemaeus (Douc langur)	48	54	9.0	18.8	44 s

Table II (contd.)

	Mean number in captivity	% bred in captivity	Mean number of births in captivity	Birth rate (%) No. born / No. in captivity	Neonatal mortality rate (%)
ARTIODACTYLS (contd.)					
Ozotoceros bezoarticus (pampas deer)	25	35	4	16.0	0 s
Pudu pudu (Chilean or southern pudu)	34	73	9	26.4	11 +
Bison bison athabascae (wood bison)	51	66	9.5	18.6	0 s
Bos frontalis (gaurus) (gaur)	82	91	13.6	16.6	18 +
Nemorhaedus goral (common goral)	26	54	5	19.2	13 s
Oryx leucoryx (Arabian oryx)	158	90	48.6	30.8	20 +
			Mean neonatal mortality rate: 14%		
CARNIVORES					
Canis lupus (Indian grey wolf)	n.d.	n.d.	242	n.d.	17 s
Speothos venaticus (bush dog)	20	63	10.6	53.3	47 s
Selenarctos thibetanus (Asiatic black bear)	n.d.	n.d.	41.0	n.d.	22 s
Tremarctos ornatus (spectacled bear)	94	41	6.5	6.9	67 –
Ursus arctos (Italian brown bear)	42	50	118.7	283	17 s
Lutra lutra (Eurasian otter)	107	34	11.7	10.9	14 s
Pteronura brasiliensis (giant otter)	21	14	7.0	33.3	52 –
Hyaena brunnea (brown hyaena)	59	46	6.3	10.7	26 s

Hylobates concolor (crested or black gibbon)	84	15	2.3	2.7	28 s
Pongo pygmaeus (orang utan)	730	48	45.6	6.2	16 +
Pan paniscus (pygmy chimpanzee)	32	40	5.0	15.6	20 +
Gorilla gorilla (lowland gorilla)	472	24	23.0	4.9	18 −
			Mean neonatal mortality rate: 26%		
PERISSODACTYLS					
Equus grevy (Grevy's zebra)	390	54	45.3	11.6	19 s
Equus przewalskii (Przewalski's horse)	315	100	64.0	20.3	18 +
Tapirus indicus (Malayan tapir)	134	38	9.0	6.7	15 s
Rhinoceros unicornis (Indian rhinoceros)	56	52	3.7	6.5	18 s
Ceratotherium simum (white rhinoceros)	394	16	18.0	4.6	17 +
Diceros bicornis (black rhinoceros)	154	35	7.3	4.8	23 −
			Mean neonatal mortality rate: 18%		
ARTIODACTYLS					
Babyrousa babyrussa (babirusa)	47	51	11.0	23.4	24 +
Vicugna vicugna (vicuna)	61	93	12.3	20.1	19 −
Cervus (Axis or Hyelaphus) kuhli (Kuhl's deer)	68	92	13.3	19.6	5 +
Cervus duvauceli (swamp deer)	247	98	76	30.7	25 +
Cervus eldi (Eld's or brow-antlered deer)	115	81	39	33.9	n.d. s
Dama mesopotamica (Persian fallow deer)	18	87	5	25.9	14 +

Acinonyx jubatus (cheetah)	554	35	47.0	8.6	24 s
Felis (Lynx) caracal (Asian caracal)	n.d.	n.d.	57.0	n.d.	19 s
Felis temmincki (Asiatic golden cat)	n.d.	n.d.	12.3	n.d.	51 s
Neofelis nebulosa (clouded leopard)	145	52	16.0	11.0	53 s
Panthera leo persica (Asiatic lion)	116	76	30.7	26.4	26 s
Panthera onca (jaguar)	n.d.	n.d.	134	n.d.	27 s
Panthera pardus (leopard)	229	62	254	111	33 s
Panthera tigris (tiger)	431	79	251	58.2	37 +
Panthera uncia (snow leopard)	175	67	41.6	23.8	26 +

Mean neonatal mortality rate: 33%

breeding records in captivity. On the other hand, several primates have been very successful in captivity. There is a large and growing population of golden lion tamarins, a high proportion of which are captive-bred and which have a high reproductive rate. This species is greatly endangered in the wild but is increasing in numbers in captivity. Amongst the great apes, reproductive rates of orang utans and gorillas (all subspecies) are low compared to chimpanzees and all three great apes listed here have in the breeding population a high proportion of animals originally caught in the wild.

Neonatal mortality rates in captive primates are highly variable, but are generally higher for the smaller species such as lemurs and the Callithricidae. The relatively low mortality rates for gorillas and orang utans are perhaps a consequence of very careful management and perhaps hand-rearing programmes. Such individual attention is not generally paid to smaller primates. The difficulty of drawing general conclusions concerning neonatal mortality patterns in captive primates is illustrated by reference to data for gorillas and orang utans. The mean mortality rate of neonates has fallen over the period 1960 to 1979 (see Table III). In both species, neonatal mortality rate is consistently lower for females than for males and in both species, female mortality rate has shown the greatest decline. Clearly, improved management practices have contributed to this decline, but the very low mortality of female neonates may in part be due to the special care which zoo staff apply to the rearing of young female great apes. Harcourt, Fossey & Sabater-Pi (1981) quote an estimated mortality rate for immature gorillas of 25% over the first year of life in the wild. Although direct comparison with zoo-bred gorillas may be inappropriate, it is probable that the neonatal mortality rates of captive-bred gorillas are well below those experienced in the wild. However, the future breeding performance of these captive-bred (and frequently hand-reared) animals is a particular cause for concern as the original wild-caught population approaches the end of its reproductive life. Despite very low neonatal mortality rates, gorillas in captivity are not increasing in number.

Amongst the ungulates, mortality rates are generally lower than figures published for wild populations (see Table I) although for some species such as the black and Indian rhinoceros, the low number of births makes estimates of mortality rate difficult to assess. Perissodactyls in general have relatively low neonatal mortality rates in captivity and despite generally low birth rates, all six species quoted here are increasing in number. With the exception of the Przewalski's horse, which is extinct in the wild, the proportion of captive-bred animals is much lower than for primates or artiodactyls. This is primarily a consequence of the low reproductive rate of perissodactyls rather than high neonatal mortality of captive-bred animals.

The 12 artiodactyl species listed here have on average the lowest rate of neonatal mortality of all four orders, the highest average birth rate (approx-

Table III. Neonatal mortality rates of captive orang utans and gorillas over the period 1960–79. Based on data from International Studbooks for these two species.

	Male			Female		
	No. born	No. dying	Neonatal mortality	No. born	No. dying	Neonatal mortality
Sumatran orang utan						
1960–64	12	3	0.25	5	1	0.20
1965–69	20	3	0.15	32	5	0.16
1970–74	35	9	0.26	43	6	0.14
1975–79	29	4	0.14	21	3	0.14
Total	105	21	0.20	112	19	0.17
Bornean orang utan						
1960–64	10	5	0.50	7	2	0.29
1965–69	16	6	0.38	15	3	0.20
1970–74	34	12	0.35	34	5	0.15
1975–79	30	5	0.17	40	4	0.10
Total	91	29	0.32	98	15	0.15
Gorilla						
1960–64	3	0	0	4	2	0.50
1965–69	4	1	0.25	18	7	0.39
1970–74	35	14	0.40	51	9	0.18
1975–76	17	4	0.24	14	4	0.29
1977–79	17	5	0.29	21	2	0.10
Total	86	27	0.31	110	24	0.22

imately 25% p.a.) and the greatest proportion of adults which were bred in captivity. Most populations are either stable or increasing in number and the neonatal mortality rates shown in Table II are low compared to wild populations. Many of the ungulate species listed here are kept in relatively large groups, frequently on grassland paddocks, and most are grazers in the wild, although some species such as the Malayan tapir, black rhinoceros, wood bison, southern pudu and Arabian oryx are primarily browsers. Amongst the seasonal breeders neonatal mortality is frequently low compared to aseasonal species.

Captive carnivore populations usually suffer high neonatal mortality rates and the figures quoted in Table II are generally higher than for primates or ungulates. Some species such as the spectacled bear with a low proportion of captive-bred animals, low birth rate, and high neonatal mortality are clearly greatly endangered and this species shows a general decline in numbers held in captivity over the four-year period 1978–81. Other bears such as the Italian brown bear frequently breed well in captivity, have a high proportion of captive-bred animals, a high birth rate and very low neonatal mortality rates. Amongst the carnivores, the high average neonatal mortality rates of some species may be primarily a consequence of the natural attrition that occurs in multiparous species. For instance, Schaller (1972) estimated that out of 79 lion cubs born in his study area in the Serengeti, 53

(67%) died as first-year cubs and of the remaining 26, only 10 survived to become sub-adults and some of these animals may have eventually died before reaching maturity. In this study, the major cause of mortality was considered to be starvation or abandonment. In general, zoo populations of big cats have a high birth rate and most zoos have sustaining or increasing populations. Some species such as the Siberian form of the tiger (*Panthera tigris*) have become very common zoo animals although they are endangered in the wild.

Although the study of the demography of captive-bred populations is now regarded as an essential management tool in future captive breeding programmes (Foose & Foose 1983; Ralls, Brugger & Ballou 1979; Senner 1980), several factors limit its general application. With the exception of a few key species covered by the studbooks, data on the age structure and survivorship of captive species is not currently recorded in a systematic form. There is little statistical information on the nature of infertility within these captive populations and whether low reproductive rates are a consequence of a general depression in fertility or a high proportion of barren individuals. Perhaps the greatest difficulty lies in interpreting neonatal mortality data, gathered from a number of different species, kept under different conditions in a large number of different zoos. Virtually no information is available describing key factors of neonatal mortality and while factors such as lactation failure, abandonment or accident are occasionally quoted, there are no data available to describe the major causes of neonatal mortality in zoos.

The data in Table II indicate that the neonatal mortality rates of captive-bred populations are highly variable. There is no statistically significant correlation between or within orders for the relationship between neonatal mortality rate and crude birth rate (numbers born/numbers of adults) or the proportion of captive-bred zoo stock. In many captive populations (e.g. gorillas) low neonatal mortality rates are frequently also associated with exceptionally low fecundity. It would seem that the demographic vigour of captive populations results from a complex interaction of neonatal mortality and fecundity whereas in the wild neonatal mortality, rather than fecundity, is frequently the key factor limiting the rate of increase of populations (Caughley 1977).

Lactation

Limitations of database

An understanding of maternal and neonatal nutrition is essential for the successful husbandry and rearing of many rare and endangered species of mammal. Although some species breed well in captivity and require little or no intervention, many species have low neonatal survival and poor postnatal growth and young animals frequently need to be rescued and hand-reared. For this reason, the attention of research workers has been drawn to studies of the energy requirements of young mammals and to a detailed examination of milk composition of a wide range of species.

In a recent review, Oftedal (1981) estimated that of over 4000 species in 18 orders, extensive data on milk composition was available for only 48 species and just half of all mammalian orders (8) are unrepresented by any reliable data on milk composition. This factor, combined with a general lack of knowledge of postnatal growth and energy requirements, means that attempts to mimic normal maternal yields frequently fail and while published records stress successful attempts, failures are seldom acknowledged. Since the database is currently limited, most research workers emphasize the need for good comparative studies which may permit generalizations of the lactation requirements of closely related unstudied species.

Gross energy requirements

The production of offspring is energetically expensive since the energy costs of reproduction are added to the overall costs of normal maintenance metabolism. Estimates of the metabolizable energy (ME) requirements for maintenance are generally only available for domesticated and for a few wild species. Amongst ungulates, typical estimates of ME requirements for cattle, sheep, goats, and horses lie between 100 and 130 kcals/kg$^{0.75}$/day, while estimates for deer are generally of the same order or slightly higher (i.e. 130–150 kcals/kg$^{0.75}$ for white-tailed deer, *Odocoileus virginianus*: Silver, Colovos, Holter & Hayes 1969; Ullrey *et al.* 1970; 100–120 kcals/kg$^{0.75}$ for red deer, *Cervus elaphus*: Kay 1969; Simpson 1976). Late gestation generally results in an increase of between 140 and 170 kcals ME/kg$^{0.75}$ for most domesticated ungulates (Robbins, Podbielancik-Norman, Wilson & Mould 1981; Clapp *et al.* 1971). Recently, Robbins (1983) has suggested that the costs of fetal production for both ungulates and small mammals peak at approximately 40% above the non-pregnant ME requirements, irrespective of body size.

In eutherians, the energy costs of lactation generally exceed all other reproductive costs (Blaxter 1964; Hanwell & Peaker 1977; Robbins 1983). In domesticated ungulates, peak lactation energy requirements are generally 2.5–3.0 times those of non-lactating females (Blaxter 1964; Oftedal 1984) while in wild herbivores such as red deer and the closely related wapiti (*Cervus elaphus nelsonii*), the ME requirements at peak lactation increase to 2.6–2.9 times those of non-lactating animals (Arman, Kay, Goodall & Sharman 1974; Robbins, Podbielancik-Norman *et al.* 1981; Loudon & Kay 1984).

Peak lactation costs for other mammalian orders are also high. Interspecies variation in the gross energy output at peak lactation has been

considered by a number of authors (Brody 1945; Linzell 1972; Hanwell &
Peaker 1977; Oftedal 1984). Although these authors have used different
databases (Brody and Linzell included dairy species while Hanwell &
Peaker and Oftedal excluded these species), all are agreed that peak energy
yields in lactation scale in proportion to metabolic weight, that is, body-
weight raised to the power 0.75. Linzell (1972) and Hanwell & Peaker
(1977) have suggested that since peak yield is related to metabolic weight, it
follows that lactation energy costs at peak are similar for all mammals,
irrespective of body size. A more recent analysis suggests that this conclusion was based on data from too narrow a range of species (Oftedal 1981,
1984). For instance, peak yields of some marine mammals are almost certainly greatly in excess of those that might be expected from comparisons
with other species (Fedak & Anderson 1983), while other species, such as
primates, with relatively slow growth rates are characterized by proportionately low milk yields (Buss & Voss 1971).

Oftedal (1981) has re-analysed available data on the peak yields of 16
non-dairy species and proposed that, on the basis of present knowledge,
three separate regressions can be established for terrestrial mammals: (1)
high yielding mammals which generally produce litters and which suckle
over relatively short periods; (2) domestic and wild ungulates with lactations of intermediate length; and (3) primates with low peak yields relative to body size, slow postnatal growth rates and long periods of
dependence upon maternal milk supply. Within each of these groups peak
yield is well correlated with metabolic weight, but there is an approximately
two-fold difference between ungulates and multiparous species and ungulates and primates. On the basis of limited current data, it seems likely that
for many marine mammals peak lactation output greatly exceeds even that
of the high-yielding terrestrial multiparous species (Bonner 1984), while
peak output for other mammals such as macropod marsupials is almost certainly below the line established for eutherian herbivores.

Although precise estimates of lactation length are difficult to obtain (see
below), it is clear that there is an inverse correlation between peak energy
yield of a mammal relative to body size and the length of lactation. Thus, ice
seals with lactations of 10–20 days (reviewed by Bonner 1984) and a primate of similar body size as typified by women with lactations of up to 2–3
years in some communities (Konner & Worthman 1980) illustrate the
extreme range of possible lactation strategy. Associated with differences in
lactation length and peak yield there are obvious phylogenetic differences in
postnatal growth and maturation rates of the offspring; an increase in the
length of dependency upon milk is associated with an extension of the
period of neonatal mortality. For this reason, generalizations of the gross
energy requirements for optimal postnatal growth based on broad interspecies comparisons are now seen as being of limited practical application

and research in the future will almost certainly concentrate on obtaining good comparative data on key groups of closely related species (Robbins, Oftedal & O'Rourke, in press; Loudon & Kay 1984).

Milk composition

The primary constituents of milk are water, fat, protein, sugars, and mineral material. There is an enormous diversity in mammals in the relative ratios of these various components with the dry matter content of milk ranging from less than 10% for many perissodactyls to over 55% for marine mammals. Oftedal (1984) in a recent major review of mammalian milk composition has observed that one of the principal limitations to composition studies lies in establishing reasonable criteria for milk sampling. Data obtained from zoos are usually biased towards samples gathered very late in lactation when the offspring is weaning or from females whose offspring have recently died. Frequency and extent of milk removal and the physiological techniques employed to obtain the samples (i.e. sedation and use of oxytocin) can have a profound effect on composition. Thus, consideration of the estimated nutrient requirements of young suckling mammals is complicated by a database limited in terms of both milk composition and appropriate volumes to be consumed at each feed.

Since peak milk production across a wide range of species is a function of metabolic size, it follows that, in relation to body weight, small species yield more milk energy than large species. Blaxter (1961) has observed that although the energy requirements of the young are proportional to metabolic size (i.e. $W^{0.73-0.75}$), gut capacity is a function of body weight. From this, it follows that the dry matter content should be proportional to energy requirements and in consequence the milk of small species should on average be more concentrated. Payne & Wheeler (1968) showed that milk energy was broadly correlated with body size (as weight $^{-0.28}$) for a wide range of species and, in a more recent analysis, Loudon & Kay (1984) showed that within the cervids gross energy output at peak yield was similarly related to body size, larger species producing proportionately more dilute milk. From this, it is tempting to conclude that reliable estimates of gross energy requirements combined with a knowledge of the approximate energy density of the milk should lead to an improved understanding of postnatal nutrition.

In general, changes in the energy density of milk tend to be associated with changes in the relative proportion of fat and proteins to carbohydrates; an increase in dry matter and gross energy content usually results in a reduction in milk sugars and an increase in the fat and protein content. Since the protein and fat content of eutherian milk generally increases with dry matter content, it follows that the protein content of mammalian milks should be

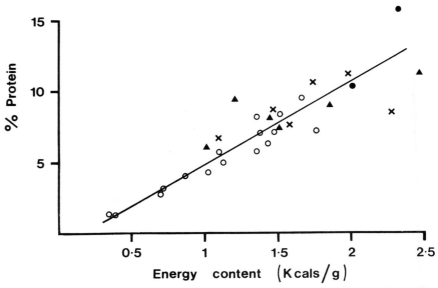

Fig. 2 The relationship between protein and energy content for a range of mammalian milks (○ ungulates, ▲ rodents, × terrestrial carnivores and ● lagomorphs). Data are mainly from Robbins (1983) quoting unpublished material from Oftedal (1981). Data for red deer and Père David's deer are from A. S. I. Loudon (unpublished). (y (% protein) = 0.365 × (kcals/g) − 0.07 for the combined orders.)

correlated with the gross energy content. Some data for four mammalian orders (rodents, lagomorphs, ungulates including elephants, and carnivores) are shown in Fig. 2. The best studied group is the ungulates and the regression line is fitted to the data for this order alone; in general a doubling in milk energy content results in a two-fold increase in the protein content.

Obvious exceptions to this general trend are the pinnipeds and primates. Pinnipeds are characterized by very high energy milks with high fat contents (between 4 and 5 kcals/g) and moderate or low protein content (7–13%) and fall well outside the general relationships for terrestrial mammals (Oftedal 1981, and unpublished cited in Robbins 1983). The high fat content of pinniped milk is an obvious reflection of the very high postnatal fattening rates (and low protein deposition) and in this respect marine mammals differ fundamentally from most terrestrial mammals studied. Primates on the other hand tend to produce dilute milks (energy values of 0.5–1 kcal/g), but with unexpectedly low protein content (1.5–2.0%) (e.g. Buss & Voss 1971). The low protein content of primate milks is reflected in very slow postnatal growth rates and long periods of dependency upon maternal milk supply.

It is intellectually attractive to propose that milk composition is uniquely tailored to suit the particular growth requirements of a species and early workers such as Bunge (1902) and Abderhalden (1908) suggested that the protein content of milk was directly related to crude postnatal growth rate. This approach is now considered to be oversimplistic. For instance, within the ungulates, species such as reindeer have surprisingly high absolute protein intakes compared to the faster growing red deer (Luick, White, Gau & Jenness 1974; Arman et al. 1974; White & Luick 1984; Loudon & Kay 1984). In a more recent analysis, Jenness & Sloan (1970) have proposed that it is more realistic to consider the proportion of energy in milk which is supplied by protein. On this basis, most mammals (excluding marine mammals) supply about 15 to 30% of the milk energy as protein. Within a species, changes in yield are normally associated with a simultaneous change in both the protein and fat content of the milk so that the relative contribution of protein to the total energy remains approximately constant (Jenness & Sloan 1970; Arman et al. 1974; Sadleir 1980).

Most mammal neonates are born with very low fat reserves and are therefore critically dependent upon the energy supplied in milk. The gross composition of a wide range of neonates including ungulates, primates and non-hystricomorph rodents are remarkably similar, with low fat reserves and relatively high protein mass. Data on the energy composition of some mammalian neonates are shown in Table IV, and it can be seen that the chemically extractable fat reserves are generally below 4%. The figure of 16% for a human neonate (Widdowson 1950) may be an overestimate. The guinea pig (10% fat) is born with substantial energy reserves which are used in the immediate postnatal period, the milk of guinea pigs being low in energy (Oftedal 1984). Of the other species, energy reserves are generally adequate for 1–2 days' survival, less in the case of smaller species. The Bennett's wallaby joey, despite its low metabolic rate, has reserves capable of lasting a mere 8h. Although the estimates of survival time are based on a number of assumptions (all non-structural lipids are available as an energy source, the animals are in a thermoneutral environment), they do indicate that newborn mammals are incapable of surviving more than a very short time without milk.

The gross efficiencies for growth in mammals which do not deposit fat reserves during the lactation period are generally considered to be constant (Robbins & Robbins 1979). Thus, Oftedal (1981) has estimated that for most mammals the range lies between 6 and 11 kcals/g live weight gain irrespective of body size, the relatively higher maintenance costs of smaller mammals being offset by higher rates of tissue deposition (Kleiber 1975). The constancy of growth efficiency has particular implications for the protein and energy requirements for young growing mammals. The relative maintenance energy requirements decline in proportion to increasing body weight since maintenance costs lie between $W^{0.75}$ (Kleiber 1975) and $W^{0.83}$ (Oftedal 1984). However, protein requirements are related to tissue deposi-

Table IV. Energy reserves of some mammalian neonates.

Species	Body weight (g)	Percent fat	Energy[a] content (kcal/g)	Days of energy[b] reserve	Reference
White-tailed deer	3574	2.2	1.03	2	Robbins & Moen (1975).
Red deer	7500	1.4	0.88	1.5	P. Wenham, A. Pennie & R.N.B. Kay, unpubl. data cited in Loudon & Kay (1984).
Roe deer	2.350	1.9	0.96	1.8	A.S.I. Loudon (unpubl.).
Domestic pig	1.460	1.1	0.71	1.6	Widdowson (1950).
Domestic cat	0.118	1.8	0.97	1.9	Widdowson (1950).
Domestic rabbit	0.054	2.0	0.78	<1	Widdowson (1950).
Human	3.560	16.1	2.11	>3	Widdowson (1950).
Bank vole	0.002	3.8	0.88	0.5	Sawicka-Kapusta (1974).
Guinea pig	0.081	10.1	1.73	3.5	Widdowson (1950).
Bennett's wallaby	0.0005	1.0	0.89	8 hours	A.S.I. Loudon & M. Stock (unpubl.).

[a] Based on 9.11 kcals/g for fat and 5.4 kcals/g for protein.

[b] Assumes maintenance energy requirement of 140 kcals/kg$^{0.75}$/day for eutherians and 9.3 kcals/kg$^{0.75}$/day for newborn marsupials (Loudon, Rothwell & Stock, 1985), and that all neonates are in a thermoneutral environment (see text).

tion rates and these are constant for any given growth rate. Young mammals deposit large protein masses relative to their body size so that the protein requirements are very high in relation to energy requirements. With a constant postnatal growth rate and increasing body size, energy requirements rise faster than those for protein. Since the protein/energy ratio of milks remains relatively unchanged with advancing lactation, it follows that with an increase in body size there is an increase in the extent to which the protein component of milk is deaminated and utilized as a primary energy source. The composition of mammalian milks therefore represents a compromise between the needs to maintain high rates of protein deposition and an adequate supply of energy for body maintenance. For this reason, attempts to model mammalian postnatal growth rates to protein or gross energy consumption are likely to be unsuccessful unless comparisons are made at strictly equivalent developmental stages.

Summary and Conclusions

Demographic studies of wild mammal populations all indicate high neonatal mortality rates, with a steep decline in mortality as the weaned offspring approaches puberty. Comparable data on captive-bred populations are not currently available since precise age at death is not recorded for the majority of species listed in the *International zoo yearbook*. Mean neonatal mortality (expressed as a crude percentage) is highly variable. Although in some orders such as primates the mortality rates are generally high, many primate species, through careful management and hand-rearing programmes, have low neonatal mortality. In the great apes, mortality is generally low and in orang utans and gorillas an improvement in management has reduced neonatal mortality over the last 15 years. Mortality rates of captive carnivores are also highly variable but this may be a general feature of multiparous orders. The ungulates (artiodactyls and perissodactyls) have the lowest mortality of the four orders examined and in these two orders mortality is frequently lower than that observed in comparable wild populations.

An essential element in the future captive management of endangered species will be the development of realistic hand-rearing programmes for vulnerable neonates which may be rejected by their mothers at birth. This programme will require a greatly improved understanding of milk composition and energy requirements of many endangered species. Significant advances in our understanding of lactation and growth have occurred in some species (i.e. ungulates), but other groups such as marsupials, insectivores, rodents, and primates are very poorly understood. Our ability successfully to hand-rear many species is frequently determined as much by luck as by solid scientific understanding of lactation.

Acknowledgement

I would like to thank Dr G. Mace (Institute of Zoology for assistance with data contained in the ISIS inventory and for access to her unpublished analysis of great ape neonatal mortality.

References

Abderhalden, E. (1908). *Textbook of physiological chemistry*. Wiley, New York.

Altmann, J. (1980). *Baboon mothers and infants*. Harvard University Press, Harvard.

Arman, P., Kay, R.N.B., Goodall, E.D. & Sharman, G.A.M. (1974). The composition and yield of milk from captive red deer (*Cervus elaphus* L.). *J. Reprod. Fert.* **37**: 67–84.

Blaxter, K.L. (1961). Lactation and the growth of the young. In *Milk: the mammary gland and its secretion*: 305–61. Kon, S.K. & Cowie, A.T. (Eds). Academic Press, New York.

Blaxter, K.L. (1964). Protein metabolism and requirements in pregnancy and lactation. In *Mammalian protein metabolism* **2**: 173–223. Munro, H.N. & Allison, J.B. (Eds). Academic Press, London.

Blaxter, K.L. & Hamilton, W.J. (1980). Reproduction in farmed red deer: 2. Calf growth and mortality. *J. agric. Sci., Camb.* **95**: 275–84.

Bonner, W.N. (1984). Lactation strategies in pinnipeds. *Symp. zool. Soc. Lond.* No. 51: 253–72.

Brody, S. (1945). *Bioenergetics and growth*. Reinhold, New York.

Bunge, G.V. (1902). *Text-book of physiological and pathological chemistry*. P. Blakiston & Sons, Philadelphia.

Buss, D.H. & Voss, W.R. (1971). Evaluation of four methods for estimating the milk yield of baboons. *J. Nutr.* **101**: 901–10.

Caughley, G. (1966). Mortality patterns in mammals. *Ecology* **47**: 906–18.

Caughley, G. (1970a). Eruption of ungulate populations, with emphasis on Himalayan thar in New Zealand. *Ecology* **51**: 53–72.

Caughley, G. (1970b). Liberation, dispersal and distribution of Himalayan thar (*Hemitragus jemlahicus*) in New Zealand. *N.Z. J. Sci.* **13**: 220–39.

Caughley, G. (1971). Demography, fat reserves and body size of a population of red deer *Cervus elaphus* in New Zealand. *Mammalia* **35**: 369–83.

Caughley, G. (1976). Wildlife management and the dynamics of ungulate populations. *Appl. Biol.* **1**: 183–246.

Caughley, G. (1977). *Analysis of vertebrate populations*. Wiley, London.

Caughley, G. & Birch, L.C. (1971). Rate of increase. *J. Wildl. Mgmt* **35**: 658–63.

Clapp, J.E., Abrams, R.M., Caton, D., Cotter, J.R. & Barron, D.H. (1971). Fetal oxygen consumption in late gestation. *Q. Jl exp. Physiol.* **56**: 137–46.

Clutton-Brock, T.H., Guinness, F.E. & Albon, S.D. (1982). *Red deer: The behaviour and ecology of two sexes*. Chicago University Press, Chicago.

Cook, R.S., White, W., Trainer, D.O. & Glazener, W.G. (1971). Mortality of young white-tailed deer fawns in South Texas. *J. Wildl. Mgmt* **35**: 47–56.

Dapson, R.W., Ramsey, P.R., Smith, M.H. & Urbston, D.F. (1979). Demographic differences in contiguous populations of White-tailed deer. *J. Wildl. Mgmt* **43**: 889–98.

Dittus, W.P.J. (1975). Population dynamics of the Toque monkey, *Macaca sinica*. In *Socioecology and psychology of primates*: 125–51. Tuttle, R.H. (Ed.). Mouton Publishers, The Hague & Paris.

Fedak, M.A. & Anderson, S.S. (1983). The energetics of lactation; accurate measurement from a large wild mammal, the Grey seal *Halichoerus grypus*. *J. Zool., Lond.* **198**: 473–81.

Findlay, L. & Renfree, M. (1984). Growth, development and secretion of the mammary gland of macropodid marsupials. *Symp. zool. Soc. Lond.* No. 51: 403–32.

Foose, T.J. & Foose, E. (1983). Demographic and genetic status and management. In *The biology and management of an extinct species: Père David's Deer*: 133–81. Beck, B.B. & Wemmer, C.M. (Eds). Noyes Publ., New Jersey.

Frith, H.J. & Sharman, G.B. (1964). Breeding in wild populations of the red kangaroo. *CSIRO Wildl. Res.* **9**: 86–114.

Fuller, T.K. & Keith, L.B. (1981). Woodland caribou population dynamics in northeastern Alaska. *J. Wildl. Mgmt* **45**: 197–213.

Guinness, F.E., Albon, S.D. & Clutton-Brock, T.H. (1978). Factors affecting calf mortality in red deer. *J. Anim. Ecol.* **47**: 817–32.

Hanwell, A. & Peaker, M. (1977). Physiological effects of lactation on the mother. *Symp. zool. Soc. Lond.* No. 41: 297–312.

Harcourt, A.H., Fossey, D. & Sabater-Pi, J. (1981). Demography of *Gorilla gorilla*. *J. Zool., Lond.* **195**: 215–33.

Hauge, T.M. & Keith, L.B. (1981). Dynamics of moose populations in north-eastern Alaska. *J. Wildl. Mgmt* **45**: 573–97.

Heinsohn, G.E. (1966). Ecology and reproduction of the Tasmanian bandicoots. *Univ. Calif. Publs. Zool.* **80**: 1–96.

Hickey, F. (1960). Death and reproductive rate in relation to flock culling and selection. *N. Z. J. agric. Res.* **3**: 332–4.

Hickey, F. (1963). Sheep mortality in New Zealand. *N.Z. Agriculturalist* **15**: 1–3.

How, R.A. (1976). Population strategies of four species of Australian possum. In *The ecology of arboreal folivores*: 305–13. Montgomery, G.G. (Ed.). Smithsonian Institute, Washington DC.

Jenness, R. & Sloan, R.E. (1970). The composition of milks of various species: a review. *Dairy Sci. Abstr.* **32**: 599–612.

Jewell, P.A., Milner, C. & Morton-Boyd, J. (Eds) (1974). *Island survivors: the ecology of the Soay sheep of St. Kilda*. Athlone Press, London.

Kay, R.N.B. (1969). Experimental studies on food intake and digestion. a. Studies on tame deer. In *The husbanding of red deer*: 45–6. Bannerman, M.M. & Blaxter, K.L. (Eds). Rowett Research Institute & H.I.D.B., Aberdeen.

Kleiber, M. (1975). *The fire of life: an introduction to animal energetics*. Kreiger, Huntingdon, New York.

Konner, M. & Worthman, C. (1980). Nursing frequency, gonadal function, and birth spacing among !Kung hunter-gatherers. *Science, Wash.* **207**: 788–91.

Laws, R.M., Parker, I.S.C. & Johnstone, R.C.B. (1975). *Elephants and their habitats. The ecology of elephants in the Northern Bunyoro, Uganda*. Clarendon Press, Oxford.

Leader-Williams, N. (1980). Population dynamics and mortality of reindeer introduced into South Georgia. *J. Wildl. Mgmt* **44**: 640–57.

Linzell, J.L. (1972). Milk yield, energy loss in milk, and mammary gland weight in different species. *Dairy Sci. Abstr.* **34**: 351–60.

Loudon, A.S.I. (1978). The control of roe deer populations: a problem in forest management. *Forestry* **51**: 73–83.

Loudon, A.S.I. & Kay, R.N.B. (1984). Lactational constraints on a seasonally breeding mammal: the red deer. *Symp. zool. Soc. Lond.* No. 51: 233–52.

Loudon, A.S.I., Rothwell, N. & Stock, M. (1985). Brown fat, thermogenesis and physiological birth in a marsupial. *Comp. Biochem Physiol.* **81A**: 815–9.

Lowe, V.P.W. (1969). Population dynamics of the red deer on Rhum. *J. Anim. Ecol.* **38**: 425–57.

Luick, J.R., White, R.G., Gau, A.M. & Jenness, R. (1974). Compositional changes in the milk secreted by grazing reindeer. 1. Gross composition and ash. *J. Dairy Sci.* **57**: 1325–33.

Mundinger, J.G. (1981). White-tailed deer reproductive biology in the Swan Valley, Montana. *J. Wildl. Mgmt* **45**: 132–9.

Oftedal, O.T. (1981). *Milk, protein and energy intakes of suckling mammalian young: a comparative study.* Ph.D. thesis: Cornell Univ.

Oftedal, O.T. (1984). Milk composition, milk yield and energy output at peak lactation: a comparative review. *Symp. zool. Soc. Lond.* No. 51: 33–85.

Payne, P.R. & Wheeler, E.F. (1968). Comparative nutrition in pregnancy and lactation. *Proc. Nutr. Soc.* **27**: 129–38.

Poole, W.E. (1973). A study of breeding of grey kangaroos in central New South Wales. *Aust. J. Zool.* **21**: 183–212.

Ralls, K., Brugger, K. & Ballou, J. (1979). Inbreeding and juvenile mortality in small populations of ungulates. *Science, N.Y.* **206**: 1101–3.

Reiter, J., Stinson, N.L. & LeBoeuf, B.J. (1978). Northern elephant seal development: the transition from weaning to nutritional independence. *Behav. Ecol. Sociobiol.* **3**: 337–67.

Robbins, C.T. (1983). *Wildlife feeding and nutrition.* Academic Press, London.

Robbins, C.T. & Moen, A.N. (1975). Uterine composition and growth in pregnant white-tailed deer. *J. Wildl. Mgmt* **39**: 684–91.

Robbins, C.T., Oftedal, O.T. & O'Rourke, K. (In press). Lactation, early nutrition and hand-rearing of wild ungulates with special reference to deer. In *The biology and management of the Cervidae.* Wemmer C. (Ed.). (Symposium of the Smithsonian Institution). Smithsonian Publications, Washington DC.

Robbins, C.T., Podbielancik-Norman, R.S., Wilson, D.L. & Mould, E.D. (1981). Growth and nutrient consumption of elk calves compared to other ungulate species. *J. Wildl. Mgmt* **45**: 172–86.

Robbins, C.T. & Robbins, B.L. (1979). Fetal and neonatal growth patterns and maternal reproductive effort in ungulates and subungulates. *Am. Nat.* **114**: 101–16.

Russell, E.M. (1982). Patterns of parental care and parental investment in marsupials. *Biol. Rev.* **57**: 423–86.

Sadleir, R.M.F.S. (1980). Milk yield of black-tailed deer. *J. Wildl. Mgmt* **44**: 472–8.

Sawicka-Kapusta, K. (1974). Changes in the gross body composition and the caloric value of the bank vole during their postnatal development. *Acta theriol.* **19**: 27–54.

Schaller, G,. (1972). *The Serengeti lion.* Chicago University Press, Chicago.

Senner, J. (1980). Inbreeding depression and the survival of zoo populations. In *Conservation biology*: 202–29. Soule, M. & Wilcox, B. (Eds). Sinauer Associates Ltd., Sunderland Mass.

Silver, H., Colovos, N.F., Holter, J.B. & Hayes, H.H. (1969). Fasting metabolism of white-tailed deer. *J. Wildl. Mgmt* **33**: 490–98.

Simpson, A.M. (1976). *A study of the energy metabolism and seasonal cycles of captive red deer.* Ph.D. thesis: Univ. of Aberdeen.

Thomson, J.A. & Owen, W.H. (1964). A field study of the Australian ringtail possum. *Ecol. Monogr.* **34**: 27–52.

Ullrey, D.E., Youatt, W.G., Johnson, H.E., Fay, L.D., Schoepke, B.L. & Magee, W.T. (1970). Digestible and metabolisable-energy requirements for winter maintenance of Michigan White-tailed does. *J. Wildl. Mgmt* **34**: 863–9.

Verme, L. (1977). Assessment of natal mortality in upper Michigan deer. *J. Wildl. Mgmt* **41**: 700–8.

White, R.G. & Luick, J.R. (1984). Plasticity and constraints in the lactational strategy of reindeer and caribou. *Symp. zool. Soc. Lond.* No. 51: 215–32.

Widdowson, E.M. (1950). Chemical composition of newly born mammals. *Nature, Lond.* **166**: 626–8.

Government and conservation

Symp. zool. Soc. Lond. (1985) No. 54: 211–217

The cost of conservation

F. B. O'CONNOR

*Nature Conservancy Council
Banbury
Oxfordshire OX16 8EX, UK*

Synopsis

The recent publication by the Nature Conservancy Council (1984), *Nature conservation in Great Britain*, includes revised objectives for the conservation movement, which are outlined here under ten themes: site safeguard; conservation in the wider environment; marine conservation; the science base; publicity and education; legislation for nature conservation; international conservation; and creative conservation. The two final themes deal with resources for nature conservation and the distribution of effort.

Development of nature conservation under these headings is the job of the conservation movement as a whole. NCC is preparing programmes for its own part of the task: these form the basis for the summaries given in this paper, for each of the first eight themes, of (a) present expenditure, (b) factors influencing present and future costs, and (c) future predicted costs.

NCC's budget in 1984–85 is approximately £15m overall; present evidence suggests that, if current trends continue, NCC will require at least to double its present staff and cash resources over the next five years in order to achieve inescapable conservation targets.

Introduction

This chapter presents the author's personal assessment of the future costs of maintaining the wildlife heritage of Great Britian.

The context for this assessment is provided by a series of recent publications. The *World conservation strategy* (International Union for Conservation of Nature and Natural Resources 1980) sets out the basis for natural resource conservation on a global scale, highlighting human dependence upon the rational and sustainable use of living resources. *The conservation and development programme for the UK* (1983) provides a broad assessment of how the principles of resource conservation can be applied to help meet material, economic and social needs in a well developed western society. *Nature conservation in Great Britain*, published by the Nature Conservancy Council (NCC) on 26 June 1984, is concerned with the ways in which the conservation of wildlife and physical features can contribute to the wider programme of natural resource conservation. All three publications emphasize the need for a working partnership between development

ZOOLOGICAL SYMPOSIUM No. 54
ISBN 0–19–854002–7

and conservation. For wildlife conservation, this partnership involves the NCC, the voluntary conservation bodies, land owners and managers, other Government and private agencies and both central and local Government. All of these have a contribution to make and *Nature conservation in Great Britain* provides a clear framework for them to do so, clarifying objectives for nature conservation under 10 main headings, and indicating the respective roles of the several participants in their pursuit.

The role of the Nature Conservancy Council

This chapter is concerned with the present and future costs of NCC's own contribution to the objectives of conservation. Its responsibilites and the statutory equipment it has at its disposal are determined by four main Acts of Parliament:–

(a) *The National Parks and Access to the Countryside Act 1949* set up the original Nature Conservancy, giving it the powers to:

   (i) set up Nature Reserves by purchase, lease or agreement and to schedule land as Sites of Special Scientific Interest;
  (ii) to advise Government, public and private bodies and individuals on nature conservation generally;
 (iii) to carry out research as a basis for these activities;
  (iv) to disseminate knowledge about conservation.

(b) *The Countryside Act 1968* added the power to enter into management agreements over Sites of Special Scientific Interest.

(c) *The Nature Conservancy Council Act 1973* largely re-stated the 1949 and 1968 Acts but most significantly changed the emphasis from 'in-house' to commissioned research by separating off the former research branch of the Nature Conservancy as the Institute of Terrestrial Ecology.

(d) *The Wildlife & Countryside Act 1981* served mainly to consolidate existing powers in a new framework and made two notable additions: first, the power to control agricultural and forestry activities on Sites of Special Scientific Interest through a system of notifications of potentially damaging operations and the power to pay compensation on the basis of 'profits forgone' when agricultural or forestry activities are restricted in the interests of conservation; second, the ability to create Marine Nature Reserves through byelaws limiting certain kinds of activities. These additions are most significant in determining the costs of conservation.

There is also a good deal of legislation dealing with the regulation and licensing of activities affecting a very wide range of species of plants and animals, on both the domestic and international fronts. From these statutes arise the main functions and duties of the NCC.

The present budget

To fulfil its role, the NCC currently employs 590 staff, and has an annual budget of some £15m (in 1984/5); the voluntary conservation bodies probably contribute as much again.

Future costs

The remaining parts of this chapter examine the present and future costs of the main elements of conservation practice as defined in *Nature conservation in Great Britain*. Table I summarizes present and predicted costs by 1990 for each heading.

Table I. The cost of conservation: summary of present and predicted costs

		Expenditure in 1984/5 (£ million)	Requirements	Predicted costs in 1990 (£ million)
1.	Site safeguard			
	(a) Staff & Management	7.0	×2	14
	(b) Land	1.7	×15	25 (=£5m p.a.)
	(c) Agreements	0.3	×50	15
2.	Wider Environment	1.3	×3	4.0
3.	Marine	0.1	×10	1.0
4.	Science	1.0	×4	4.0
5.	Legislation	0.5	×1.5	0.75
6.	Publicity & Education	1.0	×2	2.0
7.	International	0.2	×1.5	0.3
8.	Creative	0.2	×5	1.0
9.	Management & Capital Expenditure	2.0	×1.5	3.0
	Total	15.3		50

Site safeguard

More than half NCC's present budget goes on site safeguard including the acquisition and management of land for conservation. This is a staff-intensive activity and staff requirements absorb the greater proportion of current expenditure.

Within a total of 1.3 million ha designated as Sites of Special Scientific Interest (SSSI), some 150 000 ha is managed as nature reserves by NCC and about the same by other conservation bodies. The SSSI series is at risk from the increasing pressures of industrial, agricultural and forestry development and, if its interest is to survive, is likely to require positive safeguard measures sooner or later. The costs of these are determined largely by the impact of the Wildlife & Countryside Act 1981, which has placed conservation firmly in the market place. The high value of land, and the potential profits, combined with the present agricultural support system, provide a powerful incentive for agricultural development. Presently the Government's annual expenditure on agricultural development is ca. £200 m, and a further £13 000m on price support. Given these factors, and the basis of compensation through the Wildlife & Countryside Act in terms of 'profits forgone', conservation, either through purchase or agreements, is expensive.

Given the eventual need to protect the whole of the SSSI series, it is not easy to foresee how much will need to be purchased and how much can be achieved by agreement. However, for purposes of calculation a reasonable objective would be to double the Nature Reserve series and bring the rest of the SSSI under management agreements in five years. The cumulative capital cost over five years would be ca. £25m and the annual cost of agreements some £15m by 1990. Increased staff and management costs might add another £7m per year by 1990 representing a doubling of the present effort. These figures are summarized in Table I. These are, on the face of it, fairly startling figures, but if the purchase costs are averaged out at £5m per year then the annual cost by 1990 is some £34m. This level of expenditure would secure conservation management over some 10 per cent of the land surface. It is not perhaps a large price to pay in comparison with current annual expenditure of some £1500m on agricultural development and price support. It could be achieved by diverting less than 0.5 per cent of public expenditure on agriculture to conservation. Thus, in comparative terms, the price of conservation is not large, and the decision on how large it should be must rest with Government.

Conservation in the wider environment

Despite the very great importance attached to site safeguard, it is clear that wildlife cannot survive in the special sites alone, nor could it be readily available to a wide section of the population if confined to only 10 per cent of the land surface. Success in conserving wildlife in the wider environment must be measured in terms of securing a general matrix of habitats throughout the fabric of town and country.

From the NCC's point of view, this is best achieved through persuading land owners and managers to avoid unnecessary destruction of natural or semi-natural habitats and species in the course of development and productive use of the land. In many instances this can be achieved at low cost and without significant loss of production. The interest and enthusiasm of a substantial sector of the industrial and rural community in conservation is not in doubt. Fostering and developing the interest requires high quality advice to be readily available. NCC's present staff effort in this field is small, especially so because of recent diversion of effort to site safeguard through the Wildlife & Countryside Act. If present expenditure is assessed at £1.3m a year, then trebling it to *ca.* £4m a year would make a reasonable impact (see Table I).

Marine conservation

Marine conservation is a new area of work arising from the Wildlife & Countryside Act 1981. Although there is a substantial amount of literature on the characteristics and functioning of marine ecosystems, there is as yet no complete survey of Britain's intertidal and sub-littoral living marine resources. The major and immediate need is a full scale survey and evaluation of living near-shore marine resources as a basis for selecting Marine Nature Reserves. Meanwhile, the practical conservation management of special areas already identified is a heavy demand on both scientific and administrative staff skills. At present this new field of work commands only some £100 000 worth of effort and expenditure; at least 10 times this (£1m a year) will be required to make a significant start in this new and important field of work.

The science base

Conservation practice depends on knowledge of (i) what there is of conservation interest on the land surface, (ii) the natural ecological processes which sustain that interest, and (iii) the effects of external factors, both natural and of human origin, on the distribution, abundance, and functioning of natural systems.

The most pressing needs are for a complete national survey of wildlife resources and the establishment of the means for monitoring change. Current knowledge of ecosystem processes and the effects of external factors upon them is barely adequate for the design and implementation of management regimes for the maintenance and enhancement of conservation interest, both on special sites and in the wider environment. Present expenditure by NCC on commissioned research is about £1m a year and the whole of the total 'in house' effort is of the same order. An increase to £4m a year would be no more than adequate to meet realistic needs.

Publicity and education

At a current expenditure of under £1m a year, publicity and education is one of the most seriously under-funded areas of NCC's work. Its importance is measured in terms of awareness of conservation requirements among people at all levels from Parliament and the Government through policy-makers and managers of industries to the general public. Important changes of perception are apparent and they need to be harder driven by information flow, greater availability of conserved land and species and greater participation in conservation. An annual expenditure approximately doubling to £2m is envisaged.

Legislation for nature conservation

As indicated in the Introduction, the legislative framework is an essential basis for conservation. Both legislation concerned specifically with wildlife conservation, and also that determining the ways and means for incorporating the principles of wildlife management into a full range of other land uses, need to be kept constantly under review so that appropriate new or amending legislation can be fostered. Although very important, this activity is not large in terms of expenditure. An increase from the current annual level of about £0.5m to £0.75m would enable sound progress to be made.

International conservation

Currently comprising only some £0.2m worth of expenditure, international conservation is not a large part of NCC effort. However, its importance is increasing in relation to EEC policies for conservation including regulations and directives for species and habitat conservation and for the assessment of the environmental impacts of development. Its importance is further highlighted by the opportunities for conservation arising from re-examination of the Common Agricultural Policy (CAP) and its wide-ranging regulations which are a dominant influence on the course of rural land-use change. Small adjustments within the CAP could dramatically affect both the opportunities for and the costs of conservation. A valuable increase in NCC's capacity in this area could be achieved at relatively low cost. An annual expenditure rising to about £0.3m would meet foreseeable demands.

Creative conservation

Conservation, either on special sites or in the wider environment, cannot depend solely on protective management of what is there at the present. There must also be a component of creative or restorative management. The bits and pieces of left-over land in both rural and urban settings, disused and derelict industrial and urban land, the surroundings of industrial developments and the management of public open space and recreational areas all provide opportunities for replacing some of the past losses of wildlife. Though not a substitute for safeguarding the more natural ecosystems, they do provide an important means of participation in conservation for many industrial, urban, and leisure land-users and, perhaps most important, for a large general public. Present expenditure by NCC is small and is devoted largely to a catalytic role, stimulating the involvement of others. This is the right approach and could become a major force in the future given an increase in expenditure some five times the present levels—to, say, £1m a year.

Conclusion

The remaining headings in *Nature conservation in Great Britain* are 'Resources for Nature Conservation' and 'The Distribution of Effort'. Both of these have been subsumed within previous sections of this paper.

Table I summarizes the costs attributed to each of the eight main conservation objectives. My personal assessment is that if the NCC budget can rise to £50m by 1990, then the NCC should be in meaningful business as the leading agency for wildlife conservation in the UK. This chapter has dwelt only on NCC's part in a major partnership. Much of what is outlined above is directed towards increasing the benefits of well-managed wildlife reserves to the majority of people through ensuring availability, ready access and useful information. Above all, the need is to ensure full participation in conservation by all sectors of national activity. In the end, the success of conservation will be directly proportionate to public interest and participation and it is to that increasing interest the Government must respond in ensuring adequate funding for its own conservation agency.

References

The conservation and development programme for the UK: A response to the world conservation strategy (1983). Kogan Page, London. (Sponsoring bodies: World Wildlife Fund UK; Nature Conservancy Council; Countryside Commission; Countryside Commission for Scotland; Royal Society of Arts; Council for Environmental Conservation).

International Union for Conservation of Nature and Natural Resources (1980). *World conservation strategy: Living resource conservation for sustainable development*. IUCN, Gland, Switzerland.

Nature Conservancy Council (1984). *Nature conservation in Great Britain*. Nature Conservancy Council, Shrewsbury.

Symp. zool. Soc. Lond. (1985) No. 54: 219–239

Trade in and exploitation of endangered exotic species of animals

MICHAEL R. BRAMBELL

*The North of England Zoological Society.
Formerly Chairman of the Advisory
Committee on Animal Species
Endangered by Trade,
Nature Conservancy Council*

Synopsis

This chapter is a short review of international trade in endangered species, particularly of trade in animal species. It examines the nature of the trade itself, covers the history of international control of trade and assesses the future development of international control. It discusses the CITES Convention in relation to species which are globally endangered as well as to those which are only endangered in particular regions of their distribution.

It concludes with a warning that, simply because international trade lends itself to some degree of measurement and to concerted controls, it should not be regarded as a prime factor in the battle to preserve habitats and their constituent species; but it should be seen as an expression of the attitudes of exporting countries in particular towards their own wildlife resources.

Introduction

This chapter concerns some of the aspects and issues involved in the movement across international boundaries, by way of trade, of animals which belong to endangered species and of their parts and derivatives. It is not primarily concerned with indirect effects on endangered species through the conversion of their native habitats to meet other international commercial demands, e.g. the raising of beef for export, the growing of cash crops, the building of tourist resorts, the extraction of mineral reserves or the construction of hydroelectric schemes. Though animals and their products which have been introduced from the sea are mentioned, this paper does no more than give passing reference to the rather special issues involved.

International trade is, in most of its aspects, simply an extension of internal trade, the differences being relative rather than absolute. For example, the pressures on the environment caused by internal trade can be expected to increase proportionally with the square of the distance to the extra-territorial markets, on the assumption that the larger the area served the larger the population that is generating the demand. It must be remembered that

ZOOLOGICAL SYMPOSIUM No. 54
ISBN 0–19–854002–7

international transport is very easy, fast and relatively cheap. Indeed there is now no country in the world which need be more than 24 h travelling time from any other should sufficient demand for such ease of communication arise. There is, therefore, no guarantee that any particular species might not suddenly find itself the centre of an overwhelming international demand, unless there are enforceable controls to protect it from over-exploitation.

International trade, because it involves the crossing of international frontiers, lends itself to fuller recording (by the Customs Authorities) of what is in trade, though their records tend to be more quantitative than qualitative. Thus the financial value, the weight or the bulk of the major categories of items in trade is given greater emphasis than the taxonomy of the items themselves.

Though the differences between trade which occurs within a country, that is internal trade, and that which occurs between countries, international trade, are largely artificial and relative, there is at least one absolute difference. In internal trade, restricted as it is to one country, the producer, the middle man and the consumer are all under the same jurisdiction. In international trade the producer and the consumer are by definition under separate national jurisdictions. The middle man may be under the same jurisdiction as one or the other but he may equally well be operating under a third jurisdiction. International trade, therefore, has, through the incompatibility of legal systems, a potential for evasion of restrictions not open to internal traders.

Should one country not wish a trade in one of its products to take place, should it not want there to be any export of one of its endangered species, then any illegal shipment has only to be smuggled across the frontier, be carried out of the national airspace or reach extra-territorial waters, for the shipper to have got the goods out from under the jurisdiction of the country of origin whose wishes have been flouted. No further sanctions can be applied against him unless he tries to return to the same country or unless other countries have agreed to co-operate. It is the development of such co-operation, largely under the terms of the Washington Convention on International Trade in Endangered Species of Wild Fauna and Flora (CITES) (1975), which has been a most significant step in preventing the over-exploitation through trade of endangered exotic species throughout the world. A recent telling example of the need for such co-operation has been the recent illegal export from Brazil of about one quarter of the known world population of the golden-headed lion tamarin *Leontopithecus chrysomelas* via Bolivia to Belgium, which had no treaty obligations to Brazil at the time and whose law was not broken by the trader when he imported the same animals. If Belgium had already been a Party to CITES the import would have been illegal and sanctions could have been applied on the importer.

Nature of international trade in endangered species

Trade in animals includes the whole animal whether it be alive or dead, parts of the dead animal, occasionally parts obtained from the living animal (such as peacock feathers and deer antlers), and derivatives obtained from the animal alive or dead. Dead animals contributing to trade are usually killed deliberately for that purpose, sometimes humanely, sometimes less so. Occasionally, animals which die naturally are harvested as tradeable items. Though trade in any kind of animal could take place and almost any part or derivative could be utilized, in practice the bulk of trade in exotic species falls into the following categories.

Live animals

The pet trade

Principally in birds, reptiles and fish; some are bred in captivity but a considerable proportion are still wild-caught. Primates are also an important part of the world-wide pet trade. This trade probably relies on South America, Africa and south-east Asia for the bulk of its supplies from the wild. The size of the trade is difficult to assess, but it forms potentially the most serious threat to a wide range of species. Any species of easily transported animal may be in trade as long as the trader has a reasonable chance that individual specimens are likely to survive at least until they are in the hands of the myriads of potential pet owners throughout the world. It was because of the open-endedness of the pet trade that the IUCN, at its meeting in Ashkabad in Russia in 1978, asked all nations to prohibit or restrict as appropriate the entry of wild-caught animals into the pet trade.

Parrots are just one of the many groups of animals traded as pets. Using data collected at Schiphol Airport, Amsterdam (Van Den Berg, van den Plas-Haarsma & Wijker 1983) (almost all intercontinental trade in wild animals and their products now moves by air) the bald statistics of trade in 1980 into just one importing country are: 15 200 parrots from South and Central America, valued at 379 000 US dollars to the exporting countries and involving at least 22 species; 6 500 parrots from south-east Asia and the Pacific, valued at 188 000 US dollars, involving at least 33 species, and 11 800 parrots from Africa, valued at over 300 000 US dollars, involving over 10 species, Some, but very few, of these birds will have been captive-bred for the purpose. Some will belong to species which occur in almost pest proportions in parts of their range, but most will have been wild-caught, often as nestlings, collected, in the case of many individuals of tree-nesting species, by the felling of the trees containing suitable nesting holes, a practice which not only removes the current brood from the wild but denies the parent birds the use of the nesting site to raise further broods.

The bio-medical research trade

This can involve any species, but the primates have formed a very significant section of this trade in recent years. This trade, too, relies heavily on South America and south-east Asia for its supply of primates. Numbers can be very high in proportion to the native population, though in some instances the monkeys which are in trade occur in pest proportions. The demand has been artificially increased in western countries, frightened by the thalidomide tragedy, demanding that a wide range of products are tested in primate species before they can be licensed as suitable for sale to human beings. It is to be hoped that methods of testing develop which reduce the reliance of this form of research on wild-caught animals. However, biomedical research, with its interest in the understanding of human problems, relies heavily on the primates, being man's closest relations, for its research models. For many years it went without question that wild-caught primates were suitable research material though similar work performed on wild-caught rats, instead of on laboratory-bred rats, would have been rejected as worthless. It has only been in the last decade or so that serious efforts have been made to provide captive-bred primates for essential research purposes. In particular, the wild populations of several species of marmosets and tamarins have faced serious pressures from biomedical research demand. Strong pressures were applied on our own country's importing authorities to relax the restriction of importation of wild-caught cotton-headed tamarins *Saguinus oedipus* on the grounds that the urgency of the cancer research for which they were needed outweighed all considerations of rarity. It was only when it was pointed out that if the species was indeed as essential as was being claimed, then the research workers were, in effect, proposing to eat their own seed corn that the pressure to relax import controls was resisted and the establishment of a captive breeding programme insisted upon. As a result funds are now granted for the breeding of many of the species of primates as research stock, as well as for the research itself. Viable numbers are being born and raised without continual recourse to the collecting of wild-born animals.

The zoo trade

Historically the movement of wild animals for zoos included species of all kinds up to the size of elephants, though in the past it showed itself more likely to involve rare species than the other forms of live animal trade. Zoos have a reputation for collecting as many kinds of rare and curious animals as they can without having too much concern for the effect of this on the wild and without making sure that the stock was managed so that it could reproduce itself in captivity. There is no doubt that this criticism is justified for some zoos still, though there has been an enormous change of attitude by the major zoos of the developed world, and for them the criticism is now less justified. Even so the criticism has been overstated, for though the zoo trade has been blamed for much, it has been relatively small compared with the bulk of wildlife moving for other reasons. Nevertheless, old-fashioned zoo collecting has put significant pressures on some species, for example the mountain gorilla, *Gorilla gorilla beringei*. Zoological collections in future must endeavour to divorce themselves totally from speculative collecting of endangered wildlife. Only truly co-ordinated programmes, where zoological gardens, international conservation agencies and the competent authorities in the countries of origin are working together, should be contemplated. Zoos claim, rightly, to be potential contributors towards the conservation of some species and they should temper all their actions to see that they achieve such claims without compromise. There is no reason why in future the responsible zoos throughout the world should not be stocked with zoo-bred animals produced by themselves or by other zoos or with animals donated or lent by concerned government agencies in the countries of origin. This may be an impractical stance to take at this present stage with some of the less sensitive species, but it will not be so for long. Unless zoos take such a stance they will convince nobody, neither their own supporters and visitors, nor conservationists, nor governments, that they should be regarded as serious contributors in the field of species conservation. Once they do take this stance, the movement of animals will no longer be 'trade' and the true potential of zoos and other managing establishments will become clear.

Dead animals

The skin and leather trade
Mammal species provide furs of arctic and sub-arctic species, and also of temperate and tropical cats, especially the spotted cats. Larger species of mammals also provide leathers. Reptile species provide leathers. The skin and leather trade from wild-caught animals is enormous. It completely outweighs the trade in living specimens of most species except possibly that in aquarium fish. Imports of raw skins of all kinds in the world exceeded 5 billion US dollars in 1979. At its peak in 1968/69 the reptile skin trade from India involved over 5 million individual raw and tanned skins (Inskipp, n.d.). At a time when the United Kingdom was worrying about allowing the import of six live Canadian lynx *Felis lynx* under the Animals (Restriction of Importation) Act 1964, which only controlled live animals, there were warehouses in London piled almost to the ceiling with lynx furs, representing thousands of animals which had been killed for trade.

Other items
Other items in trade, often of critical importance to the survival of the species involved, are: plumage, wools, etc.; horns and ivory (a trade increased

in recent years by the breakdown of effective wardening of game reserves and the acceptance of raw ivory as a substitute for bullion); hunting trophies and taxidermy materials; foodstuffs, including turtle meats and whale oil; and cosmetics and jewellery including musk, tortoiseshell, coral and ambergris.

Measurement of trade

It is extremely difficult to measure trade in animals and their products in zoologically meaningful terms. Except in a very few cases there is no accurate measure of the size of the wild population, so that it is impossible to express the volume of trade as a percentage of the wild population, which would be the most meaningful statistic. Usually, the trade is expressed in monetary values. To interpret money values requires a knowledge of individual values at various stages along the trade routes, as the amounts by which value is added increase enormously with the distance goods are transported and the degree to which they have been processed. Sometimes the trade is measured by the number of items that are in trade and this usually means the number of animals that have had to be slaughtered. Numbers of animals are the most useful form of statistic, though the statistics may refer to items made up from the products of several animals as, for example, with the skins of the leopard cat *Felis bengalensis* which are too small to be useful individually as traded items and are sewn together into plates of several dozen skins. Sometimes the trade has to be expressed in terms of volume or in terms of weight. Such bulk measurements are extremely difficult to convert back into numbers of animals needed to make up the consignment.

The primary sources of information on international trade are the Customs reports of the various countries of the world; those countries which are parties to CITES are obliged to produce full annual reports of trade in species listed in the Appendices of the Convention, though this does not ensure that species not yet listed in CITES are included. Even if the volume of international trade in a particular species could be converted into the number of animals involved, it would not include any evidence of the volume of internal trade, so that CITES reports could not be used to assess the effect of all trade on the wild population of the species. Indeed the use of international trade statistics to measure pressures on wild populations is an extremely inexact science which is given a gloss of exactitude only because of bureaucratic delight in keeping tight records at international boundaries, records which are further compromised by not everywhere being kept to the same standards of taxonomic accuracy. The Wildlife Trade Monitoring Unit of IUCN has conducted several surveys on the discrepancies which occur amongst the records of importing and exporting countries on the amount of wildlife which is in trade and have shown that there must be a considerable amount of trade in endangered species which is not being correctly recorded.

What is obvious is that, as H.R.H. the Duke of Edinburgh pointed out in his introduction to this Symposium, the amount of trade in wildlife is enormous.

Classification of endangeredness

Once it had become obvious that species were becoming extinct at a faster than natural rate, because of their interaction with man and with his exploitation of the world's resources, it became necessary to devise a system to classify the degree to which the species may be so endangered. Such a system is intended to express, in easily understood categories, the almost indefinable gradation between the extremes of unthreatened abundance and the point of extinction itself. It is important to remember that all species, however abundant in global terms, become locally rare somewhere or other in their distribution; even the house mouse *Mus musculus* is rare in the polar regions. Thus there is the need for a global system and there is the need for local systems. Indeed, the world of national and international conservation can be thought of in four categories: Global, Continental, National, and Local. A glance at the organization of voluntary conservation societies shows how much effort is applied to problems which are less than global in significance. If the survival of a species is globally in a critical situation then it follows that it must be continentally, nationally, and locally critical as well. However, the reverse does not follow, that a locally critical situation has any wider significance for the species.

We have to think not only in our own national and local terms, but also in global terms, and there is the danger of much confusion and repetition of effort in species conservation when we allow local and national issues concerning species which are not continentally or globally threatened to override global needs. It should be remembered that governments represent local and national issues more strongly than international and global issues, so there is a built-in legislative bias in favour of a parochial attitude towards conservation. It would be reasonable to suggest that all systems of classifying endangeredness might use the prefix G, C, N or L to make it clear whether or not the species is categorized absolutely, i.e. globally, or relatively, i.e. continentally or less.

In 1966 the International Union for Conservation of Nature and Natural Resources produced its system for categorizing the status of species in global terms. This was updated into its present form in 1972 (IUCN 1982). There are seven listed categories and, by inference, an eighth, unlisted category.

The categories are:

1. Extinct (Ex). Species not definitely located in the wild during the past

50 years. (In my opinion the 'Ex' symbol should be replaced by the single letter 'X').

2. Endangered (E). Taxa in danger of extinction and unlikely to survive if the causal factors continue operating. Included are taxa whose numbers have been reduced to a critical level or whose habitats have been so drastically reduced that they are deemed to be in immediate danger of extinction. Also included are taxa that are possibly already extinct but have definitely been seen in the past 50 years.

3. Vulnerable (V). Taxa believed likely to move into the 'Endangered' category in the near future if the causal factors continue operating. Included are taxa of which most or all of the populations are decreasing because of over-exploitation, extensive destruction of habitat or other environmental disturbance; taxa with populations that are still abundant but are under threat from severe adverse factors throughout their range.

4. Rare (R). Taxa with small world populations that are not at present 'Endangered' or 'Vulnerable', but are at risk. These taxa are usually localized within restricted geographical areas or habitats or are thinly scattered over a more extensive range.

5. Indeterminate (I). Taxa known to be 'Endangered', 'Vulnerable' or 'Rare' but on which there is not enough information to say which of the three categories is appropriate.

6. Out of Danger (O). Taxa formerly included in one of the above categories but now considered relatively secure because effective conservation measures have been taken or the previous threat to their survival has been removed.

7. Insufficiently known (K). Taxa that are suspected but not definitely known to belong to any of the above categories, because of lack of information.

8. The unstated category is that of species which are sufficiently 'abundant' or at least not rare; for such species, which are not regarded as being under present threat, the symbol (A) could be used.

There are further complications, because the IUCN categories do not allow sufficiently for the rate of change that may be occurring to the status of a species. The status may be getting worse, i.e. going Downhill, remaining Static, or improving, i.e. going Uphill, conditions which could be classified with the suffixes D, S or U. In addition, species that are under severe threat in the wild may be breeding to profusion in captivity. This could be shown by adding the symbol (C) to the IUCN categorization.

By combining the prefixes and suffixes suggested in this paper to the IUCN Symbols a fuller description of the status of a species could be given. For example the southern white rhinoceros would be classified as G.O.U.; the common otter in Europe would be C.V.D.; the British population of golden eagles N.R.S., and the chinchilla G.E.S.(C).

The advantages and disadvantages of trade to endangered species in their countries of origin

If a trade relies on wild-caught material and the wild population is itself in grave danger of extinction, it follows that the trade itself is an adverse factor in the preservation of the species.

If a trade relies on wild-caught material drawn from a population not yet in grave danger but liable to become so, it may be that the trade itself could provide the political and economic stimulus to reverse the adverse factors that are operating, provided the trade is controlled within adequately monitored limits and provided the limits are set on conservationally valid grounds.

Therefore, we have to judge when trade is in itself adverse and when it can be used to support field conservation. Hitherto, there has been a tendency to assume all trade is adverse. It only takes a developing country to say 'if you will not let us trade in our vulnerable species, we cannot resist the demand for an income from our land surface, and therefore we cannot prevent the land surface being converted from wild habitat to domesticated use', for the danger of this approach to be obvious.

The difficulty is how to judge when inhibition should give way to permitted, but controlled, trade.

This dilemma is much more complicated when captive breeding, farming and ranching occur, especially if the costs of captive production are too high to make it economic to undercut wild-taken products entering into the market.

To take the extreme of the American alligator *Alligator mississippiensis*, there is such a large capacity available of captive-bred stock which can be produced very economically that the international trade in alligator skins poses no real threat to the endangered wild population.

However, in the case of the peregrin falcon, *Falco peregrinus* is being bred very successfully in captivity but the costs are such that illegal taking from the wild is cheaper, unless the miscreants are caught.

At the other extreme it is fairly widely held that the release of skins of captive-bred tigers *Panthera tigris* on to the market would not help the conservation of wild tiger. There are two reasons for this: firstly the presence of legitimate tiger skins in the market would make it easier for illegally obtained wild tiger skins to be slipped into the market and, secondly, the introduction of tiger skins into the market at the present stage of tiger conservation would create an 'envy' trade which captive-bred sources could not now meet.

The dilemma which faces the development of farms and ranches for species likely to bring real wealth into the countries involved, is that it will take time for production to build up to a level sufficient to meet the whole of the demand which will have to be stimulated in order to ensure the ventures are viable. Quite apart from questions of good taste, whether it is a civilized thing to be doing to be wearing tiger skins (and most human societies in the world rely on extensive use of animal products) there is a real dilemma facing those who believe that some of the pressure on wild habitats could be relieved by encouraging trade in ranched and farmed products. It is the question of when the alternative supply exceeds the envy demand.

There will be fierce debate in the next decade or so between the permissives, who will find themselves being allied to less altruistic pressure groups from the trade itself, and the inhibitors, who run the danger of having their conservation arguments diluted by those who argue from a welfare standpoint and who will find themselves accused of denying habitats their most potent weapon: that they are of value to the people who control their destinies. What has to be accepted is that trade in wildlife products cannot any longer be regarded as being *ipso facto* unacceptable in terms of conservation. It is not trade itself, but uncontrolled trade in endangered species which has to be resisted. Of course, the severity of the controls can be expected to increase with the degree of endangeredness of the habitats and of the species involved, leading inevitably to total prohibition in the most extreme cases.

Historical background to the control of international trade in endangered species

In 1900, the U.S. Congress passed the Lacey Act. In its original form it made it a federal offence to take across state borders wildlife taken illegally in a state, that is contrary to the law of the state of origin. In its later amended form, this Act was extended to include illegal export from foreign countries.

In 1911, the Pribilof Fur Seal Convention between the U.S.A., Canada (the U.K. negotiated for her), Russia, and Japan restricted the taking of northern fur seals *Callorhinus ursinus* to the U.S.A. which had to compensate the other parties on a *pro rata* basis out of the value of the take. The population of seals which had been reduced to 200 000 from 2.5 million began to rise again and can again be numbered in millions.

These two steps, both involving the U.S.A., have set the scene for later developments, the one leading to CITES, which is designed to protect species from over-exploitation by trade, and the other designed to protect the trade itself from over-exploitation.

It is these two themes, that trade should be controlled in order to protect some species, and that trade itself should be protected from over-exploitation of its basic resource, which seem to alternate in importance as international controls develop.

In 1946, the International Convention for the Regulation of Whaling was concluded, but this covered only a very small proportion (entirely marine) of all the species involved in whaling. It began as a means to protect the trade from over-exploitation and it has become a means for protecting the whales themselves from being exploited at all.

In 1960, the International Union for Conservation of Nature and Natural Resources, meeting in Warsaw, agreed on the need for international controls and, at its meeting in Nairobi in 1963, it resolved that there should be a convention on international trade in endangered species. At least four drafts were produced before the final version was agreed in 1973 when the Convention to Control International Trade in Endangered Species of Fauna and Flora was concluded in Washington. CITES was initially signed by 21 states and it came into force in 1975 when ten countries had ratified it. The United Kingdom could not ratify until 1976 on account of the need to get the prior agreement of its dependent territories, some of which were tardy in deciding whether or not to join.

The United Kingdom's comparatively late entry into CITES belied the fact that it had been operating controls since 1921 for plumage and since 1964 for certain kinds of live animals. The history of the development of these controls is set out in the *Report of the Scientific Authority for Animals, 1976–1981*, which was laid before Parliament during 1982 and is reproduced in full as Appendix I to this chapter.

Since 1981 the function of Scientific Authority for Animals has been transferred from the Department of the Environment to the Nature Conservancy Council.

CITES is concerned with trade in endangered species and the effect of that trade on the survival of the species. Trade may be a principal cause of endangeredness, but even when it is not it can compound the degree of danger in which a species is placed. In effect, CITES recognizes three global levels in the slide from abundance to the point of extinction:

(a) Species, for the most part in the IUCN 'E' Category, in which continued trade will make matters even more critical than they are at present, are listed in Appendix I to the Convention. This appendix comprises all species threatened with extinction which are or may be affected by trade.

(b) Species where trade, if it is under control, can be tolerated, roughly equivalent to the IUCN categories of 'V', 'R' and 'I', are listed in Appendix II to the Convention. Appendix II comprises all taxa which are not necessarily now threatened with extinction but which may become so unless trade in specimens is subject to strict regulation. It also includes a second category, that of taxa which need to be controlled in order to control taxa in the first category because of the risk of misidentification, i.e. what is known as the 'Look-Alike Principle'.

(c) Species which are not under any particular threat even though there is a trade in them, are not listed at all.

CITES also protects some species in local terms rather than globally. It allows sub-populations of species to be selectively protected by the inclusion of geographically defined populations in the Appendices and it allows individual countries to ask for greater protection to be accorded to their own populations of particular species by listing them on Appendix III to the Convention.

Although, when the CITES Convention was first drawn up, species were put on the various Appendices in a haphazard manner, the parties to the Convention, meeting in Berne in 1976, drew up precise criteria which would have to be met before a new species could be listed in an Appendix, or before a species could be transferred between the Appendices or removed altogether (CITES 1976).

In the United Kingdom the protection of endangered species from over-exploitation through trade is almost all within the scope of the Wildlife & Countryside Act 1981 and the Endangered Species (Import & Export) Act 1976, though many other separate pieces of legislation designed to protect particular species are also involved. The United Kingdom uses the principle of 'Reverse Listing' in its protection of birds and mammals. Reverse listing is the principle by which all species are assumed to be protected unless they are named on the list as being excepted from the controls, i.e. it is the commoner species which are listed. This is in contrast to 'Direct Listing' in which species which are rare and little known are listed and which assumes that Customs Officers and other law enforcement officers are expert at recognizing rare and little known forms. Direct listing also runs the risk of omitting species so rare that it might be regarded as pedantic to think of them in trade.

Reverse listing, whilst being extremely useful to the scientist and the conservationist, has created problems for the administrator because so many more species are subject to controls than would otherwise have been. Nevertheless reverse listing is now widely used in CITES at Order level. For example all the primate species (except man) are listed on Appendix II or on Appendix I to the Convention. The same is true of all the whales and all but three of the parrot species.

The role of captive and managed breeding of endangered species

The entry into trade of captive-bred animals belonging to species endangered in the wild is likely to become much more important than has been generally accepted hitherto. The example which resulted in the CITES Convention making a special exemption of captive-bred stock is the chinchilla.

The wild chinchilla is in great danger and could easily become extinct, but in captivity the chinchilla breeds in such abundance that it is accepted as a commercial fur-bearing species, the trading of which would have no bearing on the wild population. The Siberian tiger *P. t. altaica* is a sub-species which is vulnerable in the wild but which has bred in such profusion in captivity that it could become an embarrassment to the keeping institutions. However, its survival is assured as long as the institutions continue to co-ordinate their breeding programmes with each other. Captive breeding, or to use a term which may become more widely accepted in the future, managed breeding, (on account of programmes embracing zoos and similar institutions on the one hand and the semi-wild on the other) will become a more significant part of the conservation of the larger and the more specialized species. This is because it is these species which start to lose their habitats sooner than do the smaller and less specialized species.

Whilst one can imagine quite small tracts of land supporting small antelopes, such as some of the dik-diks and duikers, for a long time to come without the need of managed breeding, it is quite clear that large species, such as the larger antelopes, are going to be in great danger through lack of sufficient suitable and undisturbed habitat to support viable populations. The transfer of breeding stock from the wild and between the keeping institutions will be a vital part of the conservation management of many species in the future.

The future

In the short term much more precise knowledge of the factors operating against species survival is needed in order to assess what limits need to be set to prevent matters from getting worse.

It is essential that the trade in endangered species is recorded on an internationally consistent basis so that the volume of exploitation which a particular species or a particular habitat is undergoing can be assessed. Ultimately assessments must be made of the levels of exploitation which can be tolerated. In other words, what is needed is the ability to set internationally agreed quotas.

Once quotas are set the trade will have to continue to be monitored to ensure that the quotas are not being exceeded. It is not unlikely that the imposition of quotas for material originating from the wild will lead to some unfairness and distortion of trade. This might force the pace towards the next stage in the development of trade in endangered species, the development of ranches under CITES Conference Paper 3: 15 (CITES 1981) and of genuine captive breeding under CITES Conference Paper 2: 12 (CITES 1979) both of which could take much pressure off the wild habitats.

Until internationally accepted quotas are agreed there will be muddle and inefficiency in the control of exploitation. It is essential, therefore, that some uniformity of action is introduced to facilitate the use of quotas. The concept of quotas is likely to be resisted, but it seems obvious that as long as *some* trade in endangered species is tolerated by the Parties to CITES, they should at least have an agreed statement of *how much* can be tolerated.

CITES at its present stage is but a halfway house. Imports can only be permitted if it can be proved that the export has been legal, but there is no *pre-agreed* system to check whether the volume of the export trade is detrimental or not. However, there must be one overriding consideration in the setting of quotas: can the national population stand the level of exploitation envisaged? Any other criteria run the risk of a form of 'conservation imperialism' being imposed on producer countries by consumer countries. Without quotas limiting the total amount of exports in each species from each country of origin and for each mode of production CITES cannot be expected to provide much greater protection to endangered species than it is doing now.

Distasteful as it may be to some conservationists in developed countries, trade in wildlife products from undeveloped countries should not be restricted beyond the level needed to maintain truly viable wild populations of the species involved. Further restriction runs the risk of wild habitats being viewed as unproductive and therefore unacceptable alternatives to other intensive uses such as agriculture. Until whole nations can educate themselves into wanting to protect wildlife for its own sake, which cannot yet be said to have happened in the advanced countries, let alone the developing countries, monetary value can provide the governmental impetus to protect those national resources represented by endangered species.

However, where demand is so strong that the wild populations could not stand the full extent of trade the alternatives of ranching and of captive breeding must be preferred to the total banning of a trade, provided that the methods of breeding and rearing of the animals as well as the means of slaughter in the case of dead animals and the methods of transport and ultimate keeping are humane.

But a word of warning. There are great temptations to fudge issues. For example, it is sometimes tempting to use humane arguments to achieve conservation goals and vice versa. Is the bottle-nosed dolphin *Tursiops truncatus* really in need of conservation, considering the abundance with which it occurs in the oceans? Arguments based on how dangerous animals may be are sometimes put forward to achieve conservation goals. Are tamarins really dangerous animals? To muddle *disease risk* with *pest risk* with *danger risk* with *humane factors* and *conservation* only serves to confuse the minds of politicians and legislators and ultimately serves to help no-one. Everybody's interests, especially the interests of those who want to protect genuinely endangered species, are best served by clearly thought out legislative measures.

There are other dangers; for example, there must be a great temptation in producer countries to use over-restrictive controls in order to corner markets and thus corruptly increase personal and national wealth thereby bringing CITES into disrepute. Clear thinking in the setting of quotas and controls will make such practices more difficult to conceal.

Conclusion

Whether or not a species or an ecosystem will survive depends on whether or not it can remain a viable entity. It is to be hoped that, where species are concerned, this would happen within their natural habitat but, if not, then within some managed protection, which for many species means within a dedicated zoo. The removal of specimens from their natural habitats in order to meet demands of trade, or the removal of essential constituents of the habitats for trade, are incidental to the main problem, which is the political resolve of those with the power to defend the habitats themselves.

Just because *control* of international trade in endangered species is possible because machinery exists to monitor the movements of goods of all kinds at most international borders, it should not be taken that international trade is in itself the most important adverse pressure on habitats; it is not. The significance of international trade is that a lot more is known about it; the statistics provided at international borders tend to be more comprehensive and also have the advantage, at least in theory, of being open to checking, for one country's import must have been another country's export.

International trade must be controlled, it must be monitored and the trends must be identified and acted upon, but international trade must not be mistaken for being more than it is, a significant side issue (usually negative but sometimes positive) to the main problem facing conservation: the defence of the habitat.

It is the lack of political will and the existence of poor local attitudes which present the biggest threats to all habitats and to the species which occupy them.

References

Convention on International Trade in Endangered Species of Fauna and Flora, concluded in Washington 3rd March 1973. (CITES). (1975). HMSO, London. (Cmnd 5459.)

CITES (1976). Criteria for the addition of species and other taxa to Appendices I and II and for the transfer of species and other taxa from Appendix I to Appendix

II. Conference Paper Conf. 1.1 5.11.1976. Criteria for the deletion of species and other taxa from Appendices I and II. Conference Paper Conf. 1.2 5.11.1976. Deletion of species from Appendix I or II in certain circumstances. Conference Paper Conf. 1.3 5.11.1976. *Rep. First Meet. Conf. Parties C.I.T.E.S.* Berne: CITES.

CITES (1979). Specimens bred in captivity or artificially propagated. Conference Paper Conf. 2.12 30.3.1079. *Rep. Second Meet. Conf. Parties C.I.T.E.S.* CITES, San José, Costa Rica.

CITES (1981). Ranching. Conference Paper Conf. 3.15 8.3.1981. *Rep. Third Meet. Conf. Parties C.I.T.E.S.* CITES, New Delhi.

Endangered Species (Import and Export) Act (1976). HMSO, London.

Inskipp, T. (n.d.). Indian trade in reptile skins. *I.U.C.N. Wildl. Trade Monit. Unit. Traff. Bull.* (Suppl.) 3 (5).

IUCN (1982). Red Data Book categories 1966. *I.U.C.N. Mamm. Red Data Book 1982.* IUCN, Gland, Switzerland.

Van Den Berg, M., van den Plas-Haarsma, M. & Wijker, N. (1983). An analysis of psittacines imported at Schiphol Airport during 1980 and 1981. *I.U.C.N. Wildl. Trade Monit. Unit. Traff. Bull.* 5 (1).

Wildlife and Countryside Act (1981). HMSO, London.

Appendix I: Report of the Scientific Authority for Animals 1976–1981

In 1960 the General Assembly of the International Union for the Conservation of Nature passed a resolution urging control of the international trade in endangered species. This led to a growing realisation in the United Kingdom that the only way for countries to control illegal exports of their endangered wildlife was for them to be given the fullest possible support and co-operation by the importing countries.

From this impetus arose a private member's bill, largely due to the initiative of Lt. Col. C.L. Boyle, of the Fauna Preservation Society, to control the importation of certain groups. The bill was introduced by Miss Betty Harvie Anderson, M.P., and became law as the Animals (Restriction of Importation) Act 1964. This was implemented by the Board of Trade, advised by the Department of Education and Science, who appointed an Animals Advisory Committee, first under the Chairmanship of the fourth Earl of Cranbrook, who was succeeded by Sir Hugh Elliott in 1972. In 1973 the Committee was transferred to the Department of the Environment. The Committee's function was to advise on imports of live animals of certain families containing endangered species, including most primates, Australian marsupials, cats, rhinos, tapirs, iguanas, crocodiles and tortoises, these last to protect the two Mediterranean species, *Testudo graeca* and *T. hermanni*. The whole of the family Iguanidae was included in order to safeguard the land and marine iguanas of the Galapagos Islands.

In 1970, following concern expressed about the growing trade in live birds of prey at a period when these were decreasing in the wild, the Wild Birds (Importation) Order 1970, was made, under existing Customs & Excise legislation. Importation of both diurnal and nocturnal birds of prey was controlled by the issuing of licences, and advice on such licences was given to the Home Office by its Advisory Committee on the Protection of Birds Acts.

In 1973 the U.K. signed the Convention on Control of International Trade in Endangered Species of Wild Fauna and Flora in Washington D.C., and ratified it in 1976. To implement this the Animals Advisory Committee and some members of the Advisory Committee on the Protection of Birds were brought together on the 1st December, 1975 as the Scientific Authority for Animals under the Chairmanship of Professor V.C. Wynne-Edwards, F.R.S. On 1st January, 1976 the U.K. began to implement the provisions of CITES, even though the specific legislation had not yet been enacted. The first task of the S.A.A. was to advise on the drafting of the Endangered Species (Import & Export) Act which became law on 3rd February, 1977.

This Act controlled the import and export of endangered species, both animals and plants, and it controlled the trade in skins, plumage (which had been controlled for over fifty years under the Importation of Plumage (Prohibition) Act 1921, which was repealed by the passing of this Act) and certain other dead parts and derivatives. For several groups the Act incorporated the principle of reverse listing (the listing of those species for which there were *no controls* rather than the previously used method of listing species for which there *were controls*). The benefit of reverse listing is that the lists of what may be traded in are finite and contain species which are well known and easily recognised. With direct listing there is always the risk that a species which was so rare that it had been considered unlikely to enter trade (if indeed it had been considered at all) did enter trade to the detriment of its chances of survival. The disadvantage of reverse listing is that in some groups there are so many species in which there can be no objection to trade that the lists would be considerably longer than had only the species needing protection been in trade. Thus the reverse listing of most mammals and bird species is both practical and desirable whereas the reverse listing of the insects or of fish would be impractical and over-restrictive. This meant that the Scientific Authority for Animals was advising the Department of the Environment on up to 16 000 applications a year covering live animals for pet trade, scientific research and for zoos and circuses as well as the dead animal trade which included furs, turtle meat and other products, plumage and exotic leathers.

The control of trade in endangered species has three essential purposes:

(a) to inhibit trade in vulnerable species, in which any commercial exploitation would constitute an unacceptable extra threat;

(b)   to watch the trade in species known to be threatened to ensure that it does not reach dangerous levels;

(c)   to ascertain the level of trade in species about which the effect of trade is as yet unclear.

To exercise the necessary levels of control it is obvious that advice must be sought prior to any proposed trade in (a) or in (b); but in (c) it is only necessary to know what trade has taken place. However, strict interpretation of the 1976 Act resulted in the Scientific Authority for Animals having to pass judgement on all applications. This has undoubtedly led to a great deal of experts' time, given voluntarily, having to be spent reviewing cases which needed no special judgement prior to the issue of a licence.

However, the working of the 1976 Act revealed several areas where real problems existed. Firstly, it was extremely hard to be certain of the volume of trade which actually took place. The numbers of animals and their parts and derivatives licensed gave an indication of the upper limits it was intended might be in trade, but it was by no means certain that all licences would be used, nor that those which were used would be used in full. There is also an inevitable time lag (up to nine months in the case of imports and up to six months in the case of exports) between the time a licence is issued and when it is used. Thus the statistics under the Act could not be easily reconciled with those of H.M. Customs and those of the Ministry of Agriculture, Fisheries & Food, whose systems of recording have slightly different bases. Nevertheless, the size of the discrepancies was a considerable source of concern to the Scientific Authority for Animals and to the Department it advised.

Secondly, it was inevitable that from time to time live animals would arrive in this country without licences or incorrectly licensed, as when exporters had mis-identified what they were sending. To overcome the difficulty faced by Customs of what to do with a potentially valuable and rare creature in need of expert care while the paperwork was being corrected, a system of release from Customs with an undertaking to present a correct licence later was introduced, for live animals only. This system worked excellently for the genuine mistakes but came more and more to be abused by particular traders who adopted the practice of seldom applying for licences prior to importing, relying on obtaining release of the stock by Customs under an undertaking.

Thirdly, there were difficulties over living animals which might be delayed in transit being temporarily imported into this country. The Scientific Authority for Animals was uneasy that this concession for humane purposes was being misused by certain traders who appeared to be using the time of the apparent delay to find a market abroad for animals whose import into the U.K. would not have been sanctioned by the Scientific Authority for Animals. The Scientific Authority for Animals urged that a more realistic approach be taken over the granting of this concession.

Fourthly, there were several instances when living animals were imported for which the Scientific Authority for Animals felt obliged to recommend refusal of a licence. This placed a moral dilemma on the management authority which could have insisted on the return of the stock to the country of export. Though this did in fact happen on a few occasions, in most cases it was agreed that it would not be in the interests of the animals themselves to be kept in transit and to remain potentially in trade. Such stock was confiscated by Customs, who had the unenviable task of finding places where the animals could be deposited on a permanent basis in such a way that no benefit could be derived by the illegal traders. In general it fell to zoos to absorb the animals, often animals for which they had no need and in numbers which stretched their resources. There is no doubt that without this help many animals in illegal trade would have had to be destroyed or would have died as a result of being returned to countries which would not have had the facilities to have handled them properly on arrival.

Fifthly, the Scientific Authority for Animals was aware that animals and their products could be illegally exported from one country to another whose controls were less rigid than our own. Their re-export could be made to look genuine and legal by altering their paperwork, a process known as laundering. This problem was particularly likely to occur with exports from non-party states, but there were also instances when it was thought that stock apparently originating in one party state might have in fact originated in another, usually neighbouring, party state and thence been smuggled into a less restrictive country. The Scientific Authority for Animals were often able to help the management authority identify this abuse by pointing out that the known limits of distribution of some of the species involved ruled out their having originated in the exporting countries.

Sixth, there were large stocks of parts and derivatives and of live animals in various countries at the time the controls came into force. In some cases it has taken several years for these materials and animals to work through the trade. Stocks of legitimately held vicuna cloth are still in trade though no new vicuna wool is being imported. In the case of the Cayman Turtle Farm it has taken several years for pre-Convention stocks of animals to grow to a tradable size. With Ivory, Tortoise shell and antique Rhinoceros Horn it is likely that pre-Convention materials will remain in trade on a permanent basis as objets d'art are moved around the world. The Scientific Authority for Animals were not aware of any major attempt to abuse the concession allowing for the continued trade in pre-Convention stocks but it is obvious that care must be taken lest any attempt at such an abuse go undetected.

Seventh, the Scientific Authority for Animals was very concerned over the attitude of some medical scientists and research organisations over the use of primates. Frequently, applications were made to import Appendix I species as primary research animals, using the argument that the disease to be studied was such a scourge of humankind that import restrictions should be waived. The Scientific Authority for Animals did not consider it its duty to assess on the validity of the medical research, but it did consider it its duty to point out that if a rare species has a particular value to medical research then it is essential, lest an irreplaceable seed corn be consumed, that the animals are only taken from the wild to set up breeding colonies. Thus the research could continue using captive bred offspring, without further risk to the remnant wild population and without risking the future of the research should conservation efforts fail. Considerable progress in getting a better understanding on this point was made, but the Scientific Authority for Animals felt that there is still further ground to be gained before this threat to certain rare species, especially to some marmosets and tamarins, is completely removed.

The Scientific Authority for Animals has also had the duty of advising the Department of the Environment on desirable changes to the Appendices and the working practices of the Convention. The parties to the Convention (now numbering 68 ratified states) meet every two years. So far three meetings have been held: at Berne 1976, San Jose, Costa Rica 1979 and New Delhi in 1981. There was also a Special Working Session, lasting 8 days, in Geneva in 1977.

With the development of a common policy by E.E.C. member states in relation to endangered species, it had become increasingly clear to the Scientific Authority for Animals that the de facto appearance of an E.E.C. management policy should be paralleled (in accordance to the working of the Control of International Trade in Endangered Species Convention) by an E.E.C. scientific advisory panel.

With the transfer of the advisory function of the Scientific Authority for Animals to the Nature Conservancy Council under the Chairmanship of Dr. M.R. Brambell, who had succeeded Professor V.C. Wynne-Edwards as Chairman of the Scientific Authority for Animals in 1978, the outgoing Scientific Authority for Animals wishes to draw its successors' attention to the following points:

(a) The potentially damaging effect of the trinket trade in whole animal carcasses, parts and derivatives of immature specimens of endangered and vulnerable species; for example, the possible development of trade in birds' eggs, in stuffed baby turtles and baby crocodiles, etc.

(b) The furskins of several endangered species continue to be offered in trade, usually as single items, by some countries. This should be resisted wherever possible.

(c) The trophy trade involving stuffed whole specimens of birds and stuffed heads of larger animals creates a demand which may not be being met only by legally obtained animals.

(d) The falconry trade can not only lead to depletion of species of birds of prey already under threat for other reasons but can provide a cover for the taking of British native falcons.

(e) The control of trade in species which, in the opinion of the Scientific Authority for Animals, are benefitting from positive protection measures by the authorities in the exporting countries should be interpreted as the unnecessary inhibition of such trade, provided the exporting country clearly approves of such trade, with the Scientific Authority for Animals being satisfied with the reasons given and provided the products can be unequivocally identified.

The Scientific Authority for Animals as constituted as an advisory committee to the Secretary of State for the Environment, ceased to exist on 9th March, 1981 and its functions were transferred to the Nature Conservancy Council. This constituted the third major change in the execution of protective legislation for international wildlife since 1975. We earnestly hope that no further changes of such magnitude take place and that both the advisory and the executive arms can be given a chance to build up a body of expertise which would allow our country to remain in the forefront of such conservation.

Symp. zool. Soc. Lond. (1985) No. 54: 241–257

The World Conservation Strategy—an historical perspective

MARK HALLE

Conservation for Development Centre
IUCN
CH–1196 Gland, Switzerland

Synopsis

The increase in public support for conservation over the past decade poses an interesting dilemma for its practitioners. Conservationists have always derived what political influence they could muster by building up and serving a distinct constituency.
It is the expansion and diversification of this constituency over the last decade or so
that has begun to give conservation credibility in decision-making circles. But conservation must not be regarded as a discipline in its own right. Rather, there is a conservation dimension to all actions taken by society to transform and manage natural
resources in the interest of human well-being. Conservation's 'constituency base'
leads to conservationists being identified with nature lovers and renders it difficult
for them to enter the fray where their contribution is most needed and could have the
greatest effect. Yet, at the same time, expanding beyond this constituency base carries the risk of diluting its impact and dissipating the influence conservationists have
so painstakingly acquired.

Conservation is especially needed to affect development decisions in developing
countries where resources are being transformed at a more rapid pace and where the
checks and balances which limit environmental destruction are not as strong as they
are in most industrialized countries. In the poorer, more overcrowded developing
countries, sound social and economic development is a necessary precondition for
sustainable conservation. Without it, not even the most solid achievements will withstand the mounting pressure to exploit resources to meet immediate needs.

The World Conservation Strategy (WCS), launched in 1980 by IUCN, UNEP and
WWF, tries to bridge the unnecessary and counterproductive gap between conservation and development and, in so doing, brings conservation solidly into the main-
stream of social and economic development. The WCS sets the philosophical
framework for conservation within which the notions of maintenance (of biological
diversity and essential ecological services) and sustainability are introduced into
development. It aims to reinforce development achievements through forcing a
longer-term perspective on the planning of development activities.

The WCS also sets the agenda for priority actions in integrating conservation with
development. The most encouraging of these is the attempt, at the national level, to
translate the principles of the WCS into a solid programme of action. The development of National Conservation Strategies (NCS), now under way in over 20 developed and developing countries, is rapidly picking up momentum and promises to

ZOOLOGICAL SYMPOSIUM No. 54
ISBN 0–19–854002–7

show the way to the first comprehensive means of placing development on a sustainable footing.

Too many well-planned conservation activities fail in the long run because of problems 'upstream' over which the conservation sector has no control. The WCS and the development of NCSs aim to provide the fundamental framework within which all conservation and development activities can find their place.

The WCS is not a scientific document nor does its existence guarantee a broad consensus behind the principles it propounds. Yet, in a few short years, it has established its credentials as a major advance in conservation.

Introduction

We live in a period of inflation. The inflation touches not only our currencies, it affects the pace of change, the pace at which decisions must be made, the pace at which options are closed. It has also increased the pressure on science to prove its relevance to policy and to demonstrate its applicability. Nor is language immune from the inflationary trends; in the past decade or so, the world has been flooded by a proliferation of state-of-the-art reports, global action plans, strategies and blueprints—a whole literature aimed at finally coming to grips with the problems that beset us.

The World Conservation Strategy (IUCN 1980; Allen 1980), launched in 1980 by IUCN, with the participation and support of UNEP and World Wildlife Fund*, came at the height of this inflationary bubble. It was launched simultaneously in over a dozen countries around the world, in the presence of crowned heads, presidents, and prime ministers. It received the endorsement of a number of parliaments, including the European Parliament, and of several august world bodies, not the least of which was the United Nations General Assembly. Does it provide the long-awaited answer, or is it just another document, promoted with professional skill, packaged with imagination and timed to coincide with the swelling of a particularly significant enviromental wave?

This chapter seeks to demonstrate that, in conception and ambition, the World Conservation Strategy represents a true departure from traditional conservation and an ambitious if not yet fully realized approach to grappling with the fundamental problems of conservation in a way that offers significant promise for the future.

---

* The International Union for Conservation of Nature and Natural Resources (IUCN), founded in 1948 and with its secretariat in Switzerland, is the world's leading scientific conservation organization. IUCN is a Union of over 500 sovereign governments, government agencies and conservation organizations. The World Wildlife Fund (WWF) with which it shares international headquarters was founded in 1961 and has become the leading private body supporting conservation worldwide. The United Nations Environment Programme (UNEP) was founded in 1972 following the United Nations Conference on the Human Environment (Stockholm, June 1972). UNEP was designed as a small, flexible co-ordinating and catalytic agency whose mission is to stimulate environmental action within the UN system and among developing country governments. UNEP Headquarters are in Nairobi.

The conservation dilemma

If the 1970s were a period of inflation they were also commonly referred to as a period of transition. This can be attributed in part to a psychological accommodation to the ever more frightening pace of change. A period of transition suggests a period of stability before and after. My own illusions were shattered when a friend and colleague defined a period of transition as 'a period of time separating two other periods of transition'. Yet I believe history will show that the recent evolution of conservation has been truly remarkable, and that the past few years have seen the emergence of an awareness that current trends in resource use cannot be perpetuated without a collapse in our life-support systems and the attendant drop in our standard of living. We must, through whatever means, adapt the global use of resources to levels which these resources can sustain. All transition involves insecurity and suffering. But given the dangers of not adapting, conservation might well prove to be the most acceptable analgesic.

It is important to remember that the decision by IUCN's General Assembly to prepare a world conservation strategy came at a time when conservationists increasingly found themselves faced with a dilemma. This dilemma arises from the following: given the importance in all social and economic development of the wise use of natural resources and the maintenance of essential ecological services, conservationists can credibly argue that they should participate in decisions affecting major resource concerns; the conservation perspective is of obvious relevance in such decision-making. They can do so all the more credibly if they can demonstrate that the conservation position enjoys wide support among a clearly-identifiable constituency. At the same time, effective conservation action must be based on an intersectoral and multi-disciplinary approach and must strive for a delicate balance between a wide variety of different factors. However, by acting as a constituency—as a lobby—conservation runs the risk of finding itself labelled as a special interest, equivalent in political importance to perceived public support for the conservation cause. Clearly, conservationists must demonstrate that their perspective has broad relevance and central importance, and to do so they must speak from a platform which enjoys equally broad support. Yet to venture out from the safe confines of the conservation constituency and into the more treacherous realm of politics carries the risk of dissipating the constituency base through charges of 'selling out' and thereby reducing the claim to influence which a strong constituency can justify.

The 'special interest' approach should not be lightly dismissed; it has achieved notable success in some areas. Indeed, to bring about any major change in the way national policies are developed and implemented, a politically effective constituency is necessary. But to be politically effective, this constituency must base its claim for influence on a tangible programme of action. Without such a programme, 'there is no common denominator for that community of concern which makes for an effective constituency'. (L. K. Caldwell, unpublished). Thus for conservationists to make a real and lasting impact on the way decisions are reached, two conditions appear to be necessary—a powerful and identifiable constituency and a credible platform supporting the cause.

Conservation long ago met the first of these conditions. Most nature conservation organizations are club-like associations of the like-minded, who employ their leisure time in the pursuit of their interest in nature and use their force of numbers to promote their cause. Whether they are locally focused (on the model of community nature clubs), scientifically or sectorally based (like many zoological societies), or globally oriented (like IUCN and WWF), conservation societies have exhibited little variation in the essential motivation of their interests and actions.

This constituency base has also been used to good effect, and many conservation organizations have achieved significant success through lobbying and mobilizing public support for conservation issues. As a general rule, however, the conservation case will not win out over other, mostly economically-motivated political factors, which take undue precedence in an atmosphere of pressure and urgency and must be accommodated. The public can too easily be bought off by ritual lip-service paid to the conservation case, given 'the political importance of professed intentions, as contrasted with demonstrable economic and other results' (Sowell 1983).

The second condition, a credible action programme for the conservation case, formulated in terms that those with the responsibility for power could understand and appreciate, had not been met before the WCS was formulated. Until then, conservationists could seldom overcome the fact that decision makers prefer to deal with interests which they can clearly define and which are relatively harmless because they remain outside the confines of power. Attempts by conservationists to enter the corridors of power, even if accompanied by a willingness to share in the responsibilities of decision-making, were not well received. Those in power seldom appreciate sharing it with interlopers, and there was resistance to opening the doors to political change 'by incorporating various groups in society in an active participatory manner and hence raising their political expectations and making them more aware of their role in the social order' (O'Riordan 1981).

Governments and inter-governmental organizations

The attempt to broaden the base for decision-making is not exclusive to conservation or to other 'marginal' causes. It prevails also in government.

Complaints at the compartmentalization of government decision-making and at the impermeable walls between government departments are common. Fragmentation of decision-making, not surprisingly, discourages the close examination of interactions between sectors—the effect of agriculture on water resources, the effect of industrialization on human health; it also discourages an adequate focus on the long-term consequences of decisions taken today.

With the rapid growth in information available to the decision maker and with the growing understanding of the links between sectors, it is perhaps an understandable reaction to retreat into a clearly definable field and block out considerations which appear at first sight not to have central relevance or which are capable of being put off until later. One significant motivation behind the environmental movement of the 1970s was the desire to develop inter- or super- or trans-ministerial mechanisms for environmental action to reverse the disturbing trend toward increasing sub-division of decisions. Success was only partial.

Nor is the situation any happier on the inter-governmental scene. In the internationalist euphoria which took hold after the Second World War, governments enthusiastically responded to the recognition of the global nature of some problems by establishing international organizations—constituency by constituency. The World Health Organization provides the international forum for the world's ministers of health. FAO is the meeting place of the world's ministers of agriculture, forestry, and fisheries. UNESCO provides a platform for debate to ministers of education, culture and scientific research. At first this appeared to be a very effective model. With the pooling of information and expertise and the opportunity to share experience between nations, the world moved towards solution of some of its more intractable problems.

The success of WHO in eradicating smallpox is an excellent example of the results of global co-operation on a specific scale. But it is too often forgotten that eradication of smallpox required only a massive effort of organization. The prevalence of the disease was not irrevocably tied up with social problems of a more intractable nature, nor with cultural, religious or environmental problems which needed solving before the purely medical problem could be approached. The realization of the complex and interrelated nature of most development problems sent the international organizations exploring upstream, in search of the root causes of the problems whose effects they had diagnosed.

By the late 1960s, the enthusiasm for inter-governmental organizations had waned. It became apparent that the existing configuration of inter-governmental bodies, both within and outside the UN, dealt inadequately with questions of an inter-sectoral nature. The inter-governmental organizations are the international mirror of their constituent governments, so this is perhaps not suprising. But as cross-sectoral problems became increasingly pressing, it became clear that new approaches had to be found.

The solution, many of us thought, was global conferences focused on problems not adequately addressed by individual constituencies. These would concentrate attention on the topic in question to such an extent that it would take the necessary quantum leap in political importance without which the issues could not achieve the necessary support. The first and most successful of these conferences was the United Nations Conference on the Human Environment, held in Stockholm in 1972 (United Nations 1973). It was successful partly because the human environment was a long-neglected problem ripe for international attention. It was also a problem to which an adequate response required substantial international co-operation and action of an inter-sectoral nature. The 'spirit of Stockholm', recognized at the close of the conference, was genuine. Although 'spirits' tend now to be summoned forth at the end of each major global conference they are, like the conferences they close, subject to the law of diminishing returns.

However, despite the feeling that Stockholm had transcended institutional barriers, six months later (and with much misgiving), the Stockholm Action Plan was given over by the General Assembly to a new UN body. This body, the United Nations Environment Programme, was based on a sound idea—a light co-ordinating mechanism without extensive executive power, a brains-trust with sufficient funding to lubricate the sluggish UN machinery in the environment field. UNEP soon found what governments were finding in their own attempts to grapple institutionally with environmental problems—that light, co-ordinating mechanisms do not work without political power or substantial financial resources (Munro 1982). In the final analysis, the environmental constituency does not match up in political power or in purchasing power to the truly important sectors of the economy, such as agriculture, health, defence, and industry. The fact is that no-one wants to be co-ordinated by an outside body unless there is an acceptable trade-off. So UNEP began its long march towards the acquisition of greater executive powers, just as governments finally found themselves requiring ministries or departments of the environment which have taken their place in the jostle and rivalry for influence among government constituencies.

Subsequent UN conferences, though playing an important role, have tended to become increasingly dispirited. Most led to the establishment of a new inter-governmental bureaucracy—the 1974 Population Conference led to the UN Fund for Population Activities; the 1975 Conference on Women led to the establishment of an Under Secretary General post for Women's Affairs at UN Headquarters in New York, the 1976 UN Habitat Conference resulted in the foundation of the UN Centre on Human Settlements—each time over increasing resistance from the industrialized countries who support these institutions' budgets. Since then, if truth be told, most of these global mega-conferences have proved a disappointment. Yet international problems are still with us and the need for solutions is ever more urgent.

The development of modern conservation

The history of international conservation has followed a similar pattern and has suffered from some of the same constraints described above. The evolution of project activity within WWF and IUCN is characteristic of this trend. When WWF was established in 1961 to raise awareness and funding for urgent conservation activities world wide, its focus was on species and its approach expeditionary. Intrepid scientists ventured off to far corners of the world, studied rare species and formulated plans—usually the establishment of a protected area—to ensure their perpetuation. Save the Arabian Oryx, Save the Tiger, Save the Panda, became the familiar slogans of WWF's remarkably successful campaigns. Even the early non-species projects, often focused on land acquisition, reflected the contemporary approach to conservation. This was preservationist in spirit if not in reality, aimed at 'setting aside' representative samples of pristine natural beauty before it was too late. 'Before it was too late' reflects a sense of urgency, a sense of dedication which stimulated most conservationists in those days and which still does. It soon became evident, however, that species cannot be saved in the wild without their habitats and 'habitat conservation' took over as the watchword. Though more ecological, more broadly based and more realistic, this was nevertheless a preservationist approach to an urgent and still growing problem. Indeed, it focused on reversing or delaying the effects of problems rather than assessing and dealing with their causes.

An honest assessment of WWF/IUCN's accomplishments through the mid-1970s would conclude that many of their achievements, which appeared significant and gratifying at the time, carried within them the seeds of ultimate failure. Too often conservation was conceived as a holding action. But holding actions are no good unless action is also being taken or prepared against the cause of the problem. There is little value in even a successful conservation project whose achievements can be swept away by factors not remotely under the control of conservation practitioners.

Clearly, the conservation movement had to equip itself to affect the root causes of problems if it wanted real solutions. Like the international organizations, it had to paddle patiently upstream in the hope of convincing those in a position of influence that their actions often had unwanted consequences and that, with a little forethought and planning, these consequences could be avoided.

WWF/IUCN, the focus of whose action was in the developing world, had still another motivation for leaving their comfortable pattern of activity. Since Stockholm, it had become evident that the truly urgent, truly daunting environmental problems were those which arose from poorly planned development in the Third World. And in most developing countries, there was no conservation constituency to lobby for sound environmental planning in development programmes.

The Stockholm conference indeed marked a significant departure from the traditional perspective of enviromental problems. From an almost obsessive focus on pollution and the deterioration of environmental quality—problems particularly prevalent in industrial economies at an advanced stage of development—the focus began to shift to the more intractable problems of the deteriorating resource base in developing countries. Whereas the northern countries had tended to see environmental problems as one of the prices to be paid for a high standard of living, Stockholm demonstrated that the truly dramatic environmental problems were often inevitable unless sustainable patterns of development could be accelerated or misguided development corrected.

The question became, how to affect the pattern of development in developing countries to ensure that it promoted achievements which were sustainable? The obvious first place to look was at the contributions made by the rich countries to development through their aid programmes. In seeking to attribute responsibility for the negative environmental impacts of some development activities, development aid and financing organizations were singled out for particular attention (Stein & Johnson 1979; CIDIE 1980). While governments and the private sector in developing countries, and even multinational corporations, generally invest a great deal more in development activities than do development assistance programmes, the activities of the latter have a demonstration effect whose importance far outweighs the monetary value of their contributions. In addition, aid programmes are answerable to the public at home for the impact of their projects abroad. They are thus susceptible to lobbying pressure which, if applied directly in the receiving developing countries, would have little effect.

With conservation achievements increasingly being negated by development projects aimed at exploiting or modifying the very habitats that conservationists were trying to preserve, it became evident that the solution to conservation problems lay not solely in raising and spending ever more conservation funding on priority projects, but in finding ways to affect the vastly greater resources spent by development aid organizations and through national budgets. A marginal improvement in the conservation viability of development aid expenditures could have a significantly greater effect than a doubling or tripling of conservation expenditure by the small community supporting international conservation action.

The World Conservation Strategy

But how are we to influence the way development assistance is planned, to affect the way national budgets are put together and apportioned; how do we gain the ear of those who, at a high level, set the pace for development thinking? This subject was debated within IUCN and brought to its General Assembly in Kinshasa in 1975 (IUCN 1976). The resultant debate led to a decision to draft the World Conservation Strategy. At the same time, it triggered off what has become one of the fundamental debates in conservation, because the World Conservation Strategy meant a deliberate step away from constituency-based conservation. While this clearly involved the risk of dissipating the conservation lobby it offered other benefits.

For one thing, the WCS is the product of a very diverse constituency. The document represents a consensus on the part of its three sponsors—IUCN, with its global scientific constituency, UNEP with its governmental membership and WWF with its strong links to the business world. Every effort has been made to ensure the continuation of this valuable partnership which, supported by the whole range of organizations and governments who subsequently endorsed the WCS, provides a powerful statement on the importance of conservation and its links with development.

Far from being an encyclopaedic work, the World Conservation Strategy is concise, to-the-point and, perhaps most surprising, engagingly written. In 20 double-page sections, it sets forth the broad objectives of conservation and the priority requirements to meet these objectives. It then examines the priorities for action at the national level, in particular the need to support sustainable development through strategic planning of resource use, legislation, training, research and education. Finally, it draws attention to critical conservation issues whose solution requires international co-operation. The World Conservation Strategy symbolizes the renaissance of conservation and boldly offers itself to public judgement as a new departure for conservation. But to what extent does it justify so grandiose a designation? Was the title chosen to carve out a niche in the shrinking attention span of the public? The authors of the World Conservation Strategy knew very well the risks they were taking. In abandoning the safe confines of conservation's special interests they focused very hard on how to give their message a chance of being well received.

The World Conservation Strategy approaches this in four ways:

1. It aims at a *broader audience*. Too much conservation literature is aimed at the traditional conservation public. It is designed to reinforce, encourage, and console those in whom the conservation belief is solidly implanted, to inspire those wavering on the edge and, most important, to enlist those who did not realize that they are 'closet conservationists'. It is, by and large, a matter of total indifference to the far broader constituency

for whom conservation is not a central concern. Thus, to succeed, the strategy had to penetrate and achieve an impact where decisions are taken. Although conservation cannot entirely be expressed on a rate-of-return basis, conservationists must learn to express their concerns in terms familiar to planning boards and treasury ministries. Without that, conservation will never be more than marginal.

2. In order to reach these select audiences it was necessary to agree on a new *vocabulary*, on a new semantics of conservation. The authors, in addressing themselves to a wider, perhaps less sympathetic audience faced the challenge of prescibing change to those not yet convinced that change is necessary or desirable, without losing their readers in a backlash against more 'bad news'. Conservation concerns had to be expressed in terms the decision-makers could appreciate and understand and in terms that they could use, once convinced, to persuade their peers of the validity of conservation arguments. This entailed examining many of the tenets accepted as basic by conservationists. Expressing the whys and wherefores of conservation principles regarded as self-evident finally involved understanding what motivates decision-makers, what allows them to respond effectively and successfully to the short-term pressures, political and otherwise, to which they are subjected.

3. The WCS had to *elevate the target*. Conservationists were no longer arguing for increased support to its sectoral interests. They were no longer arguing simply for the maintenance of a species or the protection of a habitat. Instead they offered a subtler, riskier perhaps, but infinitely more sensible bargain. Conservation—the maintenance of biological diversity and essential ecological services and sustainability of resource use over the long term—must become part and parcel of planning and development.

4. Finally, conservation arguments increasingly had to become *quantifiable*. In a world increasingly impatient of subtle arguments, ever more inclined towards the path of least political resistance, a variety of shorthands have replaced the careful construction of a case for or against a position. Even among those who are inclined to recognize that one cannot indefinitely run an economy headlong against the resource base on which its continued viability depends, the pressure of the 'bottom line' has taken precedence over a range of concerns, ethical and cultural, which once played an important part in the balance of decisions. Conservation had to prove its relevance in the field of numbers. Conservation arguments capable of expression in the terms of cost/benefit analysis stand a chance of acceptance. Arguments which rely on awakening a moral conscience in those responsible for delivering development benefits cannot be accorded much hope of success.

I believe the WCS succeeds in these aims and does so without selling conservation out to development. It is important that conservation does not become too hard-nosed, does not accept many of the pressures which make traditional decision-making so unsatisfactory. Conservation must never lose the sense of awe, the sense of respect for life, and the firm sense that it is there because it has its place. The ethical, religious, and cultural sides of conservation are essential, but in today's world these considerations seldom play a very important part at decision time, when other considerations can bring in far more votes. Still, these can always be appreciated as a bonus; if conservation can establish a footing by arguing its case in terms of numbers, the other concerns can serve to consolidate the case.

The WCS was by and large well received. Negative comments came from traditional preservationists—on the grounds of selling out to the enemy—and from committed pessimists, cynical of the upbeat and optimistic tone which the WCS adopts. For the latter, in any event, there is nothing to be done. Corruption, population growth, indifference, and a whole army of other intractable problems will negate even the best-laid plans.

Other critics suggested that the WCS failed to address the single greatest conservation issue—the uncontrolled expansion of the human population. Perhaps this point is valid. Yet the WCS, focusing as it does on the role of living natural resources in sustainable development, recognizes that it does not begin to address the agenda of problems which must be solved if humanity is to develop on a sound, harmonious basis. It does not deal, for example, with the imbalance in trade flows, the use or misuse of international financial instruments, the consequence of military activity and increasing militarization, nor with many other issues which actually or potentially have a significant effect on the ability of the environment to sustain society. As such, the WCS can be regarded as a starting point, an attempt to sketch out in broad terms the action required to move resource exploitation onto a sustainable basis.

Does the WCS obviate the need for well-targeted conservation action aimed at specific problems? Certainly not. Such action must continue and indeed accelerate, but unless there is some means of influencing the way decisions are taken on the broader scale, these actions will have no assurance of achieving lasting benefits.

The World Conservation Strategy is a global blueprint and operates on common denominators. It is intended to serve first and foremost those countries where attention to problems is most urgent. It is intended to be used not only by governments in these countries but also by those who work with governments—development assistance agencies, conservation societies, etc. The WCS states the principles on which modern conservation is based and demonstrates that, fundamentally, conservation and development have the same long-term ambitions. Both stress the management of the resource base for long-term human well-being.

The WCS focuses on identifying priority actions, internationally and nationally. The priority international actions—attention to tropical forests, to the global commons, to the need for international conservation legislation, to the conservation of genetic diversity—have, by and large, made their way to the top of international development agendas and they continue to be followed up in a variety of ways by a variety of actors. The WCS serves to set action in these areas in context.

National Conservation Strategies

To demonstrate the impact that the WCS has on decision making regarding *national* development, it is interesting to follow the evolution of the dialogue between IUCN and developing countries with regard to implementation of the WCS. Since the launch of the WCS, IUCN has focused on developing the ability to respond to requests from developing countries who believe the WCS can point the way to ensuring the sustainability of their development investments but need advice on how to proceed.

Part of IUCN's response has been the establishment of the Conservation for Development Centre which, guided by the WCS, aims to achieve lasting development benefits through the application of sound conservation principles to development, working principally with the development funding organizations. Second, with funding from World Wildlife Fund and, increasingly, from a variety of bilateral and multilateral development assistance agencies, IUCN has developed the capability to assist developing countries in formulating their own National Conservation Strategies (NCSs) (IUCN, 1984) (see Table I).

Table I. An overview of National Conservation Strategy development (May 1984)

Australia	Inaugural meeting of Interim Consultative Committee held on 7 February 1984.
Belize	Initial NCS report completed and Phase II project under consideration. Project development mission planned for August.
Canada	Review of WCS completed and responsibilities for implementation of WCS assigned in Government.
Czechoslovakia	Sub-national strategy under preparation.
Fiji	Framework for NCS developed in collaboration with IUCN.
Honduras	Development of NCS discussed at national seminar.
India	Preliminary meetings on NCS development held.
Indonesia	National Conservation Plan (limited scope) developed by FAO in collaboration with Government. Further strategy work currently being considered by Government.
Italy	Draft NCS document expected to be completed in 1984.
Ivory Coast	Preliminary NCS report completed for Government's consideration. IUCN mission to Ivory Coast planned for summer 1984 to develop work plan and pilot projects.

Madagascar	National Commission set up by decree to develop NCS outline by July 1984. IUCN mission planned for June 1984.
Malaysia	Four state conservation strategies completed by WWF-Malaysia. Review meeting planned.
Mexico	Promotion of WCS principles in work of national organisations to follow June 1983 launch of WCS.
Nepal	Draft NCS 'Prospectus' published. Phase II to begin in summer 1984.
Netherlands	WCS review completed and study being undertaken to review national/international policies with regard to WCS.
New Zealand	Draft NCS under preparation.
Norway	Study completed by Ministry of Environment containing proposal for NCS.
Pakistan	IUCN mission visited Pakistan November–December 1983 and drew up proposal for NCS. Follow-up expected later in 1984.
Philippines	NCS document published in February 1984 at end of Phase I. Phase II expected to start later in 1984.
Portugal	Development of NCS under review by new environment foundation.
Senegal	Phase I report submitted to Government in May 1984. Follow-up talks between Government and IUCN expected in October.
Seychelles	Government has largely completed background work and has been in discussion with IUCN for further work. Mission planned for autumn 1984.
South Africa	NCS completed by Wildlife Society of Southern Africa.
Spain	NCS draft completed by Inter-Ministerial Commission on the Environment.
Sri Lanka	NCS being prepared by National Task Force.
Thailand	Early form of NCS developed by National Environment Board with IUCN and UNEP.
Uganda	NCS Phase I proposal endorsed by Government. Phase II to start in summer 1984.
United Kingdom	Agencies involved in NCS (Nature Conservancy Council, Countryside Commission for Scotland and Countryside Commission) have asked for meeting with ministers to discuss programme.
Zaire	Government working on preliminary framework with FAO assistance.
Zambia	Phase II currently in progress.
Zimbabwe	Plan of Action completed with establishment of technical Steering Committee to develop strategy.

Perhaps the most fundamental objective of the NCS process is to increase the time perspective of planning, to redress the automatic precedence given to short-term considerations in the balance of decision-making (Weiss 1983). NCSs also aim to provide countries with a mechanism for choosing among competing demands on the same resource. For example, forests are often regarded as stands of timber, but may also play a role in microclimate, in regulating the hydrological cycle and in maintaining genetic diversity of important wildlife species in addition to any amenity value they may have.

Mangroves may have considerable value as firewood; but they may also serve as commercially important fish nurseries, as an effective means of coastal erosion control and as a barrier against tropical storms which claim thousands of lives each year. Each sector can evaluate the importance of a resource in terms of its own requirements but, by and large, governments do not have an effective means of adjudicating between competing demands, direct and indirect, on the same resource when some of these demands are realized by exploitation and others by conservation (Hardin 1982).

In addition, the NCS process aims to stimulate an effective debate between the different sectors making demands on the same resources or whose demand for one resource affects the status of another. In every government, there are several agencies involved in any one resource sector and implementing every resource policy. In the case of forestry, for example, there are many agencies and institutions, governmental and non-governmental, 'other than the central forest administration, that are—or ought to be—concerned with the implementation of forest policy: planning ministries, regional planning boards, environmental agencies, water boards and water conservation authorities, river basin development boards, wildlife and game departments, parks services, agrarian reform institutions, land settlement boards, rural development commissions, industrial development corporations, forest industries—public and private, municipalities, highway authorities, power companies, railways and mines' and many more (Westoby 1983).

The NCS also provides a mechanism for determining which among the many actions needed for conservation have the greatest priority. The environmental impact assessment carried out for the major Senegal river basin development projects, for example, formulated almost 100 recommendations (Gannet, Fleming Inc. & ORGATEC 1980). The recommendations may be well thought out and worthwhile but, at a realistic costing, their implementation would require many times the budget available to the countries involved. Which, then, are central, without which the development projects will be heading for serious problems in the future? Which are also important but can be left to a second stage? And which, while also worth pursuing if opportunity permits, are not fundamental to the success of the scheme? Few countries have objective ways of deciding.

Finally, the NCS stresses the identification of *practical alternatives* to current destructive practices. It is far easier to diagnose problems and to set them within their socio-economic or ecological context than it is to find realistic ways of dealing with them. The NCS approaches this by trying to answer three sets of questions:

First, what is the resource base on which the country's development is based? Which of these resources are being exploited beyond their capacity to regenerate and which are under-exploited? What is the potential of these resources on their own or through the income their export can generate to support the country's development ambitions?

Second, what are the pressures on resources which are leading to their being exploited unsustainably? These pressures can arise from a variety of causes—population pressure, the absence of suitable legislation, the absence of a conservation constituency, lack of government commitment, lack of trained personnel.

Third, what are the steps that can be taken to remove the obstacles to sustainable utilization of natural resources and thus return resource-use to a sustainable footing?

While the thinking behind the NCS approach can be understood and appreciated, it is not always clear what one should expect the final outcome to be. Suggestions of yet another ambitious national plan, another expensively produced document, often lead to the understandable objection that what is required is action on the ground rather than more analysis and debate. If the document itself were the end result, this would be a legitimate objection. With national strategies it is the *process* rather than the product which is important. The document itself has an educational and symbolic value. The real test of the strategy is the extent to which conservation has been integrated with national development. Indeed, there could be no more satisfactory outcome to an NCS project than if the five-year national development plan served as the first stage in the Action Plan for its implementation.

Conclusion

The World Conservation Strategy, at the opening of its conclusion, states 'development and conservation operate in the same global context, and the underlying problems that must be overcome if either is to be successful are identical' (IUCN 1980). NCSs, the reflection of the WCS in action at the national level, bear this out. The national strategy process aims to overcome many of the obstacles to sound conservation action which led to the formulation of WCS in the first place. It brings the notion of sustainability into development. It promotes interministerial communication and it establishes the agenda for development assistance in contributing to development which, at long last, has a chance to be sustainable.

It would be arrogant to declare that, with the World Conservation Strategy, the conservation community has finally hit upon the ultimate solution. The NCS approach, while it has developed considerable momentum, is still new. We are still feeling our way in the dark. In a short period of time, the NCS approach has gained considerable acceptability for the World Conservation Strategy and its principles, but it is too early to say how deep its penetration is and how lasting its effects will be. The test will be to see whether future development plans and future development decisions are more conscious of the need to be environmentally sustainable, whether conservation concerns and the wisdom of taking the longer perspective on human action can overcome political pressure to sell out in favour of short-term political expediency.

The World Conservation Strategy has provided legitimacy for conservation's place among the more 'serious' human concerns. It has earned acceptability for conservation among those responsible for taking fundamental decisions on the future of societies. Its translation to the national level through development of NCSs has demonstrated that the precepts of the WCS are relevant even when tested in real-life situations. Increasingly, national strategies are providing the framework within which priorities can be identified, linkages between sectors determined, the planning of lasting conservation achievements made realistic. They do not replace traditional conservation action but supplement it and, I believe, in doing so, constitute perhaps the most significant advance in conservation of these past decades.

References

Allen, R. (1980). *How to save the world.* Kogan Page, London.

Caldwell, Lynton K. (Unpublished). *Political aspects of ecologically sustainable development.* (Paper read to the World Council for the Biosphere, Delhi, India, 1–6 June, 1984.)

Committee of International Development Institutions on the Environment (CIDIE) (1980). *The declaration of environmental policies and procedures relating to economic development.* (Declaration established by CIDIE and signed in New York on 1 February 1980 and by the African Development Bank on 10 June 1981.)

Gannet, Fleming Inc. & ORGATEC (1980). *Effets sur l'environnement des aménagements prévus dans le bassin du fleuve Sénégal.* Gannet, Fleming Inc., USA.

Hardin, Garrett. (1982). *Sentiment, guilt, and reason in the management of wild herds. Cato J.* **2**: 823–33.

International Union for Conservation of Nature and Natural Resources (1976). *Proceedings of the 12th Session of the General Assembly of IUCN, Kinshasa, Zaïre, 8–18 September, 1975.* IUCN, Gland, Switzerland.

International Union for Conservation of Nature and Natural Resources (1980). *World conservation strategy: Living resource conservation for sustainable development.* (In cooperation with the World Wildlife Fund and the United Nations Environment Programme.) IUCN, Gland, Switzerland.

International Union for Conservation of Nature and Natural Resources (1984). *National conservation strategies — A framework for sustainable development.* IUCN/Conservation for Development Centre, Gland, Switzerland.

Munro, Robert D. (1982). Twenty years after Stockholm: Past achievements and future prospects. *Mazingira* **6** (1): 46–57.

O'Riordan, Timothy (1981). Problems encountered when linking environmental management to development aid. *Environmentalist* **1**: 15–24.

Sowell, Thomas (1983). Second thoughts about the Third World. *Harper's Mag.* **267** (1602): 34–42.

Stein, Robert E. & Johnson, Brian (1979). *Banking on the biosphere: Environmental procedures and practices of nine multilateral development agencies.* Lexington Books, D.C. Heath and Company, Lexington, USA.

United Nations (1973). *Report of the United Nations Conference on the human environment, Stockholm 5–16 June, 1972.* A/CONF. 48/14/Rev.1. New York, United Nations.

Weiss, Edith Brown (1983). Principles for resolving conflicts between generations over new natural resources. *Mazingira* **7** (2): 45–56.

Westoby, Jack C. (1983). Correspondence and comment. *Commonw. For. Rev.* **62**: 140–6.

Symp. zool. Soc. Lond. (1985) No. 54: 259–268

Conservation and natural resource development

J. R. SANDBROOK

*International Institute for Environment
and Development
3–4 Endsleigh Street
London WC1H 0DD*

Synopsis

This chapter begins with a short summary of the efforts to put the World Conservation Strategy into effect in Britain. It concentrates on the component of the United Kingdom Conservation for Development plan that deals with Britain's overseas environmental policy. The author explains that no such policy is available as a written piece, but existing components and gaps can be identified.

The chapter briefly comments upon the components that have been reviewed against the objectives of the WCS: the United Kingdom's posture with respect to the UN and its agencies, the European Community and the United Kingdom aid programme.

The conclusion is that the United Kingdom has a wealth of expertise and experience to offer world-wide in the management of natural resources, but does not place special emphasis upon promoting it or upon a policy framework for it. Indeed in many instances one can see a declining interest and wasted opportunities.

The United Kingdom is not a special case, but typical of most OECD states. The chapter briefly reviews some of the reasons for this, concentrating upon the attitude of economic planners and environmental scientists. Putting the two together is seen as the priority. The chapter also admits to the growing hopelessness of the task as human population and material aspirations grow at an exponential rate. Conservation linked to development is set out as the ideal solution.

In order to illustrate what could be done the chapter takes the management of the world's uncultivated lands and the forests within that category as a case in point. The present pressures on forest lands are briefly reviewed and the components of a policy needed to address the pressures are outlined. These include development as well as conservation goals.

The final section of the chapter reiterates the major conclusions of the United Kingdom foreign environmental policy review.

Introduction

The *World conservation strategy* (WCS) published in 1980 by the International Union for Conservation of Nature and Natural Resources (IUCN) with assistance from the United Nations Environment Programme and the

ZOOLOGICAL SYMPOSIUM No. 54
ISBN 0–19–854002–7

World Wildlife Fund, was a watershed in the crusade for conservation. For the first time, two of the world's leading conservation partners, WWF and IUCN, illustrated why conservation efforts must be integrated with economic development goals. The chosen objectives—the preservation of the world's life support systems, the protection of habitat and species and the sustainable use by man of renewable and non-renewable resources were highlighted together in a compelling and readable tract, the *World conservation strategy*.

In the UK the conservation movement responded in 1982/83—with a much longer but no less valuable piece, *The conservation and development programme for the UK* (1983). Sadly the UK publication was not as much of a breakthrough as the architects of it had hoped. Its scope was broad and unfocused. As a result it did not really help in establishing a new consensus between the driving forces of development, the wealth creators, and the conservation community. But it was a valiant first effort to cover the whole ground of environment and development issues in the UK. Work on putting its recommendations into effect continues.

In the UK exercise, the author, together with an experienced review group, addressed what the UK is doing, and perhaps could do in addition, to advance natural resource conservation outside our own national boundaries. They took as their subject the UK's overseas environmental policy; or at least the notion of it, since a policy set out as a single document clearly does not exist. The paper audited or reviewed all aspects of government activity overseas, save trade policy, that have a bearing on environmental questions. It did this against the WCS objectives. In so doing it sought clear answers to a number of critical questions. For example:

Is there a coherent and positive UK approach towards the major environmental actors within the UN system? (e.g. UNEP, FAO, UNESCO).

Is there a coherent and positive policy for the component parts of the Institutions of the European Economic Community that affect the environment? (e.g. the Directorate General of the Commission for Environment (DG11) and for Development (DG8)).

Does our bilateral aid programme pursue the objectives of the WCS in any overt or even hidden way?

Is the UK's academic community encouraged to apply its knowledge and experience around the globe in pursuit of WCS objectives? What of training overseas students to the same ends?

What account does private enterprise take of environmental questions when investing overseas?

Could the non-governmental community do more to help overseas?

The report sets out detailed answers to these questions but in summary it is sad to report that on all counts little emphasis upon environmental factors, or more particularly upon conservation, was found.

This is not to suggest that the UK has any direct responsibility for what goes on overseas. The jurisdiction of this nation ends at the edge of its exclusive economic zone. But the UK belongs to that half of the world that is rich in terms of science, institutions and experience as well as relative material wealth. From this position we could, as a nation, do much for the cause of conservation worldwide.

The northern response

The UK should not be singled out as a 'villain'. The lack of emphasis it puts upon conservation outside its national borders is pretty typical of the rest of the industrialized world. Both the UK and its OECD partners appear to place a low priority upon the work of the United Nations agencies in general. Within that position sound natural resource management as a fundamental part of development counts for even less. There are some notable exceptions, but no one can be surprised to find the Minister of Overseas Development saying in response to the WCS paper that environment is much like so many other demands upon him—the plight of women, appropriate technology, human rights, etc.

Such words do not matter very much, but the policy that follows does. For example, at a time of government cuts two years ago the Centre for Overseas Pest Research, the Land Resources Development Centre, and other relevant agencies supported by the Overseas Development Administration (ODA) were cut back more severely than any norm would indicate (House of Commons, 1983). So what is it that is inhibiting both the priority of conservation and the integration of long-term natural resource planning into international development concern in this and most other countries? The author would single out three major factors which, for the sake of brevity, are titled: blind economists, inhibited scientists, and growing poverty.

Economic planners, by and large, fail to take the environmental disbenefits of development into account—not only in the obvious areas of industrial development leading to pollution, or forest clearance leading to habitat loss, but also in subtle areas such as energy-intensive agriculture (with its concomitant costs in terms of excessive use of pesticides leading to pest resistance) or the construction of high dams (leading to the displacement of people who in turn over-use the renewable resources of the catchment area. Time and again this has led to soil erosion and ultimately to a worthless dam.)

The economists of the ODA, the World Bank, UNDP, etc. often do not address these obvious environmental impacts at a project level. They never address them in the confused world of large-scale economic intervention—where, for example, a single condition imposed on a country by the IMF can lead to massive shifts in agriculture toward cash cropping. All too often this leads to driving peasants off their traditional lands toward marginal and highly vulnerable ecosystems. In short, economists do not talk to natural scientists enough when drawing up their priorities and plans.

But scientists often do not want to talk to economists. The pursuit of academic excellence inhibits scientists from helping to evaluate the obvious.

The deficit in scientific and management skills now required world-wide where development is occurring is enormous. The disciplines required are very diverse but are applied, not pure, science in character. An understanding of the natural systems that are being changed is fundamental—taxonomy, field ecology, systems dynamics. This needs to be followed by the design of systems to minimize or at least contain adverse impacts. Mobilizing the available applied scientific skills needed to achieve sustainable, that is environmentally sensitive development has not begun on any significant scale in this or other Western states.

However, the social and natural scientists have a clear excuse. The greatest threat to the world's natural resources is occurring where no real development is taking place at all. Rapidly growing human populations are increasingly causing irreversible damage to nature in a totally unplanned way. For example, only some 4 per cent of the world's forest lands in the so-called developing world come under any formal management at all. The rest are subject to a random walk to destruction. In effect the major agent of environmental damage is not development but poverty linked to growing populations. As the World Conservation Strategy suggests, so-called environmentalists and developmentalists should be on the same side.

It is the author's thesis that bringing the economic planner more directly into contact with the environmental sciences would greatly assist in overcoming the major problem—poverty. To illustrate the point the author has chosen to discuss the world's cultivated lands, on the basis of unpublished material of Professor Duncan Poore and David Burns (colleagues at the International Institute for Environment and Development (IIED)), and the work of John Spears, senior forestry adviser to the World Bank (J. Spears pers. comm.).

The southern need—forest lands as a priority

The world's uncultivated lands cover about 80 per cent of the Earth's surface. A small part is barren, near the poles, in the high mountains and in the true deserts; but the majority is forest or has been forest and could bear tree cover once again.

The exact circumstances of almost every country are special to that country. Global totals and averages may be valuable in galvanizing public and political attention, but they are often not helpful in looking for solutions. Generalization cannot, however, be avoided in the confines of this brief chapter.

Generally speaking, the position of forests in temperate and boreal zones is fairly satisfactory. They account for 45 per cent of the remaining forest cover of the globe. Their management is not leading to site deterioration and the institutions responsible for them are robust and flexible enough to respond to changing circumstances. A cloud has appeared on the horizon with the dieback in European forests, attributed to acid precipitation, but in most countries, the challenge for the future is to reconcile production from the forest with the use of this same land to provide for recreation, and to do so in such a way that it retains its value as landscape and as habitat for wild plants and animals.

The situation is very different in the rest of the world. Here the area of forest is declining: in many countries it is almost gone; in most it is under great pressure; while a fortunate few have large reserves of forest and can afford to use their forest lands in provident manner, if they choose to do so. The pressures will increase, as world population tends towards six billion people by the end of the century.

Much has been written about the rate of disappearance of tropical forests and the proportion of animal species they contain. But more important than the figures are the processes and what can be done to divert these in less harmful directions.

The main agents of change are agricultural expansion and the extraction of wood. These vary between two extremes. Where the population is low and the forest resource abundant, timber is creamed or the forest is opened up to plantation cash crops—both to provide a springboard for economic development. At the other extreme, where resources are scarce and populations are growing rapidly, forest goes to provide land for the landless and the remaining uncultivated land is degraded by overuse for grazing, fuel wood and construction wood. Each of these processes has its own economic, social and ecological characteristics. One is a result of positive development, the other a result of poverty. A colleague has described them as 'runaway' and 'treadmill' deforestation respectively. There is every gradation between—and they may be combined with all kinds of geographical circumstances, political systems, and alternative sources of development capital (from oil, mining, and so on).

The most acute problems occur in those countries with a rapidly growing population and with a long history of de-vegetation; countries which have been described as being 'in a stable state of completed erosion'. Here recovery requires a relaxation of pressures on the overused land and this has proved socially and politically very difficult to attain.

The situation in relation to industrial wood (positive development) is serious enough, but that of fuel wood (treadmill development) is dramatically worse. To quote figures given by John Spears of the World Bank Forestry Department, he considers that in 16 years' time, 27 countries will be able to sustain their domestic and industrial wood requirements from the remaining areas of natural forest; 12 will have established sufficient plantations to do so. But in contrast, what he calls a 'medium' deficit situation will exist in 46 countries and there will be a further 10 where the climate is unsuitable for rain-fed forestation. In the case of fuel wood, 18 have enough natural forest area, 21 are considered satisfactory and one (Korea) has assured its supply by re-forestation. In contrast there is a medium fuel wood deficit in 29 countries and an acute deficit in 25. When one links this with shortage of agricultural land and rising population, it is evident that the forces leading to land degradation are immense.

What is perhaps most serious is what is not happening. The process of deforestation, after all, is only that which is already complete in many industrialized countries.

For example, only a small proportion of the clearance for agriculture is planned. Most is spontaneous, has little regard for the quality or fragility of the site, and often fails. Even planned settlement is often not successful. The resettlement of over half the 250 000 families moved from Java has been a failure owing to poor soil, flooding, or soil damage caused by mechanical land clearance. New agriculture can only succeed for certain where survey, method of land clearance, agricultural systems, and later management are all appropriate and continuance is assured. These conditions are very rarely met.

To repeat one of the most alarming statistics of a recent FAO study (Lanly, 1982), only 4.4 per cent of tropical forest is under any kind of management plan, however rudimentary, and three-quarters of this is in India. Plantations might reduce the pressure; but tropical plantations still amount to only 18 million ha—1 ha being planted for every 10 destroyed per annum.

The consequences of these trends towards degradation (incidentally, in the arid regions and mountains as well as in the tropical forest) are that the sustainable production of the forest is lost, often with no commensurate gain to agriculture. The soil reserve built up by the forest is dissipated; the damage caused by erosion, floods, and water shortage can be immense, and the genetic pool is dissipated.

In contrast to the very small areas under management or plantation, the record of national parks and reserves appears quite good: 42 million ha in all in tropical moist forest. Active surveys are under way to identify the best areas for expanding this total. There is, however, a great reluctance to reserve parts of the productive lowland forest, which are biologically the richest. The areas selected often prove too small to be viable when surrounded by totally alien land use. Moreover, parks have often been established without the collaboration and understanding of local people, who seldom benefit from them and are often antagonistic toward them.

Why this failure?

Why then have forest policies failed? Among the reasons are these:

(i) The causes of deforestation and misuse of the forest usually lie outside the forest—national economic goals, and policies for population, energy, agriculture, trade, etc. The solutions therefore lie outside the forest too. This is the economist's problem.

(ii) Basic to some of the difficulties would seem to be the economic theory which underlies decisions made about forest resources. These place no value on an unexploited forest, do not recognize the build-up of capital in re-establishing forest on deforested land, and underestimate the costs of transferring capital from one form—the standing forest—to another such as industrial plant.

It is trite, but nonetheless true, to say that you cannot build a forest in a day or a year: on the steep slopes and rain-washed, lateritic soils of many parts of the tropics, you may never be able to do it at all. So it should be recognized that a planning decision to shift national capital from forest to field or from forest to factory is a very serious, often irreversible decision, deserving very careful reflection.

For countries that want to make the take-off into sustained industrial growth, there can be no doubt that converting natural, forest capital into fuel, raw materials and fertile land is an obvious route. Many northern industrialized countries did this in the 13th century. In Western Europe, for example, an iron smelter fired by charcoal consumed $25m^3$ of stacked wood to produce 50 kg of iron, and could clear forest to a radius of 1km in 40 days. The iron in turn was used in ploughshares, bringing with it substantially higher agricultural yields. This transfer of capital from forest to field lasted until a new form of energy, coal, was able to replace charcoal in the forges.

But the risks of this kind of development are enormous. Development becomes a race between the depletion of natural resources with primitive technologies and the creation thereby of enough wealth to substitute the resource-conserving technologies. The ruins of civilizations as far-flung as the Yucatan, Mauritius, and Mesopotamia are there to show what the risks involve: what happens to a resource-depleting development if the technological innovations are not forthcoming.

One of the most rapid rates of forest degradation in the world has occurred in the last 20 years in the Ivory Coast; land has been cleared for cash-cropping of coffee, cocoa and fruit; extraction of timber has been the largest export industry, rendering the Ivory Coast the largest exporter of timber in Africa. This, too, has been something of a race: it has been calculated that for every cubic metre of wood extracted by the Ivorian timber industry, $4.5m^3$ have been destroyed by agricultural clearance. As so often, large-scale land clearance has not been integrated with the forest industry. In any case, Ivory Coast has reached a point of no return. The exhaustion of the most valuable species set in in the mid-1970s, and a process of progressive exhaustion of less valuable species has commenced. Fire, responsible for major damage to the cocoa and coffee plantations in early 1983, ensures in the average dry season that forest regeneration does not occur. In the last few years, droughts have crippled the country's electricity supply, a severe setback to this hitherto successful development experience. But whether take-off in terms of fuel substitution, import-led technical innovation, and industrialization is occurring or not, Ivory Coast has reached the end of this particular runway. There is precious little forest left to gamble with.

The transfer of capital from forest to field or from forest to factory has probably always been carried out wastefully. It may in some cases be reversible. But we should not pretend that it has been a conscious, planned development strategy. This would hardly be possible: very few national planners in Asia, Africa or Latin America can have had the opportunity to use a sensible estimate of the total economic value of forests to the nation. Even if some hard-working economist in the Forestry Department has gone to the trouble of making such an estimate, it is most unlikely that he will have mustered the political clout to get it on to the national economic planner's desk. For example, the problem received its first proper airing in the Ivory Coast in 1974, by which time the area of closed forest had already declined from 12 million to 5 million ha in the space of 18 years. For most national planners in the developing world the problem they have to address is how to control the transfer of forest capital so that a part goes to the satisfaction of basic needs, a part is managed as a viable and valuable natural resource, and a part goes to build up economic capital as a motor for agricultural and industrial development.

The need to integrate environment with development concerns

Thus we need to integrate social, economic and environmental factors to arrive at a more conserving style of development. This is the challenge for the governments of the Third World. And they need help. A handful of people are now wrestling with the issues. Foremost among then is Professor Conway of Imperial College. In a public lecture at Imperial College in

March 1984 (Conway, in press) he set out the thesis that good natural resources development should be:

Productive: giving a high yield over time.

Stable: giving a constant yield over time in the face of small disturbances caused by normal climatic and other environmental variables.

Sustainable: that is, able to maintain productivity despite major disturbances such as are caused by intensive environmental stress (e.g. salination) or a large perturbation (e.g. flood or drought)

Equitable: that is, fairly sharing the benefits among the participants.

Just as with the forests he suggests a future for agriculture that must be more science-based. He suggests that sustainable agriculture will not occur without more finely tuned agricultural research and implementation. The target is a more fine-grained agriculture, based on a mosaic of varieties, inputs and techniques each fitting a particular ecological, social, and economic niche.

Such a goal has considerable implications for research policy. It requires a much greater contribution from ecology and from biological science generally. This is partly because of the need for biological substitutes for costly inputs but, more important, because the development of a fine-grained agriculture requires information on the ecological structure and dynamics of agricultural environments if inputs from outside are to be made more appropriate and indigenous resources exploited more efficiently.

But it also requires a much broader holistic approach, drawing in a wider range of disciplines in the natural and social sciences.

It is in this area that the great wealth of the North could be mobilized and put to better effect. This brings us back to the here and now in the UK.

Conclusion

As a part of the research for the WCS paper the author carried out a crude survey of UK universities and specialized institutions to establish the extent of their involvement with natural resource questions overseas. Some 40 departments were surveyed and the results highly conclusive. All complained that they could do far more but for the want of a proper broker for the work. Most indicated that overseas work enriched their department's work; most thought government (the ODA or the Crown Agents) should do more to promote the creative wealth and experience of this country in natural science disciplines to countries overseas. In short, many natural scientists appear to be ready to take part constructively in the pressing conservation issues of our time—from protecting individual species, to complex integrated planning concepts, from basic taxonomy and surveys through to remote sensing.

It is an opportunity that government should grasp as the need for bringing the best of UK science into harness with those who handle the financial levers of development has never been greater.

References

The conservation and development programme for the UK: A response to the World Conservation Strategy (1983). Kogan Page, London. (Sponsoring Bodies: World Wildlife Fund UK; Nature Conservancy Council; Countryside Commission; Countryside Commission for Scotland; Royal Society of Arts; Council for Environmental Conservation.)

Conway, G. (In press). *Rural resource conflicts in the UK and the Third World: Issues for research policy*. Imperial College, London.

House of Commons (1983). *The House of Commons fourth report from the Foreign Affairs Committee Session 1982–83: The Overseas Development Administration's Scientific and Special Units*. HMSO, London.

International Union for Conservation of Nature and Natural Resources (1980). *World conservation strategy: Living resource conservation for sustainable development*. (In co-operation with the World Wildlife Fund and the United Nations Environment Programme.) IUCN, Gland, Switzerland.

Lanly, J.P. (1982). Tropical forest resources. *FAO Forestry Pap*. No. 30: 1–106.

Symp. zool. Soc. Lond. (1985) No. 54: 269–276

Concluding comments: science and conservation

LORD ZUCKERMAN

The Zoological Society of London
Regent's Park
London NW1 4RY*

I have not been asked to sum up the whole of this symposium. What I propose to do, in accordance with the printed programme, is direct a few concluding remarks to the topic 'science and conservation'. But I must start by saying that the symposium has been a most generous and flattering birthday present. Professor Hearn, whose idea it was, and who so ably organized the proceedings, knows full well that the theme of this meeting is one which I have urged on our Society on several occasions over the past two decades and more. I see that Mr Max (E.M.) Nicholson, the first Director of the Nature Conservancy, is with us today. He will remember that my concern with the subject, like his, in fact goes back to well before the Second World War.

It was once said in this hall that the purpose of conservation is not 'to play god' but to see whether we can control, for the better, a phase in an inevitable natural process of change which over time has led not only to the extinction of species, but also to changes, sometimes catastrophic, in the land surface and oceans of the globe. We are talking about a continuous process of environmental evolution which started hundreds of millions of years before man was around to affect it, whether for better or for worse. Our concern is with the changes that are taking place now, and in which we see the influence of our own hand, and an influence which has clearly had some deleterious effects on our environment. Therefore, since this Symposium has the general title *Advances in animal conservation*, I shall assume that we are talking about the period since the end of the Second World War, that is, the period in which the conservation of nature became a matter of world-wide concern, when we started seriously to discuss the problems of over-population, and of man's encroachment into, and his destruction of, the habitats of the fauna and flora into which we, the generation living now, were born, and which we inherited.

These two issues—population and habitat—have usually dominated our discussions. This morning Professor Hearn cited some recent figures relating to the size of the human population—one billion in 1850; today something

* Present address: *The University of East Anglia, Norwich NR4 7TJ, England*

ZOOLOGICAL SYMPOSIUM No. 54
ISBN 0–19–854002–7

fewer than four billion, with a projection of eight billion by 2020—less than 40 years away. Even if Professor Hearn's final figure proves to be on the high side, as some believe will be the case, the goals of conservation will always be affected by the growth of population, for the simple reason that the pressure of social demand, as well as that of the actual number of people, goes on increasing everywhere. Mounting demand is an inevitable corollary to improvements in the means of communication, in levels of education, and in the consequent rise in standards of living. Whatever the rate of increase in population, we can be sure that more material goods will be demanded tomorrow than are today. As Mr Sandbrook has just reminded us, poverty and over-population go together. The problem of poverty demands solution, and we know that its solution will create greater social demand. In my view, therefore, there is no question of conflict about what comes first—measures to limit population growth or measures to protect our environment. We need both. Family planning programmes must march together with measures to reduce poverty. Even if current estimates for the growth of population prove to be too high, the consequences of whatever growth takes place will be the same from the point of view of the pressure on resources and of the conservation of the remaining flora and fauna of our globe.

Yesterday morning His Royal Highness, Prince Philip, briefly noted some new environmental issues that have emerged since the Society's last symposium on conservation. He referred to 'acid rain'. He mentioned the 'greenhouse effect'. There is the immediate matter of more mundane kinds of pollution, which we seem unable to control—an issue about which Dr Laws knows a great deal where it concerns the oceans. There is also a fourth issue which, while certainly not a general problem, is in some places a matter of concern; namely, an increasing level of background radiation.

A recent TV programme raised the issue of Australian aborigines who had happened to be in the area of the Maralinga atmospheric nuclear tests. I started thinking. I know Maralinga. In another capacity it was once my duty to deal with the closing-down of the test site as radiation levels fell. I ran into no aborigines, but I did see any number of kangaroos and thousands of cockatoos. What, I asked myself, had happened to these creatures since the tests—if anything had happened at all? There have been corresponding stories coming from the United States about latent effects of fall-out on human beings. An increase in background radiation levels is therefore also something that should be borne in mind when we speculate about the ways in which the environment of the future could change.

Every change could, in theory, limit or modify or encroach further upon the animal habitats with which we are concerned. Of course the problem of conservation would be very different from what it is were there no limits to the amount of available land, and no limits to the confines of the energy system within which dynamic change in the living world takes place. Dr Laws told us yesterday that the annual production of krill may be 750–1350 million tonnes. Suppose an organism could be tailor-made which could fix nitrogen in the sea, would not the result be an increase in the size of the total system within which dynamic interchanges of energy take place in and between biological sub-systems, and which in the first place would affect the oceanic biomass? I made this suggestion to Dr Anne McLaren during the break. Her reply was that were that to happen, we couldn't possibly predict the consequence. Neither could I, any more than any of us can predict the consequences of what is happening now, or what is likely to happen soon, in the finite system within which dynamic interchange of energy is taking place. But in theory, if such a nitrogen-fixing organism could be genetically designed and produced, it would remove one constraint to the potential size of the energy system with which we are concerned.

Increasing population, increasing social demand, the other new factors about which we now talk—acid rain, the greenhouse effect, straightforward pollution—press slowly but continuously on the whole energy system. As Sir William Henderson reminded us yesterday, short-term catastrophic changes which are not within our control can also occur. The catastrophic effect of rinderpest, which was one of the biblical plagues, has been brought under control, or under potential control. We can eliminate other animal disease. We should be able to eliminate malaria which, like poverty, is a major controlling factor of population growth. But we must also realize that other environmental catastrophes could occur, in the face of which we would be impotent. All that we as scientists can do is try to understand what is happening and, in so far as we can, prevent or at least retard the deterioration of our environment.

As well as dealing with what remains of the wild fauna of the world, we could perhaps try and restore some of the creatures which existed in recent time. Heinz Heck, when Director of the Tiergarten in Munich, carried out a few genetic experiments, one of which had as its aim the reconstitution of the aurochs. I had the opportunity of seeing the results of his work. But whether any reconstituted aurochs are still around as a result of his efforts, I do not know. The experiment has been tried; and could be tried again.

But whatever we do requires immediate knowledge of what is happening now. Yesterday Prince Philip told us about the enormous numbers of animals which still enter world trade, dead or alive. Today Dr Brambell told us more. Through the work of people like Dr Halle, and because there is an agreed World Conservation Strategy, we also have fairly up-to-date information about the disappearance of forests and species. Dr Halle observed that in the past his organization has sometimes been accused of 'selling out to the enemy'; I would say that it is also pretty good at making friends.

I am proud that this Society took the initiative in launching the

International zoo yearbook. I have brought with me a copy of the first number, as I did not want to discover that any of my remarks today inadvertently controverted what I said 25 years ago. It was in 1959, a time when it was all but impossible to know what was happening in other zoos, that I proposed that we should launch the *Zoo yearbook*. In the Introduction to the first volume I wrote: 'the need to encourage the conservation of the remaining wild fauna of the world becomes more urgent every day, particularly as technical and economic development gathers its inevitable force in previously undeveloped or underdeveloped areas of the world'. Today the *Yearbook* is four or five times the volume it was at the start, and my message at its launching is even more relevant. The *Yearbook* provides the kind of information which made it possible for Mr Colin Rawlins to tell us at this meeting what zoos have done for conservation over the past 20 years. It also helped Dr Loudon in his account of lactation and neonatal survival in exotic animals.

We have another measure of the help which zoos have accorded the cause of conservation. When I became the Honorary Secretary of the Society 30 years ago, we were responsible for one of the only two studbooks of exotic animals then in existence. I gather that today there are 50 or 60 which deal with rare species. They are essential tools for the co-operation between the custodians of rare and endangered species. Zoos are certainly playing a valuable role.

As the papers presented this morning also showed, there have been some remarkable advances in our knowledge of the physiology of reproduction. It is only a few years ago that the artificial insemination of exotic animals began. We now have *in vitro* fertilization, the freezing of the dividing egg, nuclear transplantation, and gene manipulation. As I listened to today's papers, I recalled that I was present at a lecture given in the twenties by Dr Chambers, who I believe was the first man to 'manipulate' the nucleus of a cell. It was at University College, and Sir Grafton Elliot Smith, then a member of the Council of this Society, was in the chair. I am sure that I was not the only one on that occasion who was amazed to learn that it was possible to lift a nucleus out of its cell. In the discussion period someone stood up and asked in a shaky voice, 'Isn't it time to call a halt? Haven't we gone far enough? Haven't we penetrated nature's secrets sufficiently without destroying the nucleus of cells?' That was 60 years ago. Today we can remove the nucleus from the cell of one species and insert it into that of another. We haven't yet come to the cloning of mature mammalian somatic cells. Maybe that will happen one day.

Whether or not Dr Benirschke's DNA-bank is also achieved remains to be seen. Only the future will tell whether our successors will be able to tap banks of frozen embryos not only of today's endangered species but of others which might become endangered. Many years ago this Society established what we then called a Gene Bank. It was a very simple affair. We collected together at Whipsnade specimens of as many disappearing domestic breeds of sheep, poultry, and cattle as we could. Unfortunately little scientific use was then made of the animals in the determination of their genetic relationships. That piece of our enterprise had to come to an end because it cost money that we could ill afford. What is now the Rare Breeds Society took over most of the animals we had collected.

But the outstanding advances that have been made over the past 20 years in our knowledge of reproductive processes, and in our ability to control the early stages of embryonic development, have not transformed any of the basic principles of the subject that were formulated and elaborated in the twenties and thirties, when people such as Joseph Needham were attempting to illuminate the processes of differentiation of the cells of the dividing fertilized ovum. Today we can use computer jargon to ask what happens to the undifferentiated cell which, as it were, is a general-purpose integrated circuit, when it becomes a specialized circuit for a particular process. We still have to learn why it is that after the eight-cell stage of the morula in the mammal—I choose the figure eight arbitrarily—cells cease being multipotent, whereas at the two-cell stage they are still unspecialized. Why is it that the cloning of mature somatic cells is possible in amphibians but not in mammals?

I was glad to hear the up-to-date account of the work that is being done in this field in the Society's laboratories by Professor Hearn and his colleagues. When I encouraged the Council to agree—which they did, provided I could find the money!—that we should establish, first, the Wellcome Institute for Reproductive Physiology, and then the Nuffield Institute of Comparative Medicine, I did so because I was concerned by the fact that any amount of potentially useful material and, *ipso facto*, information, was metaphorically being washed down the drains of the Old Prosectorium. At that time, too, we did not have the means to make proper educational and scientific use of the unique material which our animal collections comprise. My first concern was with the question of comparative medicine. I kept wondering whether tissues from dead animals were just being incinerated when their study could help in our understanding of disease processes in man. In those days, too, we knew relatively little about the diseases of exotic animals. What Mr David Jones was demonstrating yesterday, when he showed a picture of a little chimpanzee having its chest rubbed with camphor oil by that excellent keeper of chimpanzees in the twenties and thirties, Mr Shelley, was what would have been done at the time to a child suffering from a chest cold. All the improvements of recent times in animal health in this and, I presume, other zoos, reflect the advances that have been made as medical science and veterinary science have moved forward. When we established our two new laboratories, I had only a hazy vision of what this meeting has revealed. What has been achieved was well beyond the bounds of any prediction.

But this meeting has also indicated how much more waits to be learnt. For example, we have heard that the spermatozoa of only some species are amenable to freezing. Why? I do not know the number of mammalian species of different Orders that exist; I know that there are a few hundred different Primates. Each presents a different set of physiological problems for enquiry. So much more needs to be done than has already been done.

This meeting has therefore revealed how small, relatively speaking, is the foundation for all the work which takes place across the whole spectrum of the medical and veterinary sciences. Most experimental work in medicine has been based upon work on rats, on mice, on rabbits, and on monkeys. Some years ago Dr Adler, together with Dr Edward Hindle, who had worked on yellow fever in the old Medical Research Institute close by Hampstead Heath and who later did research in the Society's old Prosectorium, discovered that the hamster is a creature whose cheek-pouch takes transplants very readily. This finding was of immense importance to biological science. The multiple fetus of the armadillo is another useful tool for medical science. I do not know how many other creatures there are which have some unique quality from the point of view of the advancement of knowledge. There may be many.

We should never forget, too, that the furthest we can advance when using new technology to reach a particular end, is set by the broad principles which derive from present knowledge—unless the new techniques themselves become responsible for opening up yet another new field of basic enquiry. It is our present store of knowledge which is providing us with a base for dealing with problems of reproduction in disappearing and threatened species. It is important that its size is increased not only in our own Institute of Zoology, but also in the laboratories of the Medical Research Council and the Agricultural Research Council, and in the various units which they maintain in universities.

I have long argued that the distinction that is usually made between basic science and applied science is in any event a fiction. The two are separated mainly by the dimension of time. This morning Dr Polge reminded us that the phrase 'science fiction' applies to much that today has become scientific fact. All science is fiction to the majority of people. But scientists have to go on, trying to turn fiction into fact. That is the measure of the power of scientific enquiry.

May I conclude on another theme. In reading through the papers which Professor Hearn gave me yesterday, I find that at a conference in 1974 I remarked (Zuckerman 1974 : 45) that if—on the assumption that I had then been alive—I had been invited to be one of the company which discussed in the 1820s the desirability of establishing a zoo in London, I would probably have declined. I added, however, that today's goal of conservation could never be fully realized without the kind of scientific knowledge which can be gained only by the adequate study of zoological collections.

Zoos have had strange and varied histories. This Society was started with a very strict definition of purpose, and one that has never changed. It is: 'the advancement of zoology and animal physiology and the introduction of new and curious subjects of the Animal Kingdom'. We may have to appeal to the public for the resources to keep going, but in maintaining exotic animals, whether in cages or in gene banks or in frozen spermatozoa stores, we are helping realize a true strategy for conservation.

The fulfilment of such a strategy is going to cost a great deal of money. This morning we were told that the Nature Conservancy Council, less the research component which it once possessed, spends £15 million of public money a year, and that it needs much more if it is to do its work properly. We have also been reminded that what is done for conservation world-wide has necessarily to be politically compatible with all the measures that relate to economic and social development. I wish therefore that I could share Mr Sandbrook's optimism that all that is required in order to obtain the resources necessary to implement a conservation strategy is to bring the scientists together with the economic planners. My own experience does not encourage me to believe that the result would be very different from what it has been. About four years ago, I published a paper under the title of 'The Risks of a No-Risk Society', (Zuckerman 1980), which ended by pointing out that there are risks everywhere, that because it costs money to do any kind of social good, and because in the end it does not matter from which purse the money comes, there have to be priorities in public expenditure. Out of the blue came a long letter from Nigel Lawson, now the Chancellor of the Exchequer, commending what I had written. I wish I could feel that the Mr Lawson of today will respond both soon and favourably to the messages that are being spelt out about conservation and to the one referred to yesterday by Lord Peyton about the state of this Society's finances.

I know that other good zoos help in achieving the aims of conservation, and that they are also in difficulties. Some of their directors are here, and I would suggest to them that they wait and see what comes of the pleas to Government which the Zoological Society of London has been making over the past few years. To do so will demand some forbearance from them. But our ultimate goal is the same. Why, therefore, do we not establish a Federation of British zoos, with executive rather than the purely fraternal functions which the present Federation subserves so well? I do not mean that we should set up some new institution. We could use this Society—the oldest body of its kind in the world—as the nucleus round which to affiliate. The good zoos and societies will never achieve as much separately as they could together. As I have said, we have learnt to associate in a minor and friendly way through the present Zoo Federation. Why not try to transform the Federation into a unitary executive body for the benefit of us all?

At a seminar on zoos and conservation which took place in 1964, I said that 'The problems of animal conservation are too complicated, too important and too extensive to be solved piecemeal by isolated action. Success will come only if conservationists, the directors of zoos, and academic zoologists discuss their various difficulties and co-operate wholeheartedly with others working in the same field.' (Zuckerman 1964). May I end now by re-emphasising these words. The strategy for conservation has been set. The tactics are ours to agree and then to implement.

Finally, may I once again say how honoured and how gratified I feel that this Symposium was organized in my name. Thank you very much.

References

Zuckerman, S. (1964). Zoos and conservation. Foreword. *I.U.C.N. Pubs* (N.S.) Suppl. Pap. No. 3: 7.

Zuckerman, S. (1974). Summing up. In *The 1001 Nature Trust symposium on the contribution of zoos to the conservation of nature, held at The Zoological Gardens, Regent's Park, London, on 8th May 1974*: 45–50. World Wildlife Fund, London. (Duplicated typescript.)

Zuckerman, S. (1980). The risks of a no-risk society. In *Yearbook of world affairs*: 7–30. Keeton, G.W. & Schwarzenbertger, G. (Eds). Institute of World Affairs, London.

INDEX

DATE DUE

NOV 13 2003	

GAYLORD   PRINTED IN U.S.A.